Pontifical Administration
of the Patriarchal Basilica of St. Paul

The Popes

Twenty Centuries of History

Libreria Editrice Vaticana

The Popes - Twenty Centuries of History

English translation:
A.J. O'Brien

© Copyright 2002
  Pontifical Administration
  of the Patriarchal Basilica of St. Paul

ISBN 88-209-7317-0

Cover
Perugino, The "traditio clavum" or Consignment of the Keys to St. Peter (*detail*)
Sixtine Chapel - Vatican

Back Cover
Arms of St. Paul
Cloister of the Basilica
of St. Paul outside the Walls - Rome

Forward

A complete series of mosaic portraits of the Popes, from St. Peter to the present, is conserved in the nave of the Basilica of St. Paul Outside the Walls - which was founded by Constantine, enlarged by his successors and restored by several Popes. The series dates from the latter half of the fifth century and the pontificate of Leo the Great. It has been restored and resumed on several occasions. The iconography of the portraits which refer to antiquity and the middles ages is based on traditional sources. Nevertheless, the series is quite unique. The present volume contains reproductions of the portraits which are accompanied by a brief historical note on each of the Roman Pontiffs.

Following the series in St. Paul's, 262 Popes are represented. However, Benedict IX is portrayed three times since he was Pope on three different occasions. Leo VIII and Sylvester III are omitted probably because the validity of their elections was doubtful. In addition to 262 Popes, the history of the Church has also seen 37 anti-Popes. It is difficult to determine the exact number of Popes and anti-Popes. As can be gleaned from the *Annuario Pontificio,* edited by the Secretariat of State and published by the Libreria Editrice Vaticana, in a number of cases historical and canonical doubts persist with regard to the validity of certain elections.

Up to the latter half of the second century, historical sources for the history of the Bishops of Rome are not always reliable. Liturgical tradition and hagiography regard all the Popes up to Sylvester I as martyrs, although such can be historically verified in few cases. Sylvester I is the first Pope after the great persecutions. All Popes up to Felix IV (middle of the sixth century) are venerated as saints, with the exceptions of Liberius and Anastasius II. Several Popes from the middle ages are also venerated as saints. Seventy-eight Popes are regarded as saints and a further ten have been beatified. In these cases, the historical profiles contained in this book indicate their feast days. For the earlier period and for the middles ages, the dates of birth of most of the Popes are unknown or uncertain. Dates of birth are indicated from the reign of Alexander VI at the beginning of the modern period.

The book closes with a note on the legend of Pope Joan, a synthesis of the rules governing the election of the Popes, a chronological list of the Popes and anti-Popes, and an alphabetical list of all 262 Popes.

This book seeks to combine rigorous scholarship with easy accessibility for the general public. Its principal sources are J. N. D. Kelly's *The Oxford Dictionary of Popes*, published by Oxford University Press in 1986, and the *Enciclopedia dei Papi* published in 2000 by the Istituto dell'Enciclopedia Italiana. With the exception of Celestine V, who had none, the coats of arms for all the Popes from Urban IV, mid twelfth century, are reproduced from these sources.

The biographical texts were prepared by Professor Giovanni Maria Vian, of *La Sapienza* University, Rome, member of the Pontifical Committee for Historical Sciences, and scientific advisor for the *Enciclopedia dei Papi*.

Covering over twenty centuries, the reader of these biographies cannot but be impressed by the institutional continuity of the Papacy. It is a unique phenomenon in the history of the West. The theological significance attached to that continuity is also based on its historical importance.

29 June 2002
Feast of the Holy Apostles Peter and Paul

+ Francesco Gioia
Pontifical Administrator
of the Patriarchal Basilica of St. Paul

1. Saint Peter (+67)

Throughout its history, the papacy has always seen its origins in the mandate given to St. Peter by Christ. St. Matthew's Gospel contains the best known version of that mandate: «You are Peter and on this rock I shall build my Church» (Matthew, 16, 18). The only historical data available to us about Peter is contained in the New Testament, above all in the Gospels and in *The Acts of the Apostles*. This information can be supplemented with material drawn from numerous second century texts, the so called «apocrypha», and from the Christian writers of the first and second centuries.

Peter was a fisherman from Bethsaida, a village in Galilee on the north east shore of the lake of Tiberias. Originally, he was called Simon, his father's name being John or Jonah. He was a brother of Andrew and was already married when he became a disciple of Jesus. The New Testament mentions Peter some two hundred times. This prominence illustrates that he was the most important of the disciples of Jesus. He is the first to be mentioned in the list of the twelve apostles. In the events surrounding the arrest of Christ and his subsequent passion and death, Peter appears to occupy a primary role. After the women, Peter is the first of the disciples to witness the empty tomb and to give testimony of the resurrection. Again, *The Acts of the Apostles* underlines his importance as the head of the nascent Christian Church after the ascension of Christ.

Christian writers of the first century have conserved accounts of Peter's presence in Rome, and of his martyrdom there under Nero, about the year 67 - the same year in which St. Paul was also martyred in Rome. All of these sources agree that Peter was crucified up side down: from Pope St. Clement to Dionysius of Corinth and Origen, all of whom are sources for Eusebius of Caesarea, the great ecclesiastical historian of the third century. The patristic accounts of Peter's presence in Rome, which seems historically certain, began to be contested in the thirteenth century, firstly by heretics and subsequently by the protestants reformers for polemical reasons. The first of the two New Testament epistles ascribed to Peter was written in Rome. While this letter, whether authentic or the work of a disciple of Peter, dates from the end of the first century and recalls the tradition of the martyred apostle, the second letter would seem to date from the early decades of the second century.

Much more likely is the Roman origin of the Gospel of St. Mark which was written sometime before the year 70 and is based on the testimony of St. Peter. We know nothing of Peter's role in early the Roman Church. In the second and third centuries, two places in Rome claimed to preserve the remains of St. Peter, the *memoria apostoli*, in the Basilica of San Sebastiano on the Appian way, and that in the Vatican itself, which was the one that eventually prevailed. The excavations carried out by order of Pius XII under the floor of St. Peter's Basilica between 1939 and 1949 discovered a burial place venerated at least since the second century. In 1965, Paul VI announced that the remains of the apostle had been identified.

From the latter half of the second century, Peter has been regarded as the first Pope exercising a monarchial episcopate, with the government of the Christian community being vested in a single Bishop. Since then, references to Peter have been constantly seen as a sign of continuity with Christ and as a guarantee of the authenticity of the Christian tradition. St. Peter's feast is celebrated together with that of St. Paul on 29 June.

2. St. Linus *(68-circa 79)*

According to the first list of Popes, which dates from the end of the second century, the practice began of counting from St. Peter. Linus was once considered first Bishop of Rome. He appears to have been born in Tuscany and, perhaps, can be identified with Linus, a companion of Paul, mentioned in the New Testament *(2 Tim 4, 21)*. Very little is known of the functions he exercised in the Roman Church during this very early period in its development. His name follows those of Peter and Paul in the Canon of the Mass. There is a tradition which ascribes martyrdom to him and burial beside St. Peter. His feast day is 23 September.

3. St. Anacletus (or Cletus) *(80-circa 92)*

Anacletus was probably Greek, as his name suggests. It is a Latinised form of *anèncletos*, the irreprehensible, which was frequently used for slaves. The name is sometimes recorded as Cletus. This causes the sources erroneously to postulate two distinct individuals, Anacletus and Cletus. Very little information with regard to his pontificate is extant. Much of what is available is legendary, as for example the claim that he erected a monument at the tomb of St. Peter, which became the nucleus for the future basilica. Legend also has it that he ordained twenty-five priests. His feast day is 26 April.

4. St. Clement I *(circa 92- 99)*

A Roman, possibly a freedman of the Consul Titus Flavius Clemens, a cousin of the emperor Domitian, who was condemned for converting to Judaism and with whom he is sometimes erroneously identified. The earliest sources are unanimous in associating him with the apostles Peter and Paul. He may be the Clement whom St. Paul calls his helper in the epistle to the Philippians *(Phil 4,3)*. A priest, he was the leading exponent of the Roman Church. According to a tradition, which is not confirmed by the earliest sources, he too was martyred. His exile in the Crimea is probably legendary, as is an account of his martyrdom by downing with an anchor tied around his neck. We know very little of his role in the Roman Church. The only thing known with certainty is that he was the redactor, and possibly the writer, of an important text dating from about the year 96. This is the *First Letter to the Corinthians*, addressed to the Church in Corinth, in which he calls for the reintegration of a number of priests who had been expelled. This is the first recorded intervention of the Roman Church in an external matter. This text was widely diffused, event to the extent of having been considered a book of the New Testament. Tradition holds that the present basilica of St. Clement in Rome was build on the house of Clement. His feast day is 23 November.

5. Evaristus *(circa 99-108)*

It is possible that he was Greek, as his name would suggest. The sources disagree with regard to the dates of his pontificate. Practically everything we know of him is legendary, such as, for example, his birth in Bethlehem of a Jewish father, and his martyrdom. We know nothing of his role in the Roman Church, apart from the tradition that he divided the City into parishes under the jurisdiction of priests. The letters and decretals attributed to him are not authentic. His feast day is 27 February.

6. St. Alexander I *(circa 108-119)*

We know very little about this Pope. He was a Roman. Tradition anachronicistically attributes certain changes in the canon of the Mass to him, as well as the custom of blessing houses with water and salt. Traditionally he is supposed to have been martyred on the Via Nomentana, but this derives from a confusion with another Alexander whose tomb was discovered there in 1855. His feast day is 3 May.

7. St. Sixtus I *(circa 119-126)*

Although the original form of his name, *Xystus*, would suggest a Greek origin, the extant sources regard St. Sixtus as Roman. All information concerning him derives from legendary sources, especially his important liturgical innovations (which in fact postdate him) and his martyrdom. While the historical sources do not corroborate his martyrdom, in the Roman Canon, his name appears between the apostles and the martyrs. We know nothing of his episcopate in Rome. His feast day is 3 April.

8. St. Telesphorus *(circa 127-128)*

Telesphorus was of Greek extraction and is the first Bishop of Rome whose martyrdom is historically certain. It probably occurred under the emperor Hadrian. All other information about him is legendary: that he had been a hermit before his election, that he introduced a penitential fast of seven weeks before Easter, and that he introduced the *Gloria in excelsis Deo* into the mid-night Mass of Christmas. All of these liturgical innovations, however, date from a much later period. Nothing is known of his activities as Bishop of Rome. His feast day is 2 January.

9. St. Hyginus *(circa 138-142)*

Hyginus, a Geek, may have been a philosopher who came to Rome from Athens about the same time as St. Justin, the writer and martyr. Valentinus and Cerdo, two famous Gnostics, are said to have arrived in Rome from Egypt during the pontificate of Hyginus. Accounts of his liturgical activities and of his reorganization of the Roman clergy derive from tradition. No historical evidence exists to prove his martyrdom. His feast day is 11 January.

10. St. Pius I *(circa 142-157)*

Pius was an Italian, born in Aquileia. According to the *Muratorian Fragment*, dating from the latter half of the second century, he was the brother of Hermes, a former slave, who was the author of the famous collection of visions known, as the *Shepherd of Hermes*. As Bishop of Rome he opposed the Gnostics and other heretics, who were especially active in Rome after the arrival of Marcion. He probably presided over the synod that expelled him from the Christian community. He probably knew St. Justin Martyr who then taught in Rome. We have no proof of his martyrdom. His feast day is 11 July.

11. St. Anicetus *(circa 157-168)*

Anicetus was born in Emesa in Syria. His pontificate is remembered for the dispute concerning the date of Easter, which St. Polycarp, Bishop of Smyrna, argued should coincide with the Jewish Pasch on the 14 of *Nisan*, regardless of the day on which it fell (the so called *quartodecimana*). The Pope, however, preferred to maintain the tradition of the Roman Church of celebrating the Lord's resurrection every Sunday. He probably knew St. Justin Martyr who was martyred in the year 165. He was active against the Gnostics. It was probably Anicetus, rather than his predecessor Anacletus, who erected the small monument to St. Peter in the Vatican necropolis over which the basilica would later be erected. From the beginning of the third century this monument was a centre of pilgrimage. It was re-discovered during the excavations conducted by Pius XII between 1939 and 1949.

12. St. Soter *(circa 168-177)*

Soter was born at Fondi in the Campania. It would appear that the custom of celebrating Easter on a fixed Sunday (that following the 14 of *Nisan*) every year rather than every Sunday was introduced to Rome during his pontificate. This was in contrast with the Churches of Asia Minor which continued to observe the *quatrodecimana* (the 14 of *Nisan* regardless of the day it fell on). From Dionysius of Corinth's letter to Soter we know that the Pope took a rigorist position with regard to the readmission of penitents to the Christian community as well as in matters of sexual ethics. Contrary to sources dating from the fifth century, Soter does not appear to have written against the montanist heresy. No historical proof of his martyrdom has come down to us. His feast day is 22 April.

13. St. Elutherius *(circa 177-185)*

Elutherius was Greek. He was born at Nicopolis in Epireus. He was a deacon of his predecessor, St. Anicetus. During his pontificate, the spread of montanism in the West provoked a serious controversy and many other difficulties. In 177, Irenaeus of Lyons came to Rome to persuade the Pope, ultimately without success, to condemn this heretical movement. The tradition that he sent missionaries to convert Britain at the king's request is legendary and derives from a confusion between Lucius, king of Britain, and Lucius Aelius Septimus Megas Abgar IX, king of Edessa, both of whom were converts to Christianity. He is noted as a martyr for the first time in documents dating from the ninth century. His feast day is 26 May.

14. St. Victor I *(circa 186-197)*

Born in Africa, Victor was an important and energetic Pope under whom the Roman Church became more Latinized, and set aside the Greek culture of the Orient. He was the first Pope to attempt imposing the will of the Bishop of Rome on the other Churches. The occasion was the question of the date of Easter. Through a series of Synods, he attempted to impose the celebration of Easter in all Churches on the Sunday following the 14th. of *Nisan*. In this he encountered the opposition of the Eastern Churches which remained faithful to the observance of the *quartodecimana* (i.e. the 14th. of *Nisan*). Through Marcia, the favourite of the emperor Commodus, he maintained contact with the imperial court and succeeded in liberating a group of Christians who had been condemned to forced labour in the mines of Sardinia. There are no historical records attesting to his martyrdom. His feast day is 28 July.

9

15. St. Zephyrinus *(circa 198-218)*

Zephyrinus was a Roman. During his Pontificate, Origen, the great Alexandrian theologian, «greatly desiring to lay eyes on a most ancient Church», visited Rome. He governed the Church with the help of the deacon Calixtus, whom he had entrusted with the administration of the official cemetery of the Roman Church, and who would eventually succeed him. A mediocre theologian, he was accused by Hippolytus the priest of supporting the modalists who admitted of no distinction between the persons of the Trinity. During his pontificate, the Church was disturbed by other doctrinal controversies involving both the heretical montanists and the erroneous ideas of the adoptionists who maintained that Christ had but a human nature up to the time of his baptism. While Zephyrinus was certainly buried in his cemetery on the Appian Way, close to the catacombs of St. Calixtus, there is no evidence to suggest that he was martyred. His feast day is celebrated on 26 August.

16. St. Calixtus I *(circa 218-222)*

After a turbulent life, during which he was condemned to forced labour in the mines of Sardinia for petty crime, Calixtus became a deacon and counsellor of St. Zephyrinus, whom he eventually succeeded in the Roman See. His election, however, was contested. A group of opponents supported the candidature of Hippolytus, our main source for the biography of Calixtus. Hippolytus, who was elected Bishop of Rome, thereby becoming the first anti-Pope. He too was subsequently martyred. The dispute between the two factions derived partly from disciplinary questions and partly from Christological questions. Although the Pope had excommunicated Sabellius, the leading exponent of modalism, or monarchianism, he maintained a *via media* between the doctrinal positions of Sabellius and Hippolytus. This policy induced the latter to accuse Calixtus of supporting modalism. Contrary to the rigorist position of Hippolytus, Calixtus viewed the Church as a community that offered the possibility of reconciliation to all sinners. While it does not seem likely that the Pope was martyred, it is possible that he was killed during a riot. He was interred in the cemetery of Calepodius on the Aurelian way. His tomb, decorated with later frescos, was rediscovered in 1960. His feast day is 14 October.

17. St. Urban I *(circa 222-230)*

Urban I was Roman and governed the Church in a period of tranquillity during the reign of the emperor Alexander Severus. The schism of Hippolytus continued during his pontificate. Legend connects him with the martyrdom of St. Cecilia, and also ascribes martyrdom to him. He was buried in the cemetery of St. Calixtus where a Greek inscription from his tomb was later discovered. His feast day is 19 May.

18. Pontian *(circa 230-235)*

Pontian, a Roman, presided at the Roman Synod which confirmed the condemnation of Origen issued by Demetrius of Alexandria. With the death of the emperor Alexander Severus, in 235, his successor, Maximinus the Thracian (C. Julius Varus Maximinus), unleashed a persecution against the Church. Pontian was arrested and deported to Sardinia, as was the anti-Pope, Hippolytus. On 28 September 235, Pontian became the first Bishop of Rome to renounce the See. The date of abdication, as reported in the *Catalogus Liberianus*, is the first historically verifiable date in the history of the papacy. Reconciled with each other, Pontian and Hippolytus both died in Sardinia. Pope St. Fabian had their bodies brought back to Rome in the year 236 or 237 for burial in the catacombs of St. Calixtus. Pontian's sepulchral monument, bearing his name and episcopal title inscribed in Greek, was discovered in 1909. His feast day, and that of St. Hippolytus, is observed on 13 August.

19. St. Anterus *(circa 235-236)*

Of Anterus, a Greek, very little is known. He was Pope for less than two months. Tradition has it that he collated the acts of the martyrs. He almost certainly died of natural causes - as can be inferred from the formula *obdormivit* used to describe his death in the *Catalogus Liberianus*. He was buried in the new crypt of the Popes in the cemetery of St. Calixtus near to the burial place of St. Pontian. Fragments from his sepulchral monument have also been recovered. His feast day is 3 January.

20. St. Fabian *(circa 236-250)*

The pontificate of St. Fabian, a Roman, was highly significant since under his government the role of the Bishop of Rome was clarified and assumed a heightened importance. Origen appealed to him, and defended his orthodoxy in a letter to Fabian. The division of the Roman clergy into seven ecclesiastical districts, each ruled by a deacon assisted by a subdeacon and six ministers, dates from the time of St. Fabian. He enlarged the catacombs of St. Calixtus and had the remains of Sts. Pontian and Hippolytus interred there. These events would suggest that he maintained good relations with the imperial authorities since these had responsibility for the burial of those condemned to deportation. The emperors Gordian II (M. Antonius Gordianus Sempronianus) and Philip the Arabian (M. Julius Philippus), whose reigns coincide with the pontificate of St. Fabian, had suspended all persecution against the Church. The emperor Decius (C. Messius Quintus Decius), however, resumed the persecutions with renewed vigour in 250. Fabian was arrested and died in prison. He was interred in the papal crypt of the catacombs of St. Calixtus, where his sepulchral monument was rediscovered in 1854. The body of St. Fabian was later removed to St. Sebastiano where a sarcophagus bearing his name was found in 1915. His feast day is 20 January.

21. St. Cornelius *(251-253)*

The severity of the Decian persecution delayed the election of a successor to St. Fabian for more than two years. As many of the senior figures of the Roman Church had died in prison, the priest Novatian ruled the Church until the year 251 when Cornelius was elected bishop. He may well have belonged to the ancient Roman *gens Cornelia*. Cornelius' election succeeded despite the opposition of the supporters of Novatian, who, in turn, was elected anti-Pope. This schism in the Roman Church was partly determined by the attitude adopted to the *lapsi*, (those who had fallen away), or those who had abjured the faith during the Decian persecution and who, subsequently, desired to be re-admitted to the Church. While Novatian adopted a rigorist position in their regard and argued for their exclusion, Cornelius favoured their re-admittance after a congruent period of penance. This latter position prevailed having obtained the support of the important Churches of Carthage and Alexandria. In a synod of sixty bishops, Cornelius excommunicated Novatian, and thereby disavowed the rigorist position. Some of Cornelius' letters from the period of the schism survive. They are highly important in recovering the terms in which the debate on the *lapsi* was conducted. They also contain much valuable information on the Roman clergy. When the persecutions resumed under the emperor Gallus (Trebonianus Gallus) in 251, Cornelius was arrested and exiled to *Centumcellae*, the modern Civitavecchia, where he died. While not numbered among the martyrs, he was considered such by the Church. His body was interred in the crypt of Lucina in the catacombs of St. Calixtus. The epitaph erected in memory of Cornelius was the first written in Latin for a Pope. His feast day is 16 September.

22. St. Lucius I *(253-254)*

Lucius, a Roman, was exiled by the emperor Gallus soon after his election. With the succession of the emperor Valerian (P. Licinius Valerianus) and an initial relaxation of the persecution, Lucius was able to return to Rome. He maintained the position of Cornelius with regard to the *lapsi* and re-admitted them to the Church after a period of penance. He died of natural causes and was interred in the papal crypt in the cemetery of St. Calixtus. His sepulchral epitaph bore a Greek inscription.

23. St. Stephen I *(254-257)*

Stephen I belonged to the important Roman *gens Iulia*. His pontificate was marked by conflicts arising from the problem of the re-admission of apostates. The majority of the bishops of North Africa, Asia Minor and Syria supported the position of St. Cyprian of Carthage who maintained the invalidity of baptism administered by heretics. Cyprian advocated the necessity of a second baptism for the *lapsi* as a condition for their reconciliation with the Church. St. Stephen, on the other hand, advocated the tradition of the Roman Church, and that of the Churches of Alexandria and Palestine, which held that baptism administered by heretics was valid. Re-admission to the Church consequently required only absolution by the imposition of hands. The administration of a second baptism was regarded as contrary to tradition. This conflict is important for it illustrates the position of the Church on the sacrament of Baptism, and on the validity of the sacraments. The controversy also serves to highlight how the Roman Church at the time of Stephen I had already become a reference point for many of the Oriental Churches. During the controversy, the Pope, intransigent and authoritarian, was accused of «pride in his position of Bishop of Rome and successor of Peter, on whom the Church was founded». In fact, Stephen was the first to quote the words of the Gospel: «Thou art Peter and upon this rock I shall build my Church» (*Mt*, 16,18) in favour of the Roman primacy. Contrary to tradition, he was not a martyr. He was buried in the crypt of the Popes in the cemetery of St. Calixtus. His feast day is 2 August.

24. St. Sixtus II *(257-258)*

As his name would suggest, Sixtus was probably Greek. He resumed relations with the Church of Carthage which had been strained in the controversy between his predecessor and St. Cyprian. Sixtus held firmly to the Roman position on the question of heretical baptism, which he regarded as valid, as can be seen from the sole surviving fragment of his letter to Dionysius of Alexandria, where he tries to mediate in the controversy. The biographer of St. Cyprian describes him as «a good Bishop and a lover of peace». He was martyred during the bitter persecution of Valerian. On 6 August 258 he was surprised by soldiers while preaching in the private cemetery of Praetextatus and decapitated. Four deacons were martyred with him. The three surviving deacons, including St. Lawrence, were martyred during the following days, leaving the Roman Church without shepherds. St. Sixtus was buried in the cemetery of St. Calixtus. He was one of the most venerated martyrs in the Roman Church and his name was inserted in the Roman Canon of the Mass. His feast day is 7 August.

25. St. Dionysius *(259-268)*

Dionysius was one of the most prominent priests in Rome during the pontificate of Sixtus II. He was elected Pope following the death of the emperor Valerian and the end of the persecution. For a period of about two years the Roman Church was governed only by priests. He intervened in the doctrinal controversy concerning the Trinity which was just commencing to trouble the Church. He opposed Dionysius of Alexandria who maintained a rigid distinction between the three divine persons. During his Pontificate, he re-organized the Roman Church and established nine episcopal sees in the areas surrounding the City. Priests were assigned to the parishes and cemeteries of Rome. He resumed the practise in the Roman Church of supporting Churches in difficulty, sending money to the Church in Cappadocia for the ransom prisoners. He was interred in the papal crypt in the cemetery of St. Calixtus. His feast day is 26 December.

13

26. St. Felix I *(269-274)*

Felix was Roman. Very little is known of his Pontificate whose dates are uncertain. Felix was Bishop of Rome during a peaceful interval at the beginning of the reign of Aurelian (M. Domitius Aurelianus). He intervened in a controversy that arose in the Church of Antioch where its bishop, Paul of Samosata, had ben deposed for his Christological theories. Felix upheld the decision of the synod that had deposed Paul of Samosata. The question was resolved by the intervention of the emperor who assigned the See of Antioch and its episcopal palace to the group supported by the Bishop of Rome. A profession of faith, deriving from the Christological controversies of the period, bears his name. This may well have been part of a letter written by Felix to Maximus of Alexandria, and date from the controversy surrounding Paul of Samosata. Tradition has it that Felix was martyred. This may derive from his having been confused with other martyrs of the same name. He was buried in the papal crypt in the cemetery of St. Calixtus. His feast day is 30 December.

27. St. Eutychian *(275-283)*

Eutychian was born at Luni in Tuscia. He reigned during the peaceful interval between the persecution of Valerian and that of Diocletian which began in 303. Very little is known about him - perhaps because of the destruction of sources during the Diocletian persecution. Many traditions have been handed down about this Pope, including one which says that he personally buried many of the martyrs. It is certain, however, that Eutychian re-organized the Roman Church and expanded the Christian cemeteries. He was the last Bishop of Rome to have been buried in the papal crypt of St. Calixtus, where fragments of a Greek sepulchral epitaph survive. His feast day is 8 December.

28. St. Caius *(283-296)*

St. Caius was a native of Dalmatia. According to the *Passio* of St. Susanna, an unreliable sixth century source, he was a relative of the emperor Diocletian. Nothing is known of his pontificate. Accounts of his martyrdom are legendary. He was buried in a separate part of the papal crypt in cemetery of St. Calixtus. In the nineteenth century, fragments of his funerary epitaph, composed in Greek, were recovered. His feast day is 22 April.

29. St. Marcellinus *(296-304)*

A native Roman, little is known of St. Marcellinus' pontificate until the outbreak of the persecution of Diocletian in 303. When the emperor ordered the destruction of churches, the confiscation of the sacred books, and the offering of pagan sacrifice, it appeared that the Pope had acquiesced when he handed over the biblical texts and offered incense to the gods. This act was for long regarded as one of apostasy and the source of much controversy within the Church. At the beginning of the fifth century, the donatists, in their controversy with St. Augustine, maintained that not only Marcellinus had committed apostasy but also his clergy, including the future Popes, Marcellus, Melchiades and Sylvester I. Augustine strenuously denied their accusations. From the end of the fifth century and the beginning of the sixth century, several texts assert the apostasy of St. Marcellinus. They add, however, that he repented and redeemed himself through martyrdom in which he achieved sanctity. No extant sources, including Augustine's defence of Marcellinus, refer to the martyrdom of St. Marcellinus. There is no evidence to suggest that he was deposed. His name was, however, omitted from the official list of Popes. He was buried in the cemetery of Priscilla on the via Salaria, a private cemetery of the *gens Acilia*, since all other cemeteries had been confiscated during the persecution of Diocletian. His feast day is 2 June.

30. St. Marcellus I *(306-309)*

Marcellus, a Roman, was elected Pope in 306 at the time of the accession of the emperor Maxentius (M. Aurelius Valerius Maxentius) who ended the persecution of the Church. This date, however, is uncertain and other sources hold that his pontificate extended only from June 308 to January 309. Following the apostasy of Marcellinus, the papacy remained vacant for three years during which Marcellus play an important role in ecclesiastical affairs. The donatist claim that he apostatised is improbable, especially since he ordered the removal of his predecessor's name from the list of Popes. The new Bishop of Rome adopted a severe policy towards those who had apostatised during the persecutions. He exacted harsh penances which provoked hostility towards him among the faithful. Marcellus' policy led to public disorder in Rome which obliged the emperor Maxentius to banish him for disturbing the peace. He died shortly afterwards and his body was brought back to Rome for burial in the catacombs of Priscilla. Legend recounts that Maxentius condemned him to tend animals and converted his church into a sty. In the nineteenth century, the succession of two Popes, one called Marcellinus the other Marcellus was questioned. Without apparent foundation, it was suggested that Marcellus, a priest who had ruled the Roman Church during the long interregnum following the pontificate of Marcellinus, had never been Pope. His feast day is 16 January.

31. St Eusebius *(April - October 309)*

St. Eusebius was Greek by birth and probably a medical doctor by profession. Only the date of his death is certain. It is possible that he might have been elected in 308. In contradistinction to the severe position of his rival, and possible anti-Pope, Heracles, he adopted a moderate position with regard to the conditions for the re-admission of those who had apostatised during the persecution of Diocletian. The dispute was settled by the intervention of the emperor who deported both to Sicily. Eusebius died in Sicily but his body was returned to Rome for burial in the cemetery of St. Calixtus. The account of his martyrdom does not appear to have any foundation. His feast day is 17 August.

32. St. Melchiades (or Miltiades) *(311-314)*

An African or more probably a Roman, St. Melchiades had been a priest with St. Marcellinus. This Pope saw the victory of the Church. Shortly after his election, the emperor Maxentius ordered the restoration of all ecclesiastical goods confiscated during the persecutions. St. Melchiades made formal application to the Prefect of Rome for the restoration of all confiscated churches and property. Following the battle of the Milvian bridge and the victory of Constantine over Maxentius, Melchiades met the emperor who gave him the palace of the empress Fausta on the Coelian hill. Hence the Leteran became the residence of the Popes. During his pontificate, the controversy with the rigorist African clergy resumed. St. Melchiades supported Caecilianus, the Bishop of Carthage, against Donatus, head of the rigorist party who called for the second baptism and the second ordination of those who had apostatised. This controversy was significant not only because St. Malchiades resolved the Donatist crisis by convoking a synod that condemned Doatus and his followers, but also because it was the first decisive intervention of the emperor in ecclesiastical affairs. At the request of the Donatists and not withstanding their excommunication, Constantine arrogated to himself supreme decisional authority and convoked a further synod at Arles over which the Pope did not preside. St. Melchiades died before the synod met. His remains were buried in the cemetery of St. Calixtus. His tomb has not been identified. His feast day is 10 January.

33. St. Sylvester I *(314-335)*

St. Sylvester was probably Roman and had a long pontificate, exercised in the shadow of Constantine's imperial activity and his interventions in ecclesiastical affairs. The Pope's role was limited since he was not an ecclesiastical counsellor of the emperor. He did not participate in the synod of Arles (314) which formally established papal primacy in the Western Church. The ecumenical Council of Nicea (325), convoked by the emperor, was not attended by St. Sylvester. The Council condemned the Arian doctrine on the nature of Christ, defined the formula of Trinitarian faith, declaring the Son to be «consubstantial» with the Father. The condemnation of Arius did not prevent Constantine from associating himself with Arianism to the point of asking for Baptism on his death-bed from the Arian Bishop, Eusebius of Nicomedia, in 337. During the pontificate of St. Sylvester, the Roman Church received many important benefactions from Constantine, including the basilicas of St. John in the Lateran, St. Peter's and St. Paul's. Gradually, the aspect of the city began to be christianized. St. Sylvester was buried in the cemetery of Priscilla on the via Salaria. Subsequent accounts of his life attribute an importance to him which he never had. According to a fifth century text, St. Sylvester cured Constantine of leprosy, baptized him and obtained from him the closure of the pagan temples. According to the *Constantinian Donation*, an apocryphal document dating from the eight or ninth century but long regarded as authentic, Constantine, at the foundation of Constantinople, gave primacy over the entire West to the Pope and his successors. His feast day is 30 December.

34. St. Marcus *(January-October 336)*

St. Marus, a Roman, approved the custom whereby the Pope was consecrated by the Bishop of Ostia. Other liturgical innovations attributed to him, such as the extension to metropolitans of the pallium or the white woollen stole worn by the Pope and decorated with black crosses, are doubtful. He built two churches, Santa Balbina's on the Ardeatina, of which no trace remains, and St. Mark's , situated next to the Palazzo Venezia, which was probably his own house which he transformed into a church. During his pontificate, the official lists of the Bishops and Martyrs of the Roman Church, the *Depositio episcoporum* and the *Depositio martyrum*, were first compiled. The correspondence between him and St. Athanasius of Alexandria, conserved in a ninth century collection, is not authentic. His feast day is 7 October.

35. St. Julius I *(337-352)*

St. Julius, a native Roman, took decisive action against the Arians. With the support of Constantine they had acquired an ascendency in the Oriental Churches and succeeded in exiling the principal exponents of Catholic orthodoxy as defined at Nicea (325), Athanasius, Bishop of Alexandria, and Marcellus of Ancyra. The Pope took the part of Anthanasius and Marcellus, and received both bishops in Rome where, in a synod held in 340, he exonerated them of the accusations made against them by the Arians, who were led by Eusebius of Nicomedia since the death of Arius in 337. The Pope communicated his decision to the bishops of the East and reproved them for having passed judgement on the two bishops without reference to a general synod or the traditional prerogatives of the Bishop of Rome in the affairs of the Church of Alexandria. In 341 the Arians assembled in Antioch where they again condemned Athanasius and adopted a creedal form different to that of Nicea in its omission of the fundamental affirmation of the Son's consubstantial nature with the Father. A general council was convoked in Serdica (the present day Sofia in Bulgaria) in 341. The oriental bishops withdrew from the council and reiterated their condemnation of Athanasius and accused the Pope, who was not personally present, of having provoked the controversy. The council, which continued without the Arians, condemned them and attributed to the Bishop of Rome a right of appeal in the case of deposed Bishops. Before returning to Alexandria in 345, Athanasius met with the Pope in Rome and consigned to him a letter in which he expressed his satisfaction at being able to return to his rightful see. In addition to his involvement with the Arian crisis, Pope Julius I is remembered for having established the Papal Chancellery, which he organized along the lines of the Imperial Chancellery. He was also responsible for the building of the Basilica Julia (Santa Maria in Trastevere). He was buried on the Appian Way, in the cemetery of St. Calepodius. His feast day is 12 April.

36. St. Liberius *(352-366)*

The Pontificate of Pope St. Liberius, a Roman, was marked by increasing imperial pressure on the papacy in the controversy between the Arian Oriental clergy and the supports of Nicean orthodoxy. The Oriental Bishops had indeed asked his predecessor to support the condemnation of Athanasius. Liberius asked the emperor Constantius II to convoke a general council at Aquileia to resolve the conflict between the Eastern and Western Churches. Constantius II, who had two Arians amongst his counsellors, Uracius and Valente, convoked a synod in Arles which condemned Athanasius. Under duress, the papal legates approved the condemnation. A second council was held in Milan in 355 which once again condemned Athanasius. Liberius was forcefully brought to Milan and subsequently exiled to Berea in Thrace and to Sirmio (the modern Mitrovica in Kosovo). Finally, Liberius was pressurised into accepting the condemnation of Athanasius and a further profession of faith, the so-called creed of Sirmio, which regarded the Son as similar to the Father in essence and in all things in contrast with that of Nicea which declared the Son to be consubstantial with the Father. This compromise subsequently gave rise to the fourth century legend that Liberius had betrayed the faith. Liberius was permitted to return to Rome, where Felix, who is considered an anti-Pope, had been elected bishop. He was received in the city with shouts of «One God, one Christ, one Bishop». In Rome, Liberius was in reality deprived of any power and constrained to exercise a form of joint government with Felix. Liberius was not invited to attend the synod of Rimini and did not send legates. The Oriental Bishops, under pressure from the emperor, accepted an Arian profession of faith. With the death of Constantius II in 361, Liberius resumed the government of the Roman Church. He annulled the decisions of Rimini but instituted a policy of pacification which led to the Oriental Bishops being readmitted to communion with the Roman See in return for their acceptance of the Nicean profession of faith. Liberius built a basilica on the Esquiline hill which, from the fifth century, would take the name of Saint Mary Major. In 354, the important list of emperors, consuls, Popes, and martyrs known as the *Chronographicon,* was completed.

37. St. Damasus I *(366-384)*

The son of a priest, St. Damasus was born in Rome circa 305. He was ordained a deacon by Liberius whom he accompanied into exile. On return to Rome, he supported the anti-Pope Felix, but broke with him and was reconciled with Liberius in 358. Following the death of Liberius, a group of his supporters elected Ursinus as anti-Pope to Damasus. The supporters of Damasus mounted an armed attack on those of Ursinus. According to the pagan historian Ammianus Marcellinus, they killed more than a hundred of them. The Pope subsequently made recourse to the Prefect of Rome to have his rival Felix sent into exile. This was the first appeal made to the civil power by the Bishop of Rome. Damascus governed the diocese of Rome in close collaboration with the court and the Roman aristocracy. While this contributed much to the conversion of the Roman aristocracy to Christianity, it led to many charges being levelled against Damasus - including that of being an «enchanter of matrons». In 371, a scandalous accusation, probably of adultery, was made against him by a convert Jew. He was able to assert his innocence only with the assistance of the emperor. Damasus was severe in the repression of any deviation from orthodoxy and condemned the Appolinarians and the Macedonians. He lent no support to the reestablishment of orthodoxy in the East. No efforts were made to court the Eastern Church which, at that time, was led by St. Basil of Caesarea. Although regarded as the second ecumenical council, Damasus took no part in the Council of Constantinople of 381. He strongly defended the primacy of Rome, using the term «Sedes Apostolica» to denote the papal see, and established the principle that a profession of faith was only rendered orthodox by being approved by the Roman Pontiff. He persuaded the imperial authorities to recognize the exclusive jurisdiction of the Roman See over the western episcopate. He failed, however, in efforts to obtain immunity from the imperial courts for the Pope. He obtained the official recognition of Christianity, in the form professed in Rome, from the emperor Theodosius I, thereby giving effect to a decision already reached in the edict of Thessalonika of 381. Damasus held that the primacy of the Bishop of Rome was based on his being the direct successor of Peter, and not on any synodal decision, as the emperor held. He did much to Christianize the city of Rome, especially through the building of many churches, including San Lorenzo in Damaso, the restoration of the catacombs and the promotion of the cult of the martyrs. He reorganized the papal archives. St. Jerome was appointed his secretary. It is likely that the Pope charged Jerome with the revision of the early Latin translations of the Gospels, which would serve as the basis for the Vulgate, the Latin version of the Bible commonly ascribed to St. Jerome. Damasus dictated many important epigrams celebrating the martyrs and his papal predecessors which were elegantly transcribed by Philocalus. Many of these have survived to the present. Buried initially on the via Ardeatina, his remains were subsequently transferred to the basilica of San Lorenzo in Damasus. His feast day is 11 December.

38. St. Siricius *(384-399)*

St. Siricius, a Roman, had been a deacon under his predecessors Liberius and Damasus I. His election was supported by the emperor Valentinian II. He came into conflict with St. Jerome, who described him as «frank and easily fooled», as well as with St. Paulinus of Nola. He pursued the policies of his predecessors to consolidate the primacy of Rome. He introduced the use of decretals, which have the force of edicts and are as binding as synodal canons. The earliest one to survive, addressed to the Bishop of Tarragona and subsequently transmitted to all of the western bishops, dealt with ecclesiastical discipline. In 386, he convoked a synod which determined that no bishop could be nominated without the recognition of the Bishop of Rome. He laid the foundation of the papal vicariate in Illyricum and conceded regional jurisdiction for all episcopal nominations to the Bishop of Thessalonika. This measure was intended to stem the influence of the Church of Constantinople in eastern Illyricum. He opposed the heresy of the Spanish bishop, Priscillianus, but disapproved of his execution by the imperial authorities, and refused to grant communion to those bishops who had, for the first time in the Church's history, pronounced the death sentence for heresy. Siricius also intervened in the dispute on the virginity of the Blessed Virgin Mary and condemned those who maintained that she had had other children after the birth of Jesus. He was buried in the basilica of St. Sylvester, near the cemetery of Priscilla. On the basis of the St. Jerome's criticisms, Siricius was initially omitted from the *Martyrologium Romanum,* but added to it in 1748 by Benedict XIV who had written a pamphlet demonstrating his sanctity. His feast day is 26 November.

39. St. Anastasius I *(399-401)*

St. Anastasius was born in Rome. During his pontificate a controversy broke out between St. Jerome, by then settled in Bethlehem, and Rufinus of Aquileia concerning Origen. Rufinus had translated the *De Principiis* into Latin and was intent on rehabilitating the great third century theologian. However, the Pope accepted the criticisms of Origen made by St. Jerome and had Origen's thought again condemned in synod. Anastasius intervened, with little success, in the Donatist controversy which was then raging in the Church of Africa. He maintained good relations with St. Jerome and with St. Paulinus of Nola, both of whom had been critical of his predecessor. He was buried in the cemetery of Pontian on the via Portuense. His feast day is 19 December.

40. St. Innocent I *(401-417)*

According to St. Jerome, Innocent I was the son of Anastasius I. Innocent was an important Pope and vigorously defended the Roman primacy. Thirty-three surviving decretals clearly indicate that Innocent did not limit himself to the various questions addressed in them, but also asserted the doctrinal primacy of the Roman Church. This primacy was not confined to the West. Innocent sought firmly, but without much success, to extend it to the Eastern Church. An opportunity arose in 404 to further this policy with the exiling of St. John Chrystosom, Bishop of Constantinople. Innocent strongly protested and sent a delegation to the emperor. Chrystosom, however, died in exile. Similarly, he made interventions to protect the monastery founded by St. Jerome in Bethlehem which was attacked by armed bands and accused the Bishop of Jerusalem of having allowed the situation to develop. At the insistence of St. Augustine and the African Church, he condemned the pelagian heresy which asserted a primacy of free will over grace. In 408, Alaric the Goth lay siege to Rome. The Pope rejected calls from the starving population for the offering of public sacrifices to the gods but tolerated private sacrifices. Innocent was at Ravenna imploring the assistance of the emperor Honorius when, on 24 August 410, Alaric conquered and sacked Rome. He returned to Rome only in 412, his absence having been interpreted as an act of providence to save the life of the head of the Church. He was interred alongside of his father, Anastasius I, in the cemetery of Pontian. His feast day is 12 March.

41. St. Zosimus *(417-418)*

St. Zosimus was a Greek, possibly of Jewish origin. His was a pontificate much troubled by controversy. He attempted to assert papal authority in an authoritarian manner. He alienated the bishops of Gaul by conceding wide powers to his supporter, Patroculus. He intervened in the pelagian controversy without taking into account the condemnation issued by his predecessor, and even criticized that same condemnation. Subsequently, the African bishops made appeal to the emperor, and forced Zosimus to change his opinion of the Pelagians whom he eventually condemned in a document, the *Tractoria,* which was circulated among the Eastern and Western bishops. His conflict with the African bishops was reignited when he attempted to impose his jurisdiction on the African dioceses. His authoritarianism also created difficulties in Rome, where he died shortly before he was due to excommunicate a group of his opponents. He was buried in San Lorenzo in via Tiburtina. His name does not appear in the fifth century *Martyrologium Hieronyminianum* but only in the ninth century martyrology of Adon. His feast day is 26 December.

42. St. Boniface I *(418-422)*

The son of a priest, Boniface was born in Rome. His election was contested by the election of the anti-Pope Eulalius who had the support of the pagan Prefect of Rome, Symmachus, who exiled the Pope from Rome. Following two synods, the emperor Honorius, whose sister Galla Placidia knew Boniface, declared him rightful pontiff. Modifications of the rules governing the election of the Pope were introduced which required an unanimous election. During his Pontificate, there was a firm consolidation of the Roman primacy and decisions in matters placed before Apostolic See could not be contested. Boniface attempted to extend the Roman primacy to the Oriental Churches when the emperor tried to have the diocese of Illyricum subjected to the Church of Constantinople. He fought strenuously against the pelagian heresy and obtained the emperor's approval for measures requiring all bishops to subscribe to the *Tractoria* of his predecessor. He was buried in the cemetery of St. Felicity on the via Salaria. His feast day is 4 September.

43. St. Celestine I *(422-432)*

Celestine, archdeacon of Rome, was born in the Campania. He was elected without controversy. Celestine was a correspondent of St. Augustine. As with his predecessors, he was in conflict with the African bishops whose traditional autonomy he failed curb. Through a system of vicars, he imposed Roman authority on Eastern Illyricum. He sent Germanus of Auxerre to Britain to combat the pelagian heresy. In 431, he consecrated the deacon Palladius as first Bishop of Ireland. He firmly imposed Roman authority on the dioceses of Southern Gaul. Celestine succeeded in expelling the principal supporters of pelagianism from the East. To a letter to the bishops of Gaul on the subject of pelagianism, the so called *Capitula Caelistina* was appended which contained a digest of various Augustinian positions on grace which was probably written by Prosper of Aquitaine. At the outbreak of the Christological controversy between Nestorius of Constantinople and Cyril of Alexandria, both appealed to the Pope: Nestorius held that the divine and human natures were separate in Christ, thereby questioning the validity of the term «*theotokos*» or «Mother of God». In a synod held in Roma, Celestine condemned Nestorius and threaten him with excommunication. He deputed Cyril of Alexandria to obtain a retraction from his adversary Nestorius. The emperor Theodosius II attempted to resolve the problem by convoking an ecumenical council, the third in the Church's history, which was held at Ephesus in 431. The council was decisively led by Cyril who excommunicated and exiled Nestorius to Antioch before the arrival of the Papal legates. The Pope approved the condemnation of nestorianism while attempting to save John of Antioch for the orthodox party since his moderate nestorian positions had also been condemned by the council. Celestine restored the Basilica Julia (Santa Maria in Trastevere) which had been damaged during Alaric's sackage of Rome, and he built Santa Sabina. He was buried in the cemetery of Priscilla where his mausoleum was decorated with frescos, now lost, depicting the Council of Ephesus. His feast day is 27 July.

44. St. Sixtus III (432-440)

St. Sixtus, a Roman, exerted much diplomatic effort to extend the Roman primacy in the East. Together with the emperor Theodosius II, he attempted to resolve the conflict between Cyril of Alexandria, the principal exponent of orthodoxy Christology, and John of Antioch, who held a moderate nestorian position. Reconciliation was achieved in 433 with the so called *formula unionis*, a profession of faith drawn up by the Antiochiens and accepted by St. Cyril of Alexandria. He succeeded in retaining Roman jurisdiction in the Illyrian provinces which Proclus, Bishop of Constantinople, had attempted to annex. At San Sebastiano on the Appian way, he founded the first documented monastery in Rome and began a building project in the City which saw the construction of a new Baptistery at the Lateran. He decorated the Basilica Liberiana (Santa Maria Maggiore) with mosaics and inscriptions celebrating the Church's triumph over pelagianism. He first appears as a saint in the ninth century *Martyrologium* of Adon. His feast day is 19 August.

45. St. Leo I (the Great) 440-461

St. Leo was born in Rome to a family of Tuscan origin. He was a highly influential deacon under his two immediate predecessors. Elected Pope while on a diplomatic mission to the emperor in Gaul, his was a most important pontificate. Alone with Gregory I he shares the appellative of «great». His pontificate was governed by the principle that the Church's authority had been given to Peter by Christ, and had passed directly to his successors, the Bishops of Rome. The Pope was thus «primate of all bishops». Leo the Great exercised an unrivalled authority throughout the West. He was vigilant against heresy and concerned to control the activities of the bishops so as to eradicate abuses, unify practice, and pacify controversy. The African bishops accepted his authority. He encouraged the imperial authorities to reactivate legislation against the Manichaens, and exercised firm control in the Illyrian vicariate. His relations with the East were more difficult and dominated by the outbreak of the monophysite heresy, led by the monk Euthycius, according to whose teaching Christ had but one nature which was divine. Condemned by his bishop, Flavian of Constantinople, Eutychius appealed to the Pope who also condemned him and reaffirmed the doctrine of the two natures in one person of Christ with the *Tomus*. In 449 the emperor accepted the thesis of Eutychius in a synod and imprisoned those who had opposed the monk. With difficulty, the Papal legates succeeded in escaping. The Pope reacted vehemently and in 451 the emperor convoked the fourth ecumenical council at Chalcedon on the Bosphorus. The Council annulled the decisions of the synod of Ephesus and reaffirmed doctrinal orthodoxy as expounded in the *Tomus Leonis*. «Peter has spoken through Leo» said the bishops present at the Council. The Council of Chalcedon, however, did not accept the papal claims to jurisdiction over the Oriental dioceses. Rather it emphasized the privileges of the See of Constantinople which, like Rome, was also an imperial city. This decision was rejected by Leo who declared it contrary to the canons of the Council of Nicea of 325. Leo's preoccupation with maintaining some jurisdiction over the Oriental bishops led to the nomination of a papal vicar, or *apocrisarius,* in Constantinople. The name of Leo the Great is inexorably linked with his famous meeting in Mantua with Attilla the Hun where he persuaded him to abandon his march towards the South, thereby saving Rome. His efforts to persuade Genseric, the king of the Barbarians, to abandon his siege of Rome failed, and the City was duly sacked and devastated in 455. Ninety-six sermons and four hundred letter of Leo survive, most of them the work of his chancellery. The *Sacramentarium Leonianum* , a collection of liturgical texts dating from the sixth and seventh centuries, is not the work of Leo, although ascribed to him. In 1754, he was declared a doctor of the Church by Benedict XIV. Rather than being a theologian, Leo the Great was a brilliant preacher and a lucid codifyer of Christian orthodoxy. His remains were initially interred in the atrium of St. Peter's but removed to the interior of the basilica in 688. His feast day is 10 November.

46. St. Hilary *(461-468)*

St. Hilary was born in Sardinia and had been archdeacon of Rome under Leo the Great. Hilary had also attended the synod of Ephesus as Papal legate, and only succeeded in avoiding arrest through the intervention of St. John the Evangelist. He continued many of the policies of his illustrious predecessor. His relations with the Oriental Churches were marked by his concern to reassert the Roman primacy and reaffirm the decisions of the Council of Chalcedon in relation to the monophysite heresy. In the West he struggled against the increasing influence of Arianism which was promoted by the barbarians, and had even succeeded in having an Arian church built in the City and a bishop installed there. He opposed the emperor Anthemius who encouraged heretical groups in the Rome. He made frequent interventions in Gaul and Spain to uphold the authority of the Roman See and ecclesiastical discipline. He forbade bishops to designate their successors. Hilary built three chapels in the Lateran Baptistery and restored many of the churches damaged during the sack of Genseric. He founded the monastery at San Lorenzo fuori le Mura where he was interred. His feast day is 28 February.

47. St. Simplicius *(468-483)*

St. Simplicius was born in Tivoli. During his pontificate, the last of the western emperors, Romulus Agustulus, was deposed, Odoacer the German became king of Italy, and roman-barbarian kingdoms were formed throughout the West. The Pope, concerned to maintain the Roman primacy in the West, established a Spanish vicariate which he entrusted to the Bishop of Seville. During the pontificate of Simplicius, the Oriental bishops extracted themselves almost completely from papal influence. This process was facilitated, on the one hand, by the decision of the Council of Chalcedon which emphasised the privileges of the See of Constantinople and tended to set the Eastern Patriarch on a par with the Bishop of Rome, and on the other, by the emperor in Constantinople actively promoting autonomy in the East where the monophysite heresy raged with the open support of the usurper Basilicus, and that of the restored emperor Zenon after 476. In 482, Acacius, Bishop of Constantinople, published, with the consent of Zenon, a formula of reconciliation between the Monophysites and the Calcedonians (the so-called *Henoticon*) making many concessions to the Monophysites. The Pope protested, but to no avail, and was eventually excluded from all decisions taken in the East, about which he was no longer even informed. He continued the policy of building churches in Rome. He re-structured a private pagan house on the Esquiline and converted it to Christian worship, dedicating it to Saint Andrew. It was demolished in 1684. He also built Santo Stefano Rotondo on the Coelian hill. He was buried beside St Leo the Great in the atrium of St. Peter. His feast day is 10 March.

48. St. Felix III (II) *(483-492)*

A Roman of aristocratic birth and the son of a widower who subsequently became a priest, St. Felix was also a widower with two children. He was elected in accordance with the wishes of his predecessor, St. Simplicius, and with the support of Odoacer. He is called Felix III, and not Felix II, because of the inclusion in the list of Popes of Felix, who had been anti-Pope at the time of Liberius. He was severe and rigid. During his pontificate the first schism between East and West took place and lasted for thirty-five years (484-519). His election was officially communicated to the emperor Zenon. Felix was the first of the Roman Pontiffs to make such a communication, and used the occasion to denounce the monophysite heresy to which both the emperor Zenon and Acacius, Patriarch of Constantinople, subscribed. Acacius was excommunicated and schism declared when the sentence was made public. This schism was long protracted because of the obstinacy of both the Pope and the Patriarch. The Pope refused to enter into any form of agreement, even when Odoacer was anxious to improve his relations with the emperor, neither after the death of Acacius nor after that of Zenon. Neither would he hear the pleas of the new orthodox Patriarch who tried in vain to reestablish the unity of the Church, especially following the accession of the monophysite emperor Anastasius I in 491. The Vandals, who were Arians and had assumed dominance in North Africa, unleashed a bitter persecution of the Church during this pontificate. Following the persecution, the Pope issued very severe norms for the readmittance of those who had been forcefully re-baptized by the Arians. He was buried in St. Paul's near to his father, his wife and to his children. His feast day is 1 March.

49. St. Gelasius I *(492-496)*

Of African origin, Gelasius was born in Rome and had been one of his predecessor's closest advisors. At the time of his election, Theoretic, king of the Goths, was laying siege to Ravenna, while Rome was gripped by famine. The Pope maintained good relations with the Gothic sovereign, who was Arian but tolerant of the Church. He also provided the City with food supplies and fed the poor from his personal patrimony. Gelasius temporarily made priestly ordination more easily accessible so as to alleviate the shortage of priests in the Roman Church. His relations with the Eastern Church were marked by deep intransigence which further embittered the schism initiated by his predecessor. Gelasius fought with the monophysite emperor Anastasius I. He consistently asserted the Roman primacy and was the first of the Popes to use the title *Vicar of Christ*. Gelasius also provided a systematic exposition of the theory of the two powers, that of the Pope and that of the emperor, both of whom were sovereign and independent in their respective spheres, and which asserted the superiority of spiritual over temporal power. He tried actively to extend his authority to the Eastern Church where, he feared, political disintegration would be followed by ecclesiastical disintegration. In Rome he countered an attempt by some of the aristocracy to revive the pagan *Lupercalia*. Gelasius was an accomplished theologian who has left some one hundred letters and six theological tracts. The *Sacramentarium Gelesianum* and the *Decretum Gelesianum* are not, however, his works. Much loved by the Romans, Gelasius was buried in St. Peter's. His feast day is 20 November.

50. Anastasius II *(496-498)*

A Roman, Anastasius was elected because of his more conciliatory line with the Oriental Church. He immediately set about healing the schism that had begun during the pontificate of St. Felix III. His embassy to the emperor was accompanied by a delegation from the Gothic king Theoderic, led by the head of the Roman Senate, Festus, which sought recognition of Theoderic as king of Italy. The emperor took advantage of this request to open negotiations with the Pope for concessions in relation to the *Henoticon*, the formula at the root of the schism that had never been accepted by Rome, in exchange for recognition of Theoderic as king of Italy. The Papal legates entered into an arrangement which was highly compromising. The episode aroused strong opposition to the Pope in Rome and threatened to create a schism within the Roman Church until Anastasius unexpectedly died, struck by divine retribution as his opponents maintained. Medieval tradition lists Anastasius as a traitor and a heretic. No cult was ascribe to him. Dante places him among the heresiarcs (*Inferno*, IX, 6-9). He was buried in the atrium of St. Peter's.

51. St. Symmachus *(498-514)*

A convert from paganism, St. Symmachus was born in Sardinia. He was elected Pope in the Lateran by the anti-Byzantine faction while Lawrence was elected anti- Pope at the Basilica of St. Mary Major by the pro-Byzantine faction, led by Festus. Theoderic, although an Arian, decided the election in favour of Symmachus who immediately introduced norms reserving such election to the clergy of Rome, but which also provided for the possibility of the Pope to designate his successor. In 501, the pro-Byzantine party returned to the fray, accusing the Pope before Theoderic of lapses of chastity and dispersal of ecclesiastical goods. The Pope took refuge in St. Peters while Theoderic appointed a bishop to rule the See until Symmachus could be tried. The synod convoked by Theoderic absolved Symmachus of the charges brought against him, on the grounds that no tribunal could pass judgment on him since he was the lawfully elected Pope. The acquittal, however, did not resolve the problem because Theoretic, who was allied with the Byzantines, refused to confirm the decision. For four years, the anti-Pope Lawrence governed the See of Rome from the Lateran while the Pope remained confined to St. Peter's. The situation was resolved in 506 when Theoretic recognised the sentence of the synod he had convoked and restored rightful power to the Pope. From then on, the Pope governed energetically, expelling the Manichaens from the City, and intervening in episcopal elections in Gaul. He adopted a rigid attitude to the Eastern Church and to the emperor who refused to recognise him as the legitimate Pope. He increased the size of St. Peter's and introduced the *Gloria in excelsis Deo* to Masses celebrated by bishops. He was buried in the atrium of St. Peter's. His feast day is 19 July.

52. St. Hormisdas (514-523)

Born of an aristocratic family in Frosinone, Hormisdas was a widower whose only son, Silverius, would in turn also become Pope. He was a close advisor of St. Symmachus and was probably designated by him. During this pontificate, the schism with the Eastern Church was finally ended. The initiative for this move came from the emperor Anastasius at a time when Chalcedonian orthodoxy was once again in the ascendant. The Pope, however, imposed severe terms on the emperor which were conveyed to Constantinople by two embassies. These reasserted the profession of faith established by the Council of Chalcedon, and the jurisdictional primacy of the Roman Church. The impasse was resolved by the emperor's death. His successor, Justin, was orthodox and immediately accepted the Christological doctrine of Chalcedon. In 519, a further papal embassy brought a profession of faith to Constantinople which was signed by the Patriarch, John of Constantinople, and by the entire Eastern hierarchy on the emperor's instruction. This profession of faith also contained an acknowledgement of the Roman primacy, the text of which was incorporated into *Pastor aeternus* by the First Vatican Council in 1870. Signature of the profession of faith was deemed sufficient to sanate the schism and restore the Eastern Church to Catholic orthodoxy. It did not, however, resolve the question of Roman jurisdiction in the East. Further conflict arose with the efforts of the emperor Justinian to have the theopaschite formula (one of the persons of the Trinity suffered in the flesh) accepted, so as to exclude nestorian interpretations of the Chalcedonian formula. St. Hormisdas' interest in matters relating to the Eastern Church is evident in his having charged the Scythian monk, Dionysius, with the preparation of a Latin translation of the canons of the Greek Church. He was buried in St. Peter's, his epitaph, in elegiac verse, was composed by Silverius, his son and subsequent successor in the See of Rome. His feast day is 6 August.

53. St. John I (523-526)

St. John was born in Tuscany and already old at the time of his election. John, who had at one time supported the anti-Pope Lawrence and the pro-Byzantine party, was a friend of the philosopher Boethius who dedicated three theological works to him before his master, Theoderic, executed him. During his pontificate, the Alexandrian method of calculating the date of Easter was adopted by the Roman Church and subsequently extended to whole Western Church. In Italy, John's pontificate was much troubled by the persecution of the Arians begun by the emperor Justin. All Arian churches in the Byzantine empire were confiscated, Arians were expelled from all public offices and many of them forcibly converted. Many of the Arians were Goths. These events caused Theoderic to have the Pope lead a delegation to Constantinople to obtain an end to the persecution, the restitution of confiscated goods and the possibility of those forcibly converted to the Church to return to Arianism. This was the first voyage to the East undertaken by the Roman Pontiff and he was accompanied by bishops and senators. His arrival in Constantinople was a triumph -the emperor prostrated himself before the Pope. On Easter Sunday, the Pope presided at Mass, celebrated in the Latin Rite, on a throne higher than that of the Patriarch. Most of Theoderic's demands were met except that permitting converts to revert to Arianism. Furious with the outcome of the embassy, Theoderic imprisoned the delegation on its return to Italy and detained the Pope in Ravenna where he died a short time after. He was buried in the nave of St. Peter's where his epitaph described him as a «victim for Christ». He was immediately venerated as a saint. His feast day is 18 May.

54. St. Felix IV *(526-530)*

Born in Sammnium, Felix had been a member of the delegation sent to Constantinople by Hormisdas. He was elected in accordance with the will of Theoderic, who died shortly afterwards, leaving Athalric as his successor under the regency of his mother Amalasontha. The new Pope continued to maintain good relations with the court, as can be seen from the donations of the king to the papacy. He ordained very many priests, which can be interpreted as an attempt to renew the Roman clergy. With the support of Caesarius, Bishop of Arles, he intervened against the semi-pelagians, sending twenty-five doctrinal propositions on grace and free will which were mainly taken from the writings of St. Augustine. Their adoption by the synod of Orange marked the end of the pelagian heresy. The Pope continued to transform pagan temples into churches. A mosaic of Felix is to be found in the Basilica of Ss. Cosmas and Damien which was heavily restored in the sixteenth century. He designated the archdeacon Boniface as his successor on his death bed. His feast day is 22 September.

55. Boniface II *(530-532)*

Boniface was Roman of German origin. His designation as Pope by his predecessor provoked a reaction in the pro-Byzantine Senate which elected an anti-Pope, Dioscurus. The most significant act of this pontificate was a synod convoked in Rome in 531 in which the Pope designated the deacon Vigilius, a supporter of the Goths, as his successor, and the subsequent retraction of this act as a result of the reactions it had provoked. He was buried in St. Peter's but no cult was ever ascribed to him.

56. John II *(533-535)*

John, a Roman, was elected after a vacancy of more than two months. His election was a compromise in a context dominated by massive corruption which was, however, unable to secure the election of any candidate. He was a priest of St. Clement's called Mercury. He changed his pagan name to assume a Christian one - the first of the Popes to change his name. The problem of the papal election reached such a state that the Gothic king, Athalaric, issued a decree prohibiting irregularities in papal elections and strictly limiting the amounts of money that could be used for electoral expenses. John succeeded in maintaining good relations with the Gothic court and the emperor Justinian during his pontificate. The Pope accepted an imperial decree which included the doctrines formulated by the four ecumenical councils, held in Nicea (325), Constantinople (381), Ephesus (431) and in Chalcedon (451), as well formulations of the teopaschite which some years earlier had been rejected, though not condemned, by Saint Hormisdas. The emperor was anxious to have these formulas accepted so as to win over the moderate Monophysites to orthodoxy. John continued to support the imperial formulas even when some of the monks of Constantinople (the so-called *acemeti*), who were allies of Rome, appealed to the Pope against the emperor. John excommunicated the monks and declared orthodox the decree of Justinian who included both the papal decision and the papal decree in his code of law. John II is often cited as an example of a Pope who adopted a position differing from that of his predecessors in doctrinal questions.

57. St. Agapitus I *(535-536)*

Agapitus was the son of a priest of aristocratic birth who had been killed by the supporters of the anti-Pope Lawrence. He was a strict and energetic Pope who opposed the practice of successors being designated by their immediate predecessors. He was a cultured man who assembled an important library in his family palace on the Coelian. Together with Cassidorus, he intended to found a Christian academy in Rome along the lines of those in Alexandria, and Nisbi in Mesopotamia. During his brief pontificate, he opposed Justinian's design for the reintegration of the Arian clergy following his victory over the Vandals in Africa. At that time, Justinian was preparing an invasion of Italy to annex it for the Empire. The Gothic king, Theodatus, who had come to the throne by murdering the widow of Theoretic, sent the Pope to Constantinople to persuade Justinian to abandon his threatened invasion of Italy. The Roman Church was in poor economic circumstances at this time and the Pope was forced to pledge the sacred vessels to finance the journey. The Pope was received with triumph in Constantinople but he failed to convince the emperor. His mission, however, was successful in other respects, especially in having Antemius, who enjoyed the empress' protection, removed as Patriarch of Constantinople having accused him of monophysitism. Agapitus confirmed the teopaschite formula approved by his predecessor John II. The Pope died in Constantinople. His body, sealed in a leaden coffin, was returned to Rome for burial in St. Peter's. His feast day is 22 April.

58. St. Silverius *(536-537)*

St. Silverius, son of St. Hormisdas, was born at Frosinone and elected Pope on the insistence of the Gothic king Theodatus, after news of Agapatus' death in Constantinople reached Rome. Theodatus was most anxious to ensure the election of a pro-Gothic Pope so as defend his interests against the ambitions of Justinian. Meanwhile, the empress Theodora, who supported Antemius, the deposed Patriarch of Constantinople, made a pact with Vigilius, the Papal representative in Constantinople, whereby he agreed to re-instate Antemius as Patriarch of Constantinople in return for his own election to the papacy. Vigilius returned to Rome where he found that a Pope had already been elected. At this point, the Byzantine general, Belisarius, occupied Rome, having failed to persuade the recently elected Pope to vacate the papal throne. Silverius was accused of plotting with the Goths who were then laying siege to the City. The accusation was false that the Pope, together with the Senate, had persuaded the Romans to open their gates to the Byzantines. The pretext was sufficient for Belisarius who deposed Silvarius, stripping him of the pallium and reducing him to the status of a monk. The Pope was deported to Patara in Lycia, an act which aroused the anger of Justinian who ordered that the Pope should be tried in Rome and restored to his throne should his innocence be proven. Vigilius, however, who had become Pope, had him deported to the island of Ponza where he was forced to abdicate. He died shortly afterwards of privation. He was buried on the island and his tomb became a place of cult. He has been venerated as a martyr since the eleventh century. His feast day is June 20.

59. Vigilius *(537-555)*

A Roman of noble birth, Vigilius had been designated Pope by his predecessor Boniface II but was constrained to decline designation. He was nominated *apocrisarius*, or papal delegate, in Constantinople where he made a pact with the empress Theodora which won him the papal throne. He was responsible for the deportation of his predecessor, St. Silverius. This pontificate was characterized by violent conflict with the emperor. The problem began in 543 when Justinian, desiring to win over the Monophysites to Catholic orthodoxy, published an edict in which he condemned three theologians of the fifth century rigorously faithful to the Christology of Chalcedon, accusing them of Nestorianism, and called on the Pope and the Patriarchs to confirm the decree. This amounted to the abandonment of the Christology settled on at the Council of Chalcedon in 451. After some initial resistence, the Oriental bishops succumbed and accepted the imperial decree. Initially, Vigilius refused to accept Justinian's imposition but, having been arrested while celebrating Mass in Santa Cecilia and deported to Constantinople via Sicily, he submitted and issued a verdict in 548, the *Iudicium*, in which he accepted the condemnation. The Western episcopate reacted with great indignation. At this point, both Pope and emperor decided to convoke a council to resolve the matter, and Vigilius retracted the *Iudicium*. The emperor, however, did not yield and issued a new condemnation in 551 on the advice of his theologian Askidas. Vigilius refused to accept this second condemnation and excommunicated Askidas. Following arrest and flight, he took refuge in the conciliar church in Chalcedon from which he issued an encyclical letter defending the *Tria Capitula*. An ecumenical Council, the fifth, was held in Constantinople in 553 without papal participation. It was dominated by the emperor who obtained the condemnation of the *Tira Capitula* and coerced the Pope into approving the condemnation, having imprisoned him and his counsellors. After much negotiation, the Pope ceded and approved the decisions of the Council. In return for his agreement, Vigilius obtained the *Pragmatic sanction* from the emperor which granted notable concessions to the Roman Church in those areas of Italy still under Byzantine dominion. On the return journey to Rome, Virgilius died at Syracuse. Given the reputation he had enjoyed in life, he was not buried in St. Peter's but in the cemetery of Priscilla on the via Salaria.

60. Pelagius I *(556-561)*

Pelagius was Roman and born of a noble family. He had accompanied St. Agapitus I on his mission to Constantinople in 536. He was *apocrisarius* of Pope Vigilius in Constantinople and one of the counsellors of Justinian, to whom he recommended the condemnation of the writings of Origen in 543. He was vicar for Vigilius in Rome from 544 to 551 while the Pope was in Constantinople. He ruled during the siege and capture of the City by Totila, the Goth in 547. During the most difficult stage of the *Tria Capitula* controversy he was present in Constantinople and supported the Pope in his conflict with the emperor. When the Pope capitulated, he violently attacked Vigilius in an work entitle *In defence of the Three Chapters*. In his turn, however, Pelagius succumbed and accepted the imperial edict, in return for which he became the imperial candidate for the papacy. Following Vigilius' death, Pelagius, who was not thought guiltless of it, succeeded as Pope, without election, though possibly with the approval of the Latin clergy in Constantinople. No bishop could be found to consecrate him, until eventually those of Perugia and Ferentino could be prevailed upon to do the deed. Having been consecrated, flanked by Narsetes the Byzantine governor, Pelagius made an unusual declaration affirming his loyalty to the Councils, especially Chalcedon, and swore that he had done no harm to his predecessor. Although heavily compromised and regarded as a traitor imposed by the Byzantines, Pelagius proved an energetic and capable steward of the Roman Church. In virtue of the *Pragmatic sanction*, he exercised far-reaching powers in his own right which he used to reorganize papal finances and the property of the Roman Church, to restore law and order in the City following the sieges and wars, to relieve the poor, and to improve monastic life and the morale of the clergy. In Rome, Pelagius grew in the favour of the people, but he was detested by the greater part of the Western bishops who refused to give him obedience, especially in Gaul and Nortern Italy, where the Sees of Aquileia and Milan came close to schism. In an effort to obtain the obedience of those who dissented, he called on the Byzantine governor to make armed intervention. Narsetes refused. In commemoration of the triumph of the Byzantines over the Goths, he began the construction of the Basilica of St. Philip and St. James (the present Basilica of the Twelve Apostles) which was based on the cruciform plan of the *Apostoleion* built by Justinian in Constantinople. Pelagius was buried in St. Peter's.

61. **John III** *(561-574)*

The son of a Roman Senator, John was called Catellinus prior to his election. He was doubly indebted to the Byzantines. The Lombards invaded Italy during his pontificate. Justin II, Justinian's successor, deposed Narsetes the Byzantine exarch, thereby weakening the Byzantine frontier. The Lombard invasion facilitated the resolution of the *Tria Capitula* controversy and the reconciliation of the Western and Eastern Churches. Relations were resumed with the bishops of Africa, the new Bishop of Milan returned to communion with Rome and signed the condemnation of the *Tria Capitula*; only Aquileia remained in schism. The defence of Rome against the Lombards easily convinced the Pope of the need to solicit the assistance of Narsetes. The deposed exarch settled in Rome, but the general odium which surrounded him eventually had repercussion for the Pope, who removed his residence two miles outside of the City on the Appian way in an attempt to avoid public disturbances. Thence he continued his mandate until his death which happened soon after that of Narsetes. He completed the building of the Basilica of St. Philip and St. James, begun by his predecessor in commemoration of the victory of Narsetes over the Goths. He was buried in St. Peter's.

62. Benedict I *(575-579)*

Benedict was born in Rome. Little is known of his pontificate. He attempted to strengthen the episcopate by ordaining twenty-one bishops. He created an archbishopric in Ravenna in an effort to reinforce Roman influence in the city which had become the imperial residence in Italy. In 579, as the Lombards laid siege to Rome, he despatched a delegation to Constantinople to ask for assistance. However, the Byzantine forces were neither plentiful nor sufficient. He died during the siege and was buried in the sacristy of St. Peter's.

63. Pelagius II *(579-590)*

The son of a Goth born in Rome, Pelagius was elected during the Lombard siege and consecrated without imperial confirmation. He immediately despatched his deacon Gregory (the future Gregory the Great) to Constantinople to seek imperial assistance. The emperor, who was then involved in war against the Persians, advised him to make a truce with the Lombards and to seek the help of the Franks. In 580, Pelagius vainly sought the assistance of the Frankish king. Between 585 and 589 an armistice was declared between the Byzantines and the Lombards. The Pope, unsuccessfully, attempted to reconcile the Church of Aquileia and Istria by persuasion and military force. The Visigothic king of Spain, Recaredo, converted to Christianity during this pontificate. Relations with the patriarch of Constantinople were more tense for Pelagius refused to recognise the title of *Ecumenical Patriarch* which John IV had conferred on himself in a synod held in 588. A further schism broke out. The Pope raised the floor of the Basilica of St. Peter so as to situate the altar immediately above the tomb of the apostle and re-built the Basilica of San Lorenzo fuori le Mura. In 589, following a disastrous flood, plague appeared in the City and claimed the Pope as one of its many victims. He was buried in the atrium of St. Peter's.

64. St. Gregory (I) the Great *(590-604)*

After Leo I, Gregory I is the only other Pope to bear the appellative of great. He was born, about 540, to an aristocratic Roman family that had already given two Popes to the Roman Church, St. Felix III and St. Agapitus. He had been Prefect of Rome from about 572 to 574, when he became a monk and transformed his house on the Coelian into a monastery dedicated to St. Andrew. He also erected six monasteries on his property in Sicily. Benedict I recalled him to active life and ordained him a deacon in 578. He was sent to Constantinople as *apocrisarius* in 579 by Pelagius II. On his return to Rome, he became an advisor of the Pope and was unanimously elected his successor. Gregory had no desire to abandon the contemplative life and attempted to remain faithful to the monastic life even while exercising his new roles, by living as a monk. He tried to avoid election. He regarded himself as the «*servus servorum Dei*». He was one of the Church's greatest Popes, occupying himself most competently with its spiritual and temporal administration. In an Italy devastated by the Lombards, abandoned by the Byzantines, and a helpless prey to every form of social and political disorder, Gregory assumed the responsibility of exercising the last remaining civil and political power which he transmitted to the Mediaeval Church. He moved against the Lombards firmly but with political caution, in an effort to win from them a universal peace and their conversion to Christianity which was calculated to bring them within the ambit of normal political activity. To obtain this end he negotiated, agreed truces, and paid armies. He reorganized the vast territorial possessions of the Church in Italy, Sicily, Dalmatia, Africa and in Gaul into the *Patrimony of St. Peter*, thereby laying the basis for the future Papal States. He re-organised these territories administratively and socially and ruled them through rectors who were directly responsible to the Pope. He was particularly sensitive to the plight of the poor and ensured that the administration came to their assistance. He re-organized the clergy, enforced clerical celibacy and regulated the competencies of bishops. His ecclesiastical policy in the West aimed at sanating the *Tria Capitula* schism in the Venetian region and in Istria, building relations with Visigothic Spain and Frankish Gaul, as well as with the conversion of the Angels for which purpose he despatched forty monks from his monastery on the Coelian and later nominated its prior, Augustine, as Archbishop. His relations with the East were difficult. Gregory realistically accepted the situation of ecclesiastical subordination to the political power, but never renounced the primacy of the Roman Church over all other Churches, including that of Constantinople. He continued to oppose the use of the title *ecumenical Patriarch* which had been assumed by the Bishop of Constantinople. Gregory the Great was the first monk to become Pope. During his pontificate monasticism, especially in its benedictine form, was strongly encouraged. Many of his closest advisors were drawn from the ranks of the monks. His reform of the Liturgy, especially the chant, was particularly

important. He founded a school for chant. Gregory was a man of wide ranging theological and canonical culture. Many of his works have come down to us, including some eight hundred letters which document his ecclesiastical and political activity. So great was the influence exercised by his writings that Gregory was numbered among the four great doctors of the Western Church, together with Ambrose, Jerome and Augustine. His *Liber Regulae Pastoralis*, on the office of bishop, remained a basic text throughout the middle ages, as did his homilies on the Gospel and the Prophet Ezekiel, and his *Dialogues* recounting the life of St. Benedict and those of other Italian saints. Gregory was also responsible for a vast commentary on the Book of Job, the *Moralia in Iob*, which was much read in the middle ages. He died in Rome as it faced yet another threat from the Lombards and famine from food shortages. He was buried in St. Peter's, his epitaph describing him as the *Consul Dei*. His feast day is 3 September.

65. **Sabinian** *(604-606)*

Born in Volterra, Tuscany, Sabinian had been appointed *apocrisarius* in Constantinople for Gregory the Great but was recalled because he lacked the necessary firmness in opposing imperial policy. He was on a mission in Gaul when Gregory died. He was elected possibly because of a certain discontent that had arisen during the final years of his predecessor's pontificate. He supported the secular clergy, and not the monks as had been the case during Gregory's rein. He may have been involved in negotiations for a truce between the Lombards and the Byzantines. Sabinian, instead of distributing free grain during the famine, sold it, thereby incurring the odium of the people. His funeral cortege, prudently avoiding the Roman mob, was obliged to arrive at St. Peter's by way of a long detour outside of the City walls.

66. Boniface III *(February-November 607)*

Born in Rome to a Greek family, Boniface was nominated *apocrisarius* of Gregory the Great to the emperor Phocas in 603. Following his election, he obtained formal recognition of the Roman primacy, even over Constantinople, from the emperor, and won a more consistent imperial policy towards countering the *Tria Capitula* schism in the Venetian region and in Istria. A synod convoked by Boniface imposed severe norms for the papal election, and prohibited any speculation with regard to a successor while the Pope was still alive. Nothing else is known of him.

67. Saint Boniface IV *(608-615)*

Boniface, son of a doctor, was born in Marsica and had been deacon and administrator of Gregory the Great whom he took as his model. Following his election, he converted his house into a monastery and surrounded himself with monks. He transformed the Roman Pantheon into a church dedicated to Our Lady and all Martyrs. He was much interested in the ecclesiastical condition of Anglia. A letter survives addressed to him by the Irish monk St. Columbanus sent at the behest of the Lombard king, in which he calls on the Pope to withdraw the condemnation of the *Tria Capitula* and to convoke a Council. He was buried in St. Peter's. His cult can be traced to the thirteenth century and the pontificate of Boniface VIII. His feast day is 8 May.

33

68. St. Adeodatus I *(or Deusdedit)* *(615-618)*

Adodatus, also known as Deusdedit, the son of a subdeacon, was born in Rome. He was already old when elected, and was the first priest to accede to the papacy since the reign of John II, almost a century earlier. In outlook, he belonged to the anti-Gregory the Great party and did not favour the monks. He ordained fourteen priests and introduced the recitation of an evening office for the clergy, with which he was most taken. He was faithful to the emperor through earthquakes, famine, and revolt among the troops in Ravenna. He was the first Pope to grant an allowance to his clergy in his will. His feast day is 8 November.

69. Boniface V *(619-625)*

Boniface was born in Naples. He continued the antimonastic policies of his predecessor and favoured the diocesan clergy. He issued norms concerning the right to sanctuary in churches. Boniface was especially interested in the affairs of the English church. He completed the cemetery of St. Nicomedes on the via Nomentana.

70. Honorius I *(625-638)*

Honorius was born of an aristocratic family in the Campania. He took as his model St. Gregory th Great and transformed his house near the Lateran into a monastery. He exempted the abbey of Bobbio from episcopal jurisdiction - the first documented instance of such an exemption. Honorius was much interested in the conversion of the Angels and the affairs of the Church in Anglia, and encouraged the conversion of the Saxons. He maintained good relations with the Lombard kings and made notable gains in reconciling the schismatic Churches in the Veneto and in Istria. His delegate to the sixth Council of Toledo (638) encouraged the Spanish bishops to begin the work of converting the Jews in Spain. He became involved in an unfortunate theological controversy when, in an attempt to please the emperor Heraclius and Sergius, the Patriarch of Constantinople, he accepted a Christological formula proposed by Sergius that was monothelistic in tenor by claiming that in Christ there were «two distinct natures but one will». This formula was subsequently rejected as heretical by his successors and condemned by the sixth ecumenical Council held in Constantinople (680-681), which affirmed the existence in Christ of a divine and a human will. From the fifteenth century, Honorius' involvement with the monothelist heresy became a source of embarrassment, particularly as he had been regarded as more imprudent than heretical. Honorius was an able administrator and busied himself with the civil administration of Italy, ensuring grain supplies, rebuilding the Roman aqueducts, and paying the imperial troops who had been left without funds. He restored many churches in Rome, including St. Peter's, and Sant'Agnese fuori le Mura. He was buried in St. Peter's and described in his epitaph as *dux populi*.

71. Severinus *(May-August 640)*

A Roman, Severinus belonged to the anti-monastic party and favoured the secular clergy. He was elected in 638 but had to wait over twenty months for the imperial confirmation of his election. The emperor Heraclius attempted to have him accept the document *Ekthesis* which incorporated the monothelist formula. Sevrinus refused to accept the formula, in spite of pressure from the exarchate, a siege of the Lateran palace and the confiscation of the papal treasury. Severinus died two months after his consecration without having taken a formal position on the *Ekthesis*. He was buried in St. Peter's.

72. John IV *(640-642)*

John was born in Dalmatia, the son of an official of the exarchate. He held a synod in which monothelism was condemned. In 641 the emperor Heraclius renounced monothelism on his death bed. The new Patriarch of Constantinople, Pirro, tried to support monothelism by citing the approval given to it by Honorius I. John IV replied by reinterpreting the formulas used by his predecessor so as to safeguard his orthodoxy. He tried to rescue Dalmatia after its invasion by the Slavs and the Huns, sending large sums of money to redeem Christians who had been enslaved by the invaders. He placed the relics of three Dalmatian saints in the chapel St.

Venantius in the Lateran Baptistery. His portrait is still discernable in a mosaic in the apse of the chapel.

73. Theodore I *(642-649)*

The son of a bishop, Theodore was born in Jerusalem of Greek parents. His election was secured by the support of the exarch, but he soon proved to be an energetic opponent of monothelism. He began by demanding that the emperor retract the *Ekthesis* which was still in force notwithstanding the abjuration of Heraclius. From the exiled Patriarch Pirro, who by then had been deposed from his See in Constantinople and replaced by Paul, he extracted a public renunciation of the *Ekthesis* in Rome, in return for which the exiled Patriarch received the recognition of the Pope as lawful Patriarch of Constantinople, and the excommunication of Paul who was inclined to monothelism. It proved impossible for Theodore to restore Pirro to his See in Constantinople. Pirro moved to Ravenna where he publicly embraced monothelism and was promptly excommunicated by Theodore. In 648, Constans II rejected the monothelist formulas and published the *Typos* ordering the doctrine of the Church to be limited to the teaching of the five ecumenical Councils, and prohibiting any further Christological controversy. Anastasius, the *apocrisarius*, refused to accept it and was duly arrested and exiled. The chapel of the papal legate was closed and its altar demolished. Theodore I died without having seen the *Typos*.

74. St. Martin I *(649-653)*

Born in Todi (Umbria), Martin had been *apocrisarius* in Constantinople for his predecessor. He was an energetic and courageous Pope, especially in his opposition to imperial policy. He was consecrated without imperial ratification which had been binding since the time of Justinian. The emperor refused to have him consecrated. Following his consecration, he convoked a synod in Rome, attended by over a hundred Western bishops and many exiled Eastern clergy living in Rome. The synod condemned monothelism and the *Typos*. The deliberations of the synod were transmitted both to the Eastern and Western bishops who were obliged to accept them. Paul, the Bishop of Thessalonika, refused and he was swiftly excommunicated. The Pope nominated a Vicar Apostolic for Palestine which was then the dominant centre of monothelism. When confronted by the papal demand to have the decisions of the synod accepted, the emperor ordered the exarch Olympius to arrest the Pope and bring him to Constantinople. The exarch preferred, however, to side with the Pope and, thereby, rebelled against imperial authority. In 653, another exarch arrested him in the Lateran, deposed him as an usurper, and transported him to Constantinople where he was tried and condemned to death, partly due to the treachery of Olympius. He was publicly scourged, and eventually exiled to Cherson in the Crimea where he died in 655. Martin's letters from his exile bitterly complain that the Latin clergy had abandoned him and elected a successor while he was still alive. When in 680-681 the sixth ecumenical Council - and third held in Constantinople after those of 381 and 553 - accepted the doctrine held by Martin, it could not rehabilitate him for he had been condemned not for heresy but for treason. His remains were transferred to Rome and interred in the Basilica of San Martino ai Monti. He is venerated as a martyr in both the East and West. His feast day is 13 April.

75. St. Eugenius I *(654-657)*

Eugenius, a Roman, was aged when elected Pope under pressure from the Byzantines who cared little for his person and more about ensuring the election of a successor to Martin I, who was still alive. He immediately sought reconciliation with Constantinople, and accepted a compromise formula proposed by the new Patriarch, Peter, which was agreeable to the papal delegation in Constantinople. When the formula was publicly read in St. Mary Major's, the Roman clergy and people revolted and constrained the Pope to reject it. Before Constans I could intervene with force, as he had done with Martin I, the Pope died and was buried in St. Peter's. The older martyrologies never included his name. He was inserted into the *Martyrologium Romanum* by Cesare Baronio at the end of the sixteenth century. His feast day is 2 June.

76. St. Vitalian *(657-672)*

Born at Segni, Vitalian was totally submissive to the Byzantines and refused to deal with any doctrinal questions. In 663, he sumptuously received Constans II in Rome. The emperor rendered him many honours and even had him agree to remove the archbishopric of Ravenna from papal jurisdiction. The Pope was much interested in the progress of the Church in Anglia. He developed the school of cantors founded by Gregory the Great in the Lateran, and instituted the so-called *vitaliani* to sing the new liturgical rites of very byzantine character that he had introduced to Rome. Following the assassination of Constans II in Sicily, Vitalian supported the legitimate imperial successor, Constantine IV, thereby further consolidating his links with Byzantium. His feast day is 27 January.

77. Adeodatus II *(672-676)*

Adeodatus, a Roman and a monk of the community of St. Erasmus, was already aged at the time of his election. Little is known of his pontificate, except that he rejected the monothelist profession of faith sent to him by the Patriarch of Constantinople, although his election had received imperial ratification.

78. Donus *(676-678)*

Little is known of Donus, except that he was Roman and made an agreement with the Archbishop of Ravenna to return that See to the jurisdiction of Rome. During his pontificate, the emperor Constantine IV initiated a raprochment with the Apostolic See.

79. St. Agatho (678-681)

Agatho, a Sicilian monk, succeeded in ending the schism between the Eastern and Western Churches provoked by monothelism. His election received immediate imperial ratification. It was he who received a letter from the emperor, addressed to his predecessor Donus, in which the Pope was invited to a meeting to resolve the monothelist controversy and restore the unity of the Church. The Pope prepared his delegation by convoking a series of synods so as to present a unanimous position representative of the West. The most important of these synods was held in Rome. The Roman delegation arrived in Constantinople with letters from the Pope and a condemnation of monothelism issued by the Roman synod and signed by one hundred and fifty bishops. The meeting, held in Constantinople (680-681) - subsequently regarded as the sixth ecumenical Council- in a domed (*trullos*) hall, came to be regarded as the Council of Trullo. With the emperor presiding, the Council condemned monothelism and those who had supported it, including Honorius I, and restored Christian orthodoxy. The Pope died before the closure of the Council and the emperor rendered him honour at its final session as the fathers of Chalcedon had referred to Leo the Great: «Peter has spoken through Agatho». In addition to this basic work of pacification, the Pope resumed negotiations with the Archbishop of Ravenna to end the autonomy of that See which had been granted by the emperor in 666. As treasurer of the Holy See, Agatho obtained the abolition of the taxes due to the emperor by the city of Rome for every election in return for the imperial ratification. In future, such would be paid directly to Constantinople, as was originally the case, without having to send it through the See of Ravenna. Agatho is venerated as a saint both in the East and West. His feast day is 10 January.

37

80. St. Leo II (682-683)

The Sicilian Leo II was elected in January 681. He was obliged to wait eighteen months for the imperial ratification of his election. Constantine IV delayed consent to Leo's election until the Council of Constantinople had ended and condemned all the supporters of monothelism, including Honorius I. Once the Pope had accepted the condemnation, Constantine authorized his consecration. In transmitting the decisions of the Council to the Western bishops, the Pope, however, attenuated the condemnation of Honorius by describing him as «negligent» in the defence of orthodox doctrine. This finally ended the long controversy between the Churches. The institution of *apocrisarius* was permanently established in Constantinople. The emperor reduced taxes on the patrimony of St. Peter in the Byzantine territories and the grain requisition for the army. The Pope had the acts of the Council translated into Latin and transmitted to all of the Western bishops for their subscription. The problem of the status of the See of Ravenna was also resolved when the emperor revoked the decree of 666 which had granted it autonomy from the jurisdiction of Rome. Leo was very tolerant of Macarios, the deposed Patriarch Antioch, and other supporters of monothelism whom the emperor had sent to Rome. Leo placed them in various monasteries in the City. Prior to his election, Leo had been director of the *schola cantorum* and as Pope had devoted much attention to liturgical music. He restored Santa Bibiana on the Esquiline, where he placed many relics, and San Giorgio al Velabro which he gave to the Greek community. His feast day is 3 July.

81. St. Benedict II *(684-685)*

Following two Greek speaking Sicilians, a Roman priest, Benedict, was elected in 684. He had passed through all the grades of the hierarchy. He had to wait a year for imperial ratification, following which he obtained from the emperor the concession that in future the imperial *placet* could be granted by the exarch. He was concerned to obtain the ratification of the conciliar decisions by the Western bishops, especially in Spain where he encountered notable difficulties from the Visigothic bishops. He tried unsuccessfully to have Macarios, the deposed Patriarch of Antioch, renounce monothelism. He restored St. Peter's and San Lorenzo in Lucina. His feast day is 8 May.

82. John V *(685-686)*

Born in Antioch, John had probably taken refuge in Rome in the wake of the Arab invasion. He had represented St. Agatho at the Council of Constantinople (68-681) and brought the acts of the Council to Rome. He was consecrated quickly for he used the new procedure, granted to his predecessor Benedict II, of seeking the ratification of his election in Ravenna. He came into conflict with the Bishop of Cagliari, who claimed an autonomy, but quickly asserted his authority. John was ill for the entire duration of his pontificate. He was buried in St. Peter's.

83. Conon *(686-687)*

Educated in Sicily, Conon's career had covered many ecclesiastical offices. He was a compromise between the candidate of the Roman clergy and that of the exarch, who had deployed the army to prevent the clergy from entering the Lateran for the papal election. He was a weak Pope and left the Roman Church in the grip of several grave conflicts.

84. St. Sergius I *(687-701)*

Born of an Antiochean family in Sicily, Sergius had been titular of Santa Susanna. His was a very controversial election. He was a compromise between Paschal, the candidate of the Byzantines, and Theodore, the candidate of the clergy. Since both of the rival candidates had occupied the Lateran, it became necessary to storm the palace. The exarch, John Platyn, called to Rome by Paschal to resolve the impasse in the papal election, confirmed Sergius. He was an energetic Pope and reasserted the authority of the Roman Church in the East. He was much concerned for the conversion of Anglia and baptized Caedwall, the young king of the West Saxons. He ended the schism of the *Tria Capitula*, and re-established communion with the Church of Aquileia, which had separated from Rome in 553. He renewed relations with Ravenna and, for the first time, consecrated a bishop for that See in Rome. Sergius was in conflict with the emperor Justinian II who had convoked a Council without inviting the Pope or the Western bishops. The *Quinisext* Council aimed at completing the work of the two preceding Councils. Its decrees were entirely Oriental in inspiration and conflicted with the Western norm. It eliminated clerical celibacy, the Lenten fast and accepted the claims of the Patriarchate of Constantinople to a status equiparate to that of the Roman See. When the Pope refused to sign the decrees, the emperor despatched a troop of his guard to Rome to arrest him and force him to affirm the decrees. The Byzantine army stationed in Italy revolted in favour of the Pope and pursued the emperor's envoy who was forced to seek refuge under the Pope's bed. The Byzantines had to abandon their project for the moment. Sergius restored many churches including St. Peter's, St. Paul's and Santa Susanna. He transferred the body of Leo the Great to a more dignified tomb in St. Peter's. The *Agnus Dei* was introduced into the Mass by Sergius who also introduced the custom of processions on the four principal feasts of the Blessed Virgin Mary (the Purification, the Annunciation, the Assumption, and the Nativity). He was buried in St. Peter's and enjoyed a cult immediately after his death. His feast day is 8 September.

85. John VI *(701-705)*

A Greek, John VI was elected as the empire entered into a deep crisis following the deposition of the emperor Justinian II and as Italy began to assert greater autonomy from the Byzantines. To remedy the stalemate caused by Sergius, Theophilatus, the exarch, came to Rome to arrest the Pope. A further revolt among the troops saved the Pope. The Lombards invaded the Campania and arrived at the gates of Rome. John VI was forced to pay them an enormous sum of ransom money.

86. John VII *(705-707)*

The son a Greek official of the Byzantine administration, John maintained good relations with the Lombards. Justinian II, following his restoration, sent him the canons of the *Quinisext* Council asking him to convoke a synod to discuss them and eventually approve them. Not feeling strong enough to oppose the emperor, he sent the decrees back to Constantinople, a gesture which earned him a reputation for cowardice. John VII built a new papal residence at the foot of the Palatine hill. He was buried in St. Peter's in the chapel that he had dedicated to the Blessed Virgin, to whom he had great devotion. He is represented in a mosaic conserved in the *Grotte vaticane*.

87. Sisinnius *(January-February 708)*

Of Syrian origin, Sisinnius was already in advanced ill health at the time of his election - suffering as he did from the gout. During his short pontificate, he made provision for the restoration of the City walls in anticipation of further attacks by the Lombards.

88. Constantine *(708-715)*

Again, of Syrian origin, Constantine appears to have been one of the representatives sent by St. Agatho to the ecumenical Council held in Constantinople (680-681). He returned to the Byzantine capital between 710 and 711 at the invitation of the emperor Justinian II to resolve the question of the *Quinisext* Council which the previous Popes had refused to ratify. The journey was a success for the Pope who was received with great honours. Those canons which were most at variance with Western liturgical usage and discipline he approved orally. The emperor re-affirmed all the prerogatives of the Roman See. Relations between East and West noticeably improved and were not affected by intelligence that the exarch had executed some of the papal officials after the Pope had left the City. The assassination of the emperor and the accession of Philippicos, an avowed monothelist, reopened the whole question. The emperor annulled the decrees of the sixth ecumenical Council and asked the Pope to approve the measure. Riots broke in Rome between the Romans and the imperial troops. The Pope played an active part in pacifying the situation by sending priests with crosses and the Book of the Gospel among the contending parties. The problem was resolved by the deposition of Philippicos. Anastasius II, his successor, immediately restored Catholic orthodoxy. The pontificate of Constantine was also troubled by a further eruption of the problem of the autonomy of the See of Ravenna, and also an attempt by the Bishop of Milan to arrogate to himself the Pope's traditional right to consecrate the Bishops of Pavia. This was quickly rejected by the Roman See.

89. Gregory II *(715-731)*

Born in Rome to an aristocratic family in 669, Gregory was educated at the Lateran and pursued an ecclesiastical career. He played a significant role in the delegation to Constantinople led by Constantine, his predecessor. His was the most important pontificate of the century from both an ecclesiastical and a political point of view. He sought to curb the increasing expansion of the Lombards. When the combined armies of Luitprand, and Eutychius, the Byzantine exarch, threatened Rome, Gregory entered Luitprand's camp vested in the insignia of his sacred office and obtained his submission. He had troubled relations with the Byzantines, although he considered himself a loyal subject of Byzantine dominion. Between 717 and 726, he led Italian resistence to new taxes levied by the emperor. The Byzantines sought to depose and assassinate him. In 730, the Pope supported Eutychius, the exarch, against the pretensions of an usurper. The most serious conflict with the Byzantines, however, broke out over the iconoclast campaign begun in 726 by Leo III. The Pope condemned the iconoclastic decrees of Leo as heretical. Southern Italy revolted in defence of sacred images. Gregory was particularly interested in the conversion of Germany whither he sent Wilfred, a British monk, who had taken the name of Boniface in Rome. Nominated Bishop and bound to the Apostolic See by a special oath of obedience, Boniface successfully began the conversion of Germany and the organisation of the German Church. He introduced Roman liturgical usage to Germany. In Rome, the Pope restored the City wall and many churches. He encouraged monasticism, transforming his own home into a monastery. His most important undertaking was the re-construction of the abbey of Monte Cassino which had been raised by the Lombards. He introduced a mass for the Thursdays of Lent which was a liturgical innovation. His cult is first mentioned in the ninth century *Martyrologium Adonis*. His feast day is 11 February.

90. St. Gregory III *(731-741)*

A priest of Syrian origin, Gregory was elected by acclamation of the multitude at the funeral of his predecessor. He was the last Pope to seek Byzantine confirmation of his election. The most pressing problem facing the new pontificate was that of the iconoclast heresy. In 730, Leo had prohibited making or venerating sacred images. Having unsuccessfully attempted to dissuade the emperor from this policy, Gregory convoked a synod in 730 and formally condemned iconoclasm as heretical and excommunicated its promoters. The papal letters, however, never reached Constantinople for the messengers were intercepted and arrested in Sicily by the Byzantines. At first the emperor attempted to use force to make the Pope bend. He despatched a fleet to Italy with orders to arrested the Pope. It was shipwrecked in the Adriatic. Then the emperor annexed the ecclesiastical provinces of Illyricum and Sicily to the Church of Constantinople and confiscated papal possessions in Calabria and Sicily. A truce was called in 733 when Ravenna fell to the armies of Luitprand. The Pope supported the restoration of the exarch in his efforts to retake the city. In order to resist pressure from Luitprand, Gregory entered into alliance with the Lombard dukes of Spoleto and Benevento who were in conflict with the Lombard king. He fortified the City and Civitavecchia. The Lombards captured Spoleto and invaded the duchy of Rome, capturing four of its fortresses and threatening the City. In 739 and in 740, the Pope turned to the Franks for assistance, calling on the master of the palace, Charles Martel, for assistance «for the Church of God and those closest to her». The Frankish prince, who had the support of Luitprand in his campaign against the Arabs in Provence, made no intervention. Gregory III continued a missionary policy in Germany. St. Boniface was named archbishop, «Legate of the Apostolic See» and given charge of the organization of the Church in Bavaria, Alemania, Hesse, and Thuringia. The Pope was also concerned for the Church in Anglia where he nominated the archbishop of Canterbury his Vicar for the whole of Anglia. To counteract the Eastern policy of iconoclasm, Gregory filled the Roman churches with sacred images. He founded new monasteries and supported those already existing. He restored the Roman cemeteries. He was buried in an oratory which he had build in St. Pater's and dedicated to Our Saviour and the Blessed Virgin Mary. His cult is first mentioned in the ninth century *Martyrologium Adonis*. His feast day is 28 November.

91. St. Zachary *(741-752)*

Born in Calabria of Greek origin, Zachary was the last of the Greek Popes. At the time of his election, the Lombards were at the gates of Rome and the papacy was allied with the Lombard duke of Spoleto. The new Pope broke his alliance with the duke of Spoleto and met with Luitprand at Terni where he entered into a twenty year truce and obtained the restitution of the Roman fortresses, towns and territories conquered by the Lombards. The following year, Luitprand attacked Ravenna and the exarch Eutychius called on Zachary for assistance. The Pope met for a second time with Luitprand, in Pavia, and persuaded him to abandon his expansionist policies. Zachary repeated the process in 749 with Rachis, Luitprand's successor.

With the accession of Astolphus, the brother of Rachis, the Lombard expansionist policy recommenced. Astolphus took Ravenna, expelled the exarch and moved on Rome. Notwithstanding the iconoclast controversy, the Pope maintained good relations with Constantinople. Following his election, Zachary diplomatically informed the emperor of his election, though formally he was no longer required to obtain the imperial ratification of his election. Constantine V, concerned with putting down an attempted usurpation, the advance of the arabs and Bulgars, and mindful of past support against the Lombards from Rome, abstained from any intervention in the iconoclastic controversy and bestowed on the Apostolic See important imperial possessions in Norma and Ninfa in Southern Latium. The Pope consolidated relations with the Frankish court, then governed by the sons of Charles Martel, Pepin and Charlemagne. Although these held the title of Masters of the Palace, they were in fact sovereigns in their own right. Boniface, the Apostle of Germany, was charged with the reform of the Frankish Church. With the assistance of Pepin and Carlemagne, a series of synods took place in preparation for a general synod of the kingdom which was held in 747, and began by sending a declaration of fidelity to the Pope. In 750, Pepin sent an embassy to the Pope seeking his approval for the deposition of Childerick III, the last of the Merovingian kings. The Pope made a momentous decision: it was better for the title of king to inhere in him who actually exercised political power. In 751, Pepin was proclaimed king of the Franks and consecrated by Boniface. Thus the Carolingian dynasty came to power with papal support. Zachary was politically and administratively very able. In order to reestablish the income of the Apostolic See following the Byzantine confiscations in Calabria and Sicily, he introduced a system of administration called the *domuscultae*, ecclesiastical property given to tenants who cultivated it. The Pope restored many churches in Rome, including Santa Maria Antiqua, where he is depicted in a fresco. He returned the papal residence to the Lateran having restored and enlarged it. His feast day is 15 March.

92. **Stephen II or III** *(752-757)*

The son of a Roman aristocratic family, Stephen was educated at the Lateran together with his brother, Paul, who would eventually succeed him. Immediately prior to his election, an aged priest also called Stephen was elected, but died four days later without having been consecrated. Until the 1960 edition of the *Annuario Pontificio*, his name was always inserted in the list of Popes, which explains the double numeration of Stephen II and those Popes of the same name. Although of only five years duration, his pontificate is important because during this time the Papal States were formed, the Pope having extracted himself from the dominion of Byzantium and placing himself under the protection of the Frankish kingdom. He repelled the efforts of the Lombard king, Astolphus, to annex Rome. He began his defence with diplomacy, then passed to the Roman penitential processions and finally ended by having recourse to arms. He sought the assistance of the Byzantines but had more success with the Frankish king who invited him to France. Having again failed to convince Astolphus to restore the Byzantine territories he had taken, the Pope crossed the Alps and met with Pepin at Ponthion where he solemnly called on him to become the defender of the Roman Church. In a document, the donation of Pepin, the Frankish king guaranteed the duchies of Rome and Ravenna, the exarchate and other cities and territories in the hands of the Lombards to the lawful occupant of the Apostolic See. According to some scholars, the so-called *Constantinian Donation* dates from this time although it grants dominion over Rome and the Eastern provinces and cities of Italy to St. Sylvester I. In return for his protection, the Pope solemnly consecrated Pepin, his consort and their children in the abbey of St. Denis, near Paris, and thereby legitimated the dynasty. The king's sons were granted the titles of Roman Patricians. In 754, following several diplomatic moves, Pepin defeated the Lombards and, by the terms of the first treaty of Pavia, he forced them to resign everything they had conquered from the Byzantines into the Pope's hands. A further attempt by Astolphus to take Rome was again defeated by the Franks. The second treaty of Pavia constrained Astolphus to surrender the territory of the Comacchio, the Pentapoli and Emilia to the Roman Church. The emperor called in vain for their restoration to the exarchate. Following the death of Astolphus, the Pope supported the candidature of Desiderius, Duke of Tuscany, for the Lombard throne, in return for which he was promised other territorial possessions, including the city of Bologna.

93. St. Paul I *(757-767)*

Paul was a brother of his predecessor, Stephen, and one of his closest collaborators and counsellors. He was chosen Pope in a contested election which caused his consecration to be delayed for a month because one part of the Roman Curia opposed the alliance with the Franks. Much of his pontificate was spent in consolidating the Church's newly acquired political and territorial significance. The Pope emphasised his role as the mediator between God and man. His primary occupation was to maintain the alliance with the Franks whom he immediately notified of his election (as the Roman Pontiffs had previously done with Byzantium), without however seeking their ratification. The Lombard king, Desiderius, resumed the political policies of Astolphus, and not only refused to make good his promises to Stephen II (III) in exchange for his support, but he invaded the duchies of Spoleto and Benevento, which were under papal jurisdiction, and devastated part of the Papal States. He also entered an alliance with the Byzantines to reconquer the exarchate. The Pope once again called on the assistance of Pepin who, worried by the alliance with the Byzantines, preferred to use diplomatic channels to reestablish a kind of truce between the Pontiff and Desiderius, which restricted further papal territorial ambitions. The iconoclast controversy rendered relations with the empire even more difficult. Constantine V had the condemnation of images confirmed and ratified in a synod held at Hieria, near Chalcedon, in 754. A bitter persecution of those opposed to iconoclasm ensued with many of the *iconoduli* taking refuge in Rome. The Byzantines tried to have the Franks adopt their policy of iconoclasm and to wean it from the Apostolic See. In a synod of bishops held at Gentilly in 767, which was attended by Greek iconoclast bishops, the Roman line prevailed. During his reign, Paul had the bodies of many of the Saints transferred from the catacombs to the churches in the City. Among them was the body of St. Petronella, who was much venerated among the Franks who considered her to have been the sister of St. Peter. The Pope died unexpectedly in the Basilica of St. Paul. With his death a period of grave tension began which eventually led to the election of an anti-Pope, Constantine. Paul's body was transferred to St. Peter's. His cult dates from the fifteenth century. His feast day is 28 June.

94. Stephen III or IV *(768-772)*

Born in Sicily, Stephen was educated in Rome. A member of the papal bureaucracy, he was priest of St. Cecilia at the time of his election which was in part due to the support of the notary, Christopher. The Roman See had been vacant for over a year during which chaos reigned in the Church and two anti-Popes were elected -one represented the lay aristocracy (Constantine) and lasted for a year, the other (Philip) having been imposed by the Lombards lasted for a single day. Initially, Stephen consolidated the support of the Frankish kingdom, which was ruled by the «Roman Patricians» Charles and Charlemagne, following the death of Pepin. The title had been given to them by Stephen II at the coronation of Pepin in 754. A synod was held in Rome in 769 which was attended by the Frankish bishops. It restored canonical discipline and remedied the disorders introduced by the election of the anti-Pope Constantine. The bishops who had supported the election of Constantine made a public profession of guilt and were sentenced to life-long penance. The synod also declared that only the Cardinal Deacons and Priests had the right to be elected Pope and that the laity had no vote in papal elections. In opposition to the synod of Hieria, the cult of images was re-affirmed. Preoccupied that an alliance between the Franks and the Lombards, forged by the marriage of Charles with Hermingard, Desiderius' daughter, might leave the papacy isolated, Stephen entered a pact with the Lombards which also served to mitigate the over weaning influence of Christopher and his pro-Frankish party. With the support of Christopher's worst enemy, Paolo Afiarta the Papal Chamberlain and dependent of the Lombards, Stephen had Christopher assassinated, or permitted Afiarta to have him assassinated. In 771, Charles, by now sole sovereign of the Franks, put his consort Hermingilda aside. Enmities between the Franks and the Lombards resumed and the Pope found himself in the middle of the conflict.

95. Adrian I *(772-795)*

Adrian, a Roman noble, had been ordained subdeacon by St. Paul I, and deacon by Stephen III whom he succeeded. Shortly after his election, he tried to free himself from the embarrassing alliance with the Lombards and had Paolo Afiarta, Desiderius' ally in Rome, arrested. When Desiderius marched on Rome, Adrian threatened him with excommunication and called on the Frankish king, Charlemagne (Charles), for assistance. He entered Italy, took Pavia, destroyed the Lombard kingdom and took to himself the title of *Rex Lungobardorum*. Without warning, Charlemagne arrived in Rome and met with the Pope in St. Peter's. The Pope obtained from the Frankish king another donation similar that conceded by Pepin in 754 which conceded about three quarters of Italy to the papacy. Adrian immediately began to act as a sovereign striking coin and dating documents with a regnal number. After Stephen II, he is considered the second founder of the Papal States. In reality, however, the promises of Charlemagne were never completely fulfilled and the papacy had to renounce jurisdiction over Terracina, Spoleto and Tuscany. Moreover, the Frankish king took his title of «Roman Patrician» seriously and began to interfere in the affairs of the City which created friction, although it did not undermine the alliance between the Pope and the Franks. In close collaboration with Rome, a reform of the Frankish Church began. Relations between Adrian I and Charlemagne became somewhat more tense in 787 following the second council of Nicea (the seventh ecumenical Council) which restored the use of images in the Eastern Church. The Pope sent envoys to the Council and a tract on the correct use of images. His demand for the restitution of goods confiscated by Leo III and the return of the Illyrian province to Roman jurisdiction went without reply. The rapprochement between the Pope and the Byzantine emperor in the wake of the settlement of the iconoclast controversy worried Charlemagne, who had not been invited to the Council. He had his theologians prepare a refutation of the decrees of the Council, the *Libri Carolini*, which were based on a bad translation of the Council's decrees. In 794, Charlemagne held a synod of the Western Church in Frankfort to which the Pope sent his legates. Only one decision of the Council of Nicea was condemned, namely that which, according to the translations available to the synod, seemed to permit the worship of images. The synod of Frankfort also definitively condemned Spanish adoptionism, which regarded Christ as the adopted Son of God rather than His real Son. Adrian undertook an important series of works in the City and restored many churches. He restored the walls, the course of the Tiber and the aqueducts. He extended the system of *domuscultae*, or papal estates, introduced by his predecessor Zachary and founded the *diaconiae*, or monastic foundations for the relief of the poor. He appointed many of his relations to high ecclesiastical office, including his nephew Paschal, whom he appointed dean of notaries. On his death, Charlemagne dedicated a large marble slab to the Pope's memory which he had inscribed with commemorative verses. The slab is conserved in the portico of St. Peter's.

96. St. Leo III *(795-816)*

Born in Rome of a modest family, possibly from Southern Italy, Leo was Cardinal Priest of Santa Susanna at the time of his election. He announced his election to Charlemagne and sent him the keys to the Apostle's tomb and the standard of Rome in recognition of his sovereignty. He asked the Frankish king to send legates to the City to receive the oath of the Roman people. Charlemagne replied by emphasising the complementarity of their respective roles: the sovereign defended the Church and promoted the faith, the Pope prayed for his success. The Pope aroused the opposition of the Roman nobility, headed by Paschal. In 799, he was attacked, deposed and locked away in a monastery. His adversaries tried unsuccessfully to tear out his eyes and tongue. This episode has been transmitted by tradition which has Leo's speech and sight restored. The tradition was deemed sufficient to have Leo included in the catalogue of Saints in 1673. The Pope escaped and took refuge with the king, where a party of his opponents accused him of perjury and adultery. These accusations were favourably heard in some sections of the Frankish court. Alquin, the king's counsellor, maintained that no tribunal could sit in judgement on the Pope. In the circumstances, the king sent Leo back to Rome escorted by Frankish troops. A year later, Charlemagne came to Rome where he was received with the ceremonial that had been used to receive the emperors. Before an assembly of Roman and Frankish noble that had already declared that the Pope could be judged by no one, the Pope swore a solemn oath of purification in which he declared himself innocent. This completely rehabilitated Leo. On Christmas night 800, at the beginning of Mass, the Pope placed the imperial crown on the head of Charlemagne, and the populace acclaimed him as emperor. Concord reigned more or less between the Pope and emperor, notwithstanding the interference of the emperor in the affairs of the Papal States. The only papal resistence to the Franks came in 810. A request was made for a modification in the Creed concerning the «procession» of the Holy Spirit «from the Father (*ex Patre*) to bring it into line with the form used in the Frankish Church

-«and from the Son» (*filioque*). With the emperor's death in 814, the Pope regained a certain freedom of action. Leo tried and condemned those involved in a conspiracy against him without referring to Charlemagne's successor, Louis the Pious. The Pope continued the work of restoring the City, and of the papal administration begun by Adrian I. Among the significant public works of the pontificate was the building of a great hall at the Lateran palace, decorated with mosaics symbolically depicting the new relationship between the papacy and the empire. His feast day is 12 June.

97. **Stephen IV or V** *(816-817)*

Born of an aristocratic Roman family, Stephen was educated at the Lateran and ordained to the subdiaconate and deaconate by Leo III. He was the first Pope elected after the creation of the Carolingian empire. Following his election, the Pope had the Roman people pledge an oath of fidelity to the emperor. Having communicated his election, he set out to meet the emperor in Rheims. Here he anointed him and placed on his head the crown of Constantine which had been brought from Rome. For the Pope, this act signified that imperial power required consecration by the Pope for the legitimacy of its exercise. Stephen IV, in an effort to pacify the Roman populace, requested the emperor to liberate those who had been exiled to Gaul for their part in the conspiracy against Leo III. The emperor acquiesced. The Pope died three months after his return to Rome.

98. **St. Paschal 1** *(817-824)*

A Roman who had been educated in the Lateran, Paschal was abbot of the monastery Santo Stefano, near St. Pater's, at the time of his election. He was immediately consecrated to avoid imperial interference. The Frankish emperor was notified of his acceptance of election as Pope. He maintained good relations with the Frankish court practically to the end of his pontificate. Louis the Pious granted him a privilege that had already been prepared for Stephen IV while at Rheims, the *Pactum Ludovicianum*, which repeated the traditional relationship between the Frankish monarchy and the Roman Church. The emperor agreed not to interfere in the affairs of the Papal States unless asked to do so by the Pope. He also agreed not to condition the papal election. The Popes, in return, were obliged to inform the emperor of their election. In 823, Lothair, Louis' son, succeeded to the Frankish throne and journeyed to Rome where he was crowned by the Pope. A new element was introduced into the solemn ceremony whereby the emperor was given a sword symbolizing his temporal power. While in Rome, the young emperor made several lively interventions in papal affairs and gathered around himself the aristocratic opposition to the clergy and those who opposed the autocratic government of the Pope. Following his departure, two pro-Frankish papal officials, Lothair the dean of notaries, and Leo the *nomenclator*, were seized and decapitated in the Lateran. The Pope, who was suspected of having ordered their execution, swore an oath of purification and declared his innocence. He also maintained that both had been tried and condemned for treason. During this pontificate, the Byzantine emperor, Leo V, resumed iconoclast policies. Invited to intervene in the controversy by St. Theodore Studita, the Pope protested in vain against the iconoclasm of Byzantium and gave refuge to many Greek monks who had gone into exile. Continuing the work of restoring the City,

Paschal rebuilt a number of the Roman churches including Santa Prassede, Santa Maria in Domnica (the Navicella) and Santa Cecilia in Trastevere. Authoritarian and detested by the Romans, Paschal was buried in Santa Prassede, once the riots surrounding his death had been quelled and his successor installed. Cesare Baronio had him inserted in the calendar of saints at the end of the sixteenth century. His feast day is 11 February.

99. Eugenius II *(824-827)*

Following the death of Paschal, a conflict of several months' duration broke out between the supporters of the ecclesiastical bureaucracy and those of the Roman nobility. Each party promoted its own candidate for the papacy. Eventually, imperial pressure placed Eugenius on the papal throne. The candidate of the Roman nobility, he had been archpriest of Santa Sabina at the time of his election. Not only did he announced his election to the emperor, he also recognized imperial jurisdiction in the Papal States and swore fealty to the Frankish king. Shortly afterwards, Lothair promulgated the *Constitutio Romana* in the City, regulating the relationship between both powers, but submitting the Papal States to the empire and obliging the Pope to swear fealty to the emperor at his election. The entire population of the Papal States was also required to take this oath. The *Constitutio Romana* also altered the rules for the papal election, by granting a vote to the laity, a measure subsequently ratified by a synod held in the Lateran. This represented a victory for the aristocracy allied with the emperor as is evident from a number of provisions made almost immediately following the introduction of the constitution. Exiles were permitted to return to the City and those condemned by the government of Paschal I were rehabilitated. In ecclesiastical matters Eugenius was more independent of the empire. He issued a series of canons designed to reform the life of the Church, which was also extended to the Frankish Church (on subjects such as simony, monastic rules, marriage laws, and the education of the clergy). The Pope refused to accept a compromise position on the iconoclastic question which had been proposed to him by Louis the Pious who, with the emperor Michael II, had adopted a mediate position between orthodoxy and iconoclasm, which permitted the use of images but not their veneration. The Pope rejected the position and continued to support Theodore Studita in the East. Eugenius II also began the process of evangelizing Scandinavia which he entrusted the St. Oscar in 826.

100. Valentine *(August-September 827)*

From an aristocratic Roman family, Valentine was archdeacon when unanimously elected to the papacy by the clergy, nobles and people of Rome, as required by the constitution of 824. He died a month after his consecration.

101. Gregory IV *(827-844)*

Gregory belonged to an aristocratic family and was Cardinal Priest of St. Mark's at the time of his election which was effected by the votes of the Roman nobility. He awaited imperial approval before consecration and swore fealty to the emperor. Relations with the empire were complicated by the revolt of Pepin and Ludovick, the sons of Lothair, against Louis the Pious. Responding to the harsh criticism of the episcopate, Gregory IV asserted the spiritual superiority of the papacy over the empire and the legitimacy of his pacifying mission. In 833, as the armies faced each other near Colmar, the Pope intervened and attempted to mediate in the dispute. His mediation led to the deposition of Louis the Pious thanks to the treachery of Lothair. Following the restoration of Louis the Pious, the Pope resumed relations with him, though Gregory continued his associations with the circle of Lothair. Having conquered Sicily in 827, the Saracens quickly began to threaten Italy. In preparation for an invasion, Gregory built and fortified the town near Ostia which was called Gregoriopolis. He began the evangelization of Denmark and nominated Oscar legate for Scandinavia and the missions to the Slavs. He extended the feast of All Saints to all the territories of the empire. In Rome he built and beautified many churches and restored the Sabine aqueducts which bought water to the mills on the Janiculum and St. Peter's. A portrait of Gregory is still visible in the apsidal mosaic of the Basilica of St. Mark which he restored.

102. Sergius II *(844-847)*

Following the death of Gregory IV, a faction of the Roman people elected the deacon John as Pope and installed him in the Lateran with violence. The Roman aristocracy re-acted and, with the assistance of the clergy, elected Sergius, who belonged to an aristocratic family. John was deposed and confined to a monastery. Sergius was immediately consecrated without the imperial *placet*. This was seen as a gesture of independence from the Franks, but Lothair soon established his authority by naming his son Louis viceroy of Italy and by sending him to Rome. He was accompanied by his uncle Drogo, Bishop of Metz, and a large army which devastated the Papal States. Sergius was forced by Louis to accept the convocation of a synod in St. Peter's to decide the legitimacy of the papal election. Having had his election confirmed, the Pope was obliged to swear fealty to the emperor, crown Louis king of the Lombards, and nominate Drogo Vicar Apostolic for all territories north of the Alps. In the government of the Papal States, the Pope devoted much energy to important public works such as the restoration of the Marcian aqueduct and the enlargement of the Lateran basilica. He procured the means for these works by allowing the practice of simony to flourish. This unfortunately diminished his moral standing. Indeed when the Saracens attacked Rome in 846 and sacked the Basilicas of St. Peter and St. Paul, which lay outside of the city walls, many of Sergius' contemporaries saw it as a divine punishment for the abuses he had tolerated.

103. St. Leo IV *(847-855)*

Leo, a benedictine monk, was a Roman probably of Lombard origin, and Cardinal Priest of the Basilica of the Ss. Quattro Incoronati, when he was unanimously elected Pope on the day of his predecessor's sudden death. He was consecrated without the imperial ratification. He was an active and energetic defender of the Church. Generally, he maintained good relations with the Franks. He adopted a posture of formal deference and always sought imperial approval for episcopal nominations and for other acts of ecclesiastical government. At Easter 850, he crowned Louis, son of Lothair, who became sole sovereign in 855. In the ensuing crisis, the Pope demonstrated great firmness: he prosecuted three imperial legates who had killed his own legate; he refused to nominate the highly influential Hincmar of Rheims as Vicar Apostolic, and he excommunicated Anastasius Bibliotecarius, Cardinal Priest of St. Marcellus and eventual anti-Pope who enjoyed Louis' protection. In 855 he refused to sanction the decisions of the synod of Soissons. In 852 Leo renovated the City fortifications and walled the area around St. Peter's, creating the leonine city, so at to ward off Saracen attacks. In 849 he succeeded in organizing the fleets of the republics of Amalfi, Naples and Gaeta so as to clear Ostia of muslim pirates. *Centumcellae* (Civitavecchia), which had been sacked by the Saracens, he rebuilt on a new site called Leopolis. He was also concerned for the reform of ecclesiastical discipline as can be seen from the acts of the Roman synod of 853. He encouraged sacred music and instituted the octave of the Assumption of the Blessed Virgin Mary. In 853 he crowned Alfred, future King of England. He restored many churches. His portrait appears in the frescos of the lower basilica in San Clemente. His feast day is 17 July.

49

104. Benedict III *(855-858)*

Benedict, a Roman educated at the Lateran, had been nominated Cardinal Priest of St. Mark's by St. Leo IV. He was elected by the clergy and people, but while awaiting ratification of his election, the imperial party elected a Pope at Orte, Anastasius Bibliotecarius, whom Leo IV had excommunicated. Anastasius was installed in the Lateran while Benedict was deposed and imprisoned. The attempt, however, did not succeed. The people rose against the election of an excommunicate while the Bishops of Ostia and Albano refused to consecrate him. The emperor ceded and re-instated Benedict who was consecrated, having undertaken not to pursue the anti-Pope, and having agreed to accept the authority of the imperial representative in Rome, a certain Arsenius who was a close relative and major supporter of Anastasius. From what we know of his pontificate, Benedict was an active and energetic Pope whose ecclesiastical policy was much concerned with re-asserting the authority and primacy of the Roman Church. In this he was ably assisted by his counsellor and successor Nicholas I. He inherited the problems facing his predecessor: a bitter conflict with the duke of Brittany who had deposed four Breton bishops; the problem of the synod of Soissons, which he finally ratified; a controversy with the Bishop of Constantinople who had deposed the Bishop of Syracuse without having consulted the Bishop of Rome. Benedict promoted relations with the Church in England. He restored many of the Roman churches and cemeteries. The Tiber flooded repeatedly throughout his pontificate.

105. St. Nicholas I *(858-867)*

Born in Rome in 820, Nicholas ha been counsellor to Benedict III. He was elected Pope in the presence of the emperor Louis who had come to Rome for the event. He included Anastasius, the former anti-Pope, in his government and rehabilitated him. He forcefully defended the primacy of the Pope and rejected state interference in ecclesiastical matters. He began a policy of imposing Roman authority on the metropolitans who traditionally had exercised a certain autonomy. The policy made appeal to the *False Decretals*, which had been attributed to Isodore of Seville, but turned out to have been composed in the Frankish empire around the year 850. These asserted the preeminence of the Roman Church over synods and metropolitans. The Pope obtained the complete submission of the Archbishop of Ravenna, having deposed and excommunicated him for disobedience. He intervened in a number of instances against Hincmar of Rheims, the most powerful cleric in the Frankish empire, reexamining the cases of clerics deposed by Hincmar. He restored the Bishop of Soissons. Nicholas came into direct conflict with the emperor on the question of a divorce imposed on his brother Lothair's wife that had been confirmed by a synod of the Frankish bishops held in Aachen. Lothair II then had had his marriage with his concubine, Waldrada, ratified by another synod held in Metz, where the papal legates had also given their approval. In defence of the sanctity of marriage, the Pope annulled the decisions of both synods and excommunicated Waldrada. Along with her, for their complicity in bigamy, he excommunicated the Bishops of Trier and Cologne who had come to Rome with the synodal acts. The emperor's threats to descent on Rome with an army were to no avail. Nicholas took refuge in St. Peter's and reiterated his decisions. The emperor ceded and Lothair was reconciled, at least temporarily, with his wife. In the power vacuum created by the division of the Frankish empire the role of the Pope continued to grow dominant. Another controversy was to have grave consequences for the Oriental Church. The problem began with the deposition of the Patriarch Ignatius of Constantinople and his replacement with a layman, called Photius. The incident further embittered relations between the two Churches. The Pope protested to the Byzantine emperor. He deposed and excommunicated Photius in a synod held in 863. Nicholas sent missionaries to Bulgaria at the request of Boris I. Among these was Formosus, the future Pope. Formosus' mission in Bulgaria was successful and Boris asked that he should be nominated Archbishop and Metropolitan of Bulgaria. The Pope refused the request on the grounds that Formosus was already Bishop of Porto. Constantinople regarded the mission an unacceptable interference since Bulgaria had been evangelized by Constantinople and naturally gravitated towards the Eastern sphere of influence. In 867, Photius called a synod in Constantinople that deposed and excommunicated the Pope. News of these events arrived in Rome after the Pope's death. Nicholas' name was inserted in the *Martyrologium Romanum* only in 1620, but his successor, Aadrian II, had already had his name included in the prayers of the Mass. His feast day is 13 November.

106. Adrian II *(867-872)*

Born in 792 to an aristocratic Roman family, Adrian had been married and, subsequent to ordination, had occupied several important positions in the Lateran. He was Cardinal priest of St. Mark's at the time of his election. He had already twice declined election (855 and 858), but accepted it unwillingly in 867 since he was a compromise candidate between rival factions. Louis II, who was fighting the Saracens in Southern Italy, immediately ratified his election. In difficult times for the Church, Adrian II had neither the energy nor prestige of his predecessor. He nominated Anastasius, the former anti-Pope, his secretary and archivist and immediately fought with him. Having deposed and excommunicated him, Adrian subsequently restored him to office. Adrian's pontificate began with the Duke of Spoleto's sacking Rome. On the question of Lothair's marriage, he was much weaker than his predecessor had been. He readmitted the king to communion, lifted the excommunication his predecessor had placed on Waldrada and postponed any decision on their marriage to a future synod. Lothair died in 869 and the Pope made several unsuccessful interventions in the question of his successor. The same impotence was demonstrated in his dealing with Hincmar of Rheims on the question of jurisdiction in the Frankish Church, especially when Adrian repudiated the trenchant letters written by his secretary Anastasius on the subject. In relation to the Eastern Church, he convoked a synod in which he confirmed his predecessor's excommunication of Photius, but aspired to arrive at an accord with Constantinople. In 867, the emperor Basil convoked a council which, in the East, was regarded as the eight ecumenical Council. Two Papal legates attended the Council and the condemnation of Photius was repeated. The Church of Constantinople succeeded in introducing an order of hierarchical precedence among the great Patriarchates which, up to then, Rome had refused accept: Rome, followed by Constantinople, Alexandria, Antioch and Jerusalem - the problem had been to determine a precedence between Alexandria and Constantinople. Relations with the Eastern Church quickly deteriorated with the annexation of Bulgaria to the Church of Constantinople which the imperial delegates had supported as well as the emperor. The Latin clergy were expelled. Moravia was left with the West. The Pope received Cyril and Methodius in Rome. Both are known as the «apostles of the Slavs». Adrian recognised the use of the Slav language in the liturgy. Methodius was nominated Bishop of Sirmio (present day Mitrovica, in Kosovo) and Papal Legate to the Slavs. In 872, as Louis was imprisoned by the Duke of Benevento, the Pope renewed his coronation in St. Peter's in an effort to increase his prestige.

107. John VIII *(872-882)*

John, a Roman, had been a close advisor of St. Nicholas I. He was an energetic Pope and resolute in reaffirming the primacy of the Roman See. As the Saracens began numerous incursions into the Southern part of the Papal States, John tried to unite the Southern states which raised a fleet. He also walled the Basilica of St. Paul. The desertion of his allies obliged him to maintain an uneasy peace with the muslims and pay a heavy annual tribute. In 875 a struggle broke out for the imperial succession. John supported Charles the Bald rather than Louis the German. Charles was acclaimed emperor by the Roman Senate and People. John crowned him emperor at Christmas 875. In exchange, Charles renounced control of Rome and withdrew his legates. He agreed not to interfere in the papal elections and to extend the frontiers of the Papal States. Reinforced by this situation, John was enabled to depose, exile and excommunicate many of his Roman enemies, among the them Formosus, the future Pope. The revolt of Charlemagne, son of Louis the German, radically altered the situation. Charles the Bald fled and died. Charlemagne claimed the imperial crown. His supporters, the dukes of Tuscany and Spoleto, invaded the City and those prelates exiled or excommunicated returned to Rome. While imprisoned, John resisted pressure to recognise Charlemagne. Eventually he embarked for Provence where he tried to find an alternative successor for the imperial throne. Eventually, he crowned Charles the Fat, second son of Louis the German, king of Italy (879) and emperor (881). While John was unfortunate in his choices, at the same time, events showed that the support of the papacy was a decisive factor in any imperial election. The need to deal with the muslims obliged the Pope to enter a peace with the Byzantines. This, however, did not address the question of Photius who had been restored to office following the condemnation of 879, nor that of jurisdiction in Bulgaria. The Pope agreed to accept Photius and subsequently he sent his legates to attend a synod in Santa Sofia in 879. The decisions of the council, however, ignored the conditions set by the Pope and proceeded to annul the condemnation of Photius, and to reaffirm the *Creed* of the Council of Constantinople of 381. The Roman delegation agreed. A compromise was reached with regard to the Bulgarian question according to which Bulgaria would return to the jurisdiction of Rome which would not expel the Greek missionaries. The accord was not activated because of the autonomy of the Bulgarian Church. The Pope supported Methodius, the apostle of the Slavs, in his controversy with the German bishops. John maintained a firm control of episcopal elections and was a strenuous defender of the indissolubility of marriage. He is, perhaps, the first Pope to have died violently having been poisoned and beaten by a group of conspirators.

108. **Marinus I** *(882-884)*

Born at Gallese in Northern Latium, Marinus was the son of a priest and sometimes figures erroneously in the list of Popes as Martin II. Of the three legates present at the Council of Constantinople in 869, he was by far the most intransigent and fought with the emperor Basil. He had been Archdeacon and treasurer (*arcarius*) of the Church of *Caere* (Cervteri), and had undertaken many important missions to the emperor and in the South of Italy. He was the first bishop to be elected Pope, in contravention of the ancient ecclesiastical norm which prohibited transferring bishops from one See to another. St. Nicholas I had applied this norm when he refused permission for Formosus to accept a bishopric in Bulgaria. Marinus I was elected without reference to the emperor, Charles the Fat. The Pope met with him in 883 at Nonantola and obtained his ratification at that point. The Pope and emperor announced a pardon for those who had conspired against John VIII, especially the Bishop of Porto, Formosus, who was restored to his See. Marinus also maintained good relations with the Patriarch Photius, whose most important supporter in Rome, Zaccaria di Anagni, he appointed to the important position of papal librarian. The Pope also maintained good relations with Alfred the Great of England.

109. Saint Adrian III *(884-885)*

Adrian was born in Rome. Little is known of his pontificate. He was a supporter of John VIII and permitted bloody vendettas: he was responsible for the killing of a high official of the Lateran who had been recalled from exile by Marinus I, and had a noblewoman of the opposing party publicly flogged. He maintained good relations with the Patriarch Photius, to whom he announced his election. He was invited to the imperial diet at Worms to legitimate a son of Charles the Fat and accord him a right to the imperial succession. Adrian died, however, at Modena while journeying to Worms. He may have been assassinated. He was buried in the abbey of Nonantola where a cult developed which was confirmed in 1891. His feast day is 9 July.

110. Stephen V or VI *(885-891)*

Born of a Roman aristocratic family, Stephen was Cardinal Priest of the Ss. Quattro Incoronati when elected by acclamation of the clergy and aristocracy. In a desperate effort to raise assistance against the advancing Saracens and the feuding Roman factions, the Pope appealed to the emperor who entered Italy, but rapidly withdraw. With the death of Charles the Fat in 888, the carolingian empire dissolved. Having vainly sought aid from Arnulf, Charles' nephew, Stephen appealed to Guido, duke of Spoleto, who had become king of Italy in 899, and eventually crowned him emperor in St. Peter's. He maintained good relations with the Byzantine emperor who sent a fleet to protect the coast of the Papal States against the Saracens. He lost all influence over the Church in Moravia where, following the death of Methodius, he supported the German clergy against his successor Grazd, who promoted the use of the slav language in the liturgy -as had Methodius. Henceforth, the Slav Church in this region came within the Byzantine sphere of influence.

53

111. Formosus *(891-896)*

Formosus was born in Rome about the 815. He became Bishop of Porto in 864, and subsequently served a legate in Bulgaria, where he proved himself so well that Boris I requested his nomination as metropolitan and archbishop. Having been legate in Gaul and Germany, he played an important role in the Roman synod that excommunicated Photius. In 875, John VII charged him with the task of offering the crown to Charles the bald. In 876, he fell from favour, having been charged with disloyalty and having abandoned his diocese. He was deposed and excommunicated. Rehabilitated and restored to his See by Marinus I, he was elected successor of Stephen V (VI). The fact that he was already Bishop of Porto did not raise any controversy. As Pope, he carefully maintained good relations with the English and German Churches as well as with the Patriarch of Constantinople where he tried to mediate in a schism that had broken out subsequent to the election of the new Patriarch, Stephen I. In Italy, initially Formosus continued the policy of his predecessor and supported Guido, the duke of Spoleto, whom his predecessor had crowned emperor. Formosus crowned him emperor a second time at Ravenna, together with his son Lambert. In 893, however, he appealed to Arnulf, king of the East Franks, to save Rome form the tyranny of the dukes of Spoleto. In 896, having descended into Italy and freed Rome, Arnulf was crowned emperor in St. Peter's. Arnulf had to leave Rome almost immediately for he had become ill. Formosus died shortly after. Nine months after his death, the mummified body of Formosus was exhumed by Stephan VI (VII) and Lambert, vested in pontificals and tried in synod for perjury, ambition to succeed to the papal throne and violation of the canons which prohibited the transfer of bishops from one see to another, including the Roman See. The synod, at which the Pope presided, declared Formosus guilty. His acts were declared null, his body dumped into a common fosse and eventually into the Tiber, and the three fingers with which he had sworn and blessed were amputated. This macabre incident has entered the annals of history as the *sinodo del cadavere*. The Pope's body was retrieved from the Tiber and reburied by some monks.

112. **Boniface VI** *(April 896)*

The son of a Roman priest, Boniface was elected by the people who were in revolt. His irregular conduct had induced Gregory VIII to degrade him twice. He was not rehabilitated after the second degradation. He died after a pontificate of two weeks and was buried in St. Peter's. In 898, a synod publicly deplored the manner of his election and forbade that such an election should be repeated.

113. **Stephen VI or VII** *(896-897)*

The son of a Roman priest, Stephen had been consecrated Bishop of Anagni by Formosus, but both subsequently became bitter enemies. After his election, he made fealty to Lambert of Spoleto. The account of the macabre process conducted by Stephen against Formosus is as much as is known of this pontificate. By annulling the ordinations conducted by Formosus, Stephen was able to annul his consecration as Bishop of Angani, which relieved him of any impediment to his election. Stephen was engaged in calling on those who had been ordained by Formosus to renounce their offices when the Roman population revolted. The revolt began with the collapse of the Lateran in an earthquake and by rumours of miracles having been worked by the body of Formosus. Stephen was imprisoned and later strangled.

114. **Romanus** *(July-November 897)*

Born in Gallese in Northern Latium, Romanus had been Cardinal Priest of St. Peter in Chains when elected, following the arrest and death of Stephen. He had been a supporter of Formosus. He was confined to a monastery, probably by the followers of Formosus until such time as they were in a position to install a more energetic Pope.

115. Theodore II *(December 897)*

During his pontificate of twenty days, Theodore, a Roman, convoked a synod to annul the decisions of the *sinodo del cadavere*. Formosus was completely rehabilitated and the validity of his ordinations declared in public. The body of Formosus was once again buried in St. Peter's with full honours.

116. John IX *(898-900)*

John IX was born in Tivoli. He was a benedictine monk who was elected with the support of the Formosian party and Lambert of Spoleto, king of Italy and emperor, after the anti-Formosian party had elected and installed their candidate, Sergius, Bishop of Caere, in the Lateran. John IX tried to restore order in the feuding city. A further synod condemned the synod that had tried Formosus and decreed that the dead could not be prosecuted or tried. Sergius and his followers were excommunicated, but some who had attended the *sinodo del cadavere* were pardoned. Arnulf's coronation as emperor was annulled as it was regarded as having been extorted by force from Formosus. The principle forbidding the transfer of bishops from one see to another was reaffirmed, and Formosus' case declared exceptional. The *Constitutio Romana* of 824 governing papal elections was re-activated under John IX : the Pope would be elected by the clergy, with the concourse of the Senate and people, but his consecration would only take place in the presence of the imperial envoys. This, it was hoped, would eliminate the violent disturbances that happened during the election. A synod held at Ravenna, in the presence of the emperor Lambert, confirmed these decisions and reasserted the emperor's supreme jurisdiction over the papacy: every citizen, whether cleric or lay, had a right of appeal to the emperor. In 898, Lambert died following a hunting accident and Rome was deprived of imperial protection. John favoured a reconciliation between the Byzantine Patriarch and a group of schismatics. He tried unsuccessfully to reestablish Roman supremacy in the Bulgarian Church, mainly because of the opposition of the Bavarian Bishops. He confirmed the privileges of the abbey of Monte Cassino.

117. Benedict IV *(900-903)*

Benedict was the son of a Roman aristocratic family. He had been ordained by Formosus and was regarded as one of his supporters. The exact date of his election (between January and May 900) is not known. Feuding continued in the City between the various rival factions. Two parties were led by pretenders to Lambert's imperial title: Berengar, marquis of Friuli and king of Italy since 888, and Louis the blind, king of Provence, nephew of the emperor Louis III. Given Berengar's defeat by the Magyars in 899, the Pope crowned Louis II as emperor. Berengar defeated him and chased him out of Italy. Rome descended into anarchy.

118. Leo V *(July-September 903)*

An outsider, Leo had been Parish Priest of Ardea when, as a compromise candidate, he was elected Pope. According to the Frankish priest Auxilius, Leo was a holy and upright man. Thirty days after his coronation, he was dethroned and imprisoned by the priest Christophorus who had himself declared Pope. This represented a division in the pro-Formosian group, as both belonged to it. Christophorus suffered the same fate as Leo. He was deposed by Sergius II. Both Leo and the anti-Pope Christophorus were murdered in prison. An eleventh century legend identifies Leo V with a Breton saint, Tutwal (or Tual or Tugdual). According to the legend, Tudwal, when he arrived in Rome on pilgrimage, found the Apostolic See vacant and occupied it by divine disposition.

119. Sergius III *(904-911)*

Descendant of a Roman artistocratic family, Sergius had been consecrated Bishop of Cervetri by Formosus. Having become an enemy of Formosus, he willingly cooperated in the *Sinodo del cadavère*. When the ordinations of Formosus were declared void, he was happy to return to the deaconate and to have himself ordained a priest by Stephan VI, since the episcopate would have precluded his election as Pope. In 898, following the death of Theodore II, he was elected and installed in the Lateran. He was immediately removed and sent into exile. In 904, when the pro-Formosian party split and installed Christophorus as Pope, Sergius appealed to Albert I, the duke of Spoleto, who descended on Rome with an army. Sergius was acclaimed and consecrated Pope. Shortly afterwards he had Leo V and Christophorus murdered in prison. Sergius dated his election from 898 and considered the successors of John IX as unlawful. He re-confirmed the condemnation of Formosus and declared all of his ordinations void. This resulted in chaos in the Roman Church since the Bishops ordained by Formosus had themselves also performed further ordinations. Auxilius, the Frankish Priest, has conserved valuable information about this controversy which was energetically pursued by the Pope. Auxilius had defended the validity of the ordinations conferred by Formosus. The pontificate of Sergius was characterized by the predominance of the Roman aristocracy which was enforced by violence. Notable among these was the Teofilatto family, who were pontifical administrators, consuls and commanders of the militia. It would appear that Sergius had a son by the wife of the head of this family, Theodora, daughter of Marozia. He later succeeded as John XI. Apart from its feud with the pro-Formosian party, little else distinguishes the pontificate of Sergius III. The Byzantine emperor Leo VI, widowed for a third time and childless, decided to marry, but was excommunicated by the Patriarch of Constantinople since the Byzantine Church did not accept marriage for a fourth time. The emperor appealed to Rome and the other Patriarchates. The papal legates approved the marriage of the emperor, deposing and exiling the Patriarch, Nicholas the Mystic. Sergius III completed the restoration of the Lateran basilica which had been damaged by an earthquake in 897. He was buried in St. Peter's and a monument was placed over his grave depicting the «wolves» who had sought to deprive him of the papacy. Since the time of Adrian I, he was the first Pope to strike coin bearing his own effigy.

120. Anastasius III *(911-913)*

Little is known of this pontificate, except that Anastasius was Roman. He governed as the influence of the Teofilatto family was predominant. The chronicler Flodoard praises his meekness. He gave the pallium to the Bishop of Verona and some privileges to the Bishop of Pavia, which was situated in the dominions of Berengar, king of Italy, with whom he evidently maintained good relations. Nicholas the Mystic, restored to the Patriarchate of Constantinople, protested to Rome about the support it had given for the emperor's fourth marriage. Relations with Constantinople were broken off in 912.

121. Landus *(913-914)*

Landus, a native of Sabina, was Pope for less than six months and nothing is known of his pontificate. He was likely to have been made Pope by the all powerful Teofilatto family.

122. John X *(914-928)*

Born at Tossignano in the Romagna, John was bishop of Ravenna when elected Pope, a fact that gave rise to some objections. The canonical impediments to a bishop's being transferred from one See to another were becoming less important in relation to the special case of the Roman See. He was closely associated with the Roman aristocracy and the Teofilatto family, as well as with Berengar, king of Italy. His election was partly due to the worrying advances of the Saracens in Southern Italy. John was an energetic Pope and organized a league of the Italian states. With the aid of the Byzantine fleet he defeated the Saracens at Garigliano in 915. Shortly afterwards, he crowned Berengar emperor in St. Peter's. In addition to these political successes which helped to restore something of the autonomy of the papacy which had been lost during the more recent pontificates, John exercised papal authority in ecclesiastical matters. He intervened in the successions of Narbonne and Louvain; he sent legates to preside at the synod of Hohenaltheim which restored ecclesiastical discipline in Swabia; he attempted to bring Croatia and Dalmatia within the sphere of Roman influence; in 923 he succeeded in restoring relations with Constantinople which had been in difficulty since 912. In 928, he made an intervention with regard to the abbey of Cluny, founded in 909, and underlined its direct dependence on Rome. He rebuilt the Lateran, decorated it with sumptuous paintings and interested himself in the *schola cantorum*. Following the death of Berengar in 924, he supported the candidature of Ugo of Provence for the title of king of Italy. At this point, however, Marozia, daughter of Teofilatto, and consort of the Guido of Tuscany, was alarmed by the political independence of John. In 927 a revolt broke out during which Peter, John's brother and closest adviser, was murdered before the Pope's very eyes. John was deposed and imprisoned in 928. The Pope died in mid 929, probably having been smothered.

123. Leo VI *(May-December 928)*

This Roman, Cardinal Priest of Santa Susanna, was elected by the will of Marozia, who was by this time all powerful in the City. He died after a few months.

124. Stephen VII or VIII *(929-931)*

Cardinal Priest of Santa Anastasia, Stephen, like his predecessor, was elected by the will of Marozia, who was waiting for her own son, John, to reach canonical age to have him elected Pope. Nothing is known of Stephens's government. No sources survive for his government except for some acts confirming the privileges of monasteries in Italy and France.

125. John XI *(931-936)*

Contemporaries believed that John XI was the son of Sergius III and Marozia. He was elected at twenty years of age while Cardinal Theodora, danghter of Priest of Santa Maria in Trastevere. In support of the political ambitions of his mother, he sanctioned the nomination as Patriarch of Constantinople of the sixteen year old son of the emperor Romanus. He encouraged the cluniac reform movement, confirmed the privileges of the monastery for Odo, and extended the same privileges to other monasteries. He celebrated the marriage of his mother, then a widow, to Hugh of Provence, notwithstanding the canonical impediments arising from consanguinity. A revolt broke out in Rome, strongly encouraged by Albert II, Marozia's son by her first marriage. Albert laid siege to the Castel Sant'Angelo, where Marozia and John had installed their courts. Having taken the fortress, Albert imprisoned both his mother and his half-brother. Albert was declared Prince of Rome, Senator of all Romans, Count and Patrician. He governed the City firmly and succeeded in restoring order, until his death in 954. Of the powerful Marozia nothing further is known. John XI was excluded from all power and became a total subject of Albert. Luitprand of Cremona recounts that John was treated as a slave by Albert. The chronicler Flodoard described John XI as a Pope «without power or luster, who limited himself to administering the sacraments».

126. Leo VII *(936-939)*

Born in Rome, Leo VII was a Benedictine monk who had been Cardinal Priest of St. Sixtus at the time of his election. He was placed on the papal throne by Albert II who had absolute control of Rome. His name is connected with monastic reform strongly encouraged by Albert and promoted by Odo of Cluny, then in Rome, especially in the guise of the cluniac reform. Odo had come to negotiate an accord between Albert and Hugh of Provence, king of Italy. While there, he reformed many of the Roman monasteries, including that of St. Paul's Outside the Walls. Leo VII confirmed the privileges of Subiaco and extended those of Cluny and the monasteries of the cluniac reform in Burgundy to the abbey of Gorze in Lorraine. Frederick of Mainz was named Vicar Apostolic and Papal Legate for Germany and given the task of reforming the German clergy.

127. Stephen VIII or IX *(942-946)*

Stephen II appears to have been born in Rome despite the assertion of later sources that he was German. Cardinal Priest of Ss. Silvestro and Martino, he, like his predecessor, was placed on the papal throne by Albert II. He continued the monastic reform. He intervened in favour of Louis IV who had been crowned king of France in 936. He sent Bishop Damasus to pacify opposition to him. Conflict finally appears to have broken out with Albert who had him imprisoned, mutilated and murdered.

128. Marinus II *(942-946)*

Born in Rome, Marinus was Cardinal Priest of San Ciriaco when placed on the papal throne by Albert. He is frequently listed as Martin III which is erroneous. He confined his interest strictly to ecclesiastical matters, such as the reform of the secular clergy and the monasteries. He restored many of the Roman churches and was concerned for the poor.

129. Agapitus II *(946-955)*

Agapitus, a Roman, was the last Pope nominated by Albert II and the only one capable of exercising political as well as ecclesiastical jurisdiction. He had close relations with Otto I, king of Germany since 936, who was crowned emperor in 962. Agapitus supported the restoration of the empire (*restauratio imperii*). In 948, papal legates were sent to the German court. Flanked by Otto and Louis IV of France, he presided at a synod in Ingelheim, where Hugh of Provence, a rebel vassal of the king of France, was threatened with excommunication. In 951, Otto entered Italy, assumed the crown of Italy at Pavia, and requested to be crowned emperor. The request was turned down because of the opposition of Albert. In 954, Albert, who was dying, assembled the clergy and nobility of Rome and had them and the Pope swear a solemn oath that bound them to elect his natural son, Octavian, to the papal throne after the death of Agapitus, so as to combine in him the spiritual and temporal rule of the City in an hereditary dynasty. Agapitus died shortly after Albert and was buried in the Basilica of St. John in the Lateran.

130. John XII *(955-964)*

Octavian, son of Albert II, was barely eighteen but already a priest, when he succeeded. He took the name John. According to the sources, his lived scandalously and immorally. He had, however, a high idea of papal authority and encouraged the monastic reform, protecting the abbeys of Farfa and Subiaco in Latium. The political situation was not very promising: in 958 the Pope tried unsuccessfully to capture Capua and Benevanto in an attempt to extend the Papal States in the South; in 959 Berengar II, king of Italy, took over the duchy of Spoleto and threatened to invade the Northern parts of Papal States. In 960 John XII completely reversed his father's political policies and called on Otto I for assistance and promised to give him the imperial crown. This change had probably been imposed on him by the Roman nobility which was anxious to restore order in the City and continue the reform of the Church. On 2 February 962, the Pope anointed Otto in St. Peter's and swore fealty to him with the Roman nobility. Thus the Holy Roman Empire was established. It would endure for over eight hundred years until its dissolution in 1806. A synod was held in Rome which called on the Pope to improve his morals. The German Church was reorganised in accordance with the emperor's wishes. A new Archbishopric was created in Marburg, and its bishop entrusted with the mission to the Slavs. The *Privilegium Othonianum* defined the relationship between the Papacy and the empire. It extended the Papal States to almost two thirds of the territory of Italy and obliged Otto to defend the Church. A subsequent codicil, added probably in 963, reactivated the norms issued by Lothair II in 824 for the papal election, and reasserted the need for imperial approval and an oath of fealty from the newly elected Pope. It also rendered the Papal States an imperial feud. Relations between the Pope and Otto deteriorated almost as soon as Otto had left Rome to fight Berengar. John began to plot with the Magyars and with Adalbert, the son of Berengar. The emperor returned to Rome. John fled to Tivoli taking the treasure of the Church with him. Otto convoked a synod which declared John in contumacy for his immorality. The emperor accused the Pope of treachery. The synod deposed him, declared him apostate and called on the emperor to provide a successor. Thus Leo VII was elected. This, however, did not restore stability. John XII fomented a rebellion. He returned to Rome after the emperor's departure but only for a short while. Otto I marched on Rome, obliging John XII to flee to the Campania here he died shortly afterwards of apoplexy.

131. Leo VIII *(963-965)*

A official of the Lateran administration who had exercised the function of head of the Papal Chancellery, Leo was a lay man and had to receive all sacred orders immediately before his consecration. Up to the death of John XII in 964, the legitimacy of his pontificate was questioned by the canonists, since the deposition of his predecessor had violated the principle that no one could judge the Roman Pontiff. Leo VIII was little liked by the Romans who saw him as the emperor's instrument in the City, he fled with the return of John XII. A synod deposed him, excommunicated him and declared his ordinations invalid. Leo VIII was restored to the Papal throne by Otto, following the death of John XII. In order to succeed with this project, the emperor was obliged to surround the City with troops since the clergy and people had elected another, Benedict V, as Pope. Little information is available on the pontificate of Leo VIII. Three documents (*Cessatio donationum, Privilegium maius, Privilegium minus*) ceding parts of the Papal States to the emperor and conceding ample influence to him in episcopal nominations, formerly attributed to Leo VII, date from the eleventh century and probably from the imperial party at the height of the investiture crisis.

132. **Benedict V** *(May-July 964)*

Cardinal Deacon charged with advancing the reform of the Church, Benedict was born in Rome and of irreproachable life. He was a man of letters and his fame was consolidated during the conflict between John XII and Leo VIII, although he held aloof from the controversy. He was elected Pope following the death of John XII by the Romans who did not wish to accept Leo VIII, who was already the lawful Pope. Otto's support for Leo impeded his taking possession of the Papal throne. Deposed, and stripped of papal insignia, his crozier was broken by Leo VIII. He was exiled to Hamburg as a deacon. He died soon afterwards, honoured by the Bishop, and surrounded by the reputation of holiness. Otto III transferred his remains to Rome in 988.

133. **John XIII** *(965-972)*

A Roman educated at the papal court, John was Bishop of Terni when the imperial legates installed him on the Papal throne. His was a compromise candidature and designed to placate opposing factions which did not succeed for a popular rebellion broke out in the City immediately after his election. He was imprisoned and exiled. In 966 he was deposed by the emperor who had returned to Rome to suppress the revolt. Notwithstanding the strict controls exercised by Otto over the Pope's political policy, John XIII did show signs of being able to act independently. In tandem with the emperor, he supported the cluniac reform and defended clerical celibacy. He confirmed the erection of the archdiocese of Magdaburg, which had already been agreed but not published because of the opposition of the German bishops. The Archbishop of Magdaburg was given jurisdiction over recently converted Slavs but not all Slavs as Otto had wished. The competence to create new bishoprics was given, not to the emperor, but to the Archbishop of Magdaburg. In 967, the Pope crowned Otto II, son of Otto I, thereby linking him to the imperial succession. In an effort to establish peace, Otto I arranged a marriage for Otto II with Theophano, a niece of the Byzantine emperor, John I Tzimisces. The Pope blessed the marriage. The Pope took advantage of the occasion to extend Roman influence in the Provinces of Apulia and Calabria, thereby arousing the opposition of the Patriarch of Constantinople: when Rome raised the Sees of Capua and Benevento to the dignity of Archiepiscopal Sees, Constantinople did likewise with the See of Otranto. With the visit of the newly elected Bishop of York to Rome, the Pope began the work of extending the cluniac reform to the Church in England. While John XIII was not a member of the Crescenzi family, as some have suggested, he did, however, promote their political ascendancy in Rome. He was buried in St. Paul's Outside the Walls.

134. **Benedict VI** *(973-974)*

Benedict, born in Rome, was cardinal Priest of San Teodoro when elected Pope, probably with the support of the imperial party and those who favoured reform, and opposed the candidate of the Crescenzi family. Elected in 972, he was not consecrated until January 973 because he was obliged to await the imperial consent. Benedict VI pursued the ottonian reform in his policies by encouraging the reform of monasticism, and condemning simony under which sacred orders were sold. He confirmed the pe-eminence of the See of Trier among the German Sees. He experienced grave difficulties in asserting his authority in Rome which was plagued by internecine feuding. Following the death of Otto I in 973, the anti-imperial party led by the head of the Crescenzi family, probably incited by the Byzantines, revolted. The Pope was imprisoned in the Castel Sant'Angelo and accused of unknown crimes. The deacon Falcone, was elected and consecrated Pope with the name of Boniface VII. Sicco, the imperial representative, hastened from Spoleto and demanded the release of Benedict VI. The usurper, however, had him strangled in prison which provoked a popular revolt and the flight of the anti-Pope to Southern Italy.

135. **Benedict VII** *(974-983)*

Benedict was born of noble Roman family, a descendent of Albert II, and related to the Crescenzi family. He was Bishop of Sutri when elected Pope after the murder of Benedict VI and the flight of the anti-Pope. He was the imperial candidate but his election would seem to have had the support of the Roman nobility. He immediately convoked a synod which excommunicated the anti-Pope. In 980, however, the anti-Pope, with Byzantine support, succeed in returning to Rome and claiming the papal throne. Benedict VII returned to Rome in 981 when Otto II established himself in Italy. The anti-Pope fled to Constantinople. While supportive of imperial policy, the Pope was committed to reform and succeeded in redeeming the Apostolic See from the discredit into which it had fallen and in restoring its prestige and authority. At the emperor's request, he intervened in the question of precedence among the German bishops. He confirmed the primacy of the Bishop of Mainz and his right to crown the king of Germany. In compensation the Bishop of Trier was created Cardinal Priest of the Basilica of the Ss. Quattro Incoronati. Thus began the practice of conferring Roman titles on non-residential Bishops. He created the new diocese of Prague which would serve as the hub of the Church in Bohemia and Moravia. At the request of the emperor, he suppressed the See of Merseburg. He completely supported the monastic reform in Germany, France, and Italy. He appointed Sergius of Damascus, who had been exiled to Rome following the Saracen invasion, head of the monastery of Sts. Boniface and Alessio on the Aventine which he had re-established. He interested himself in the monastery of Subiaco and consecrated the new church dedicated to St. Scholastica there. The Pope continued to extend Roman jurisdiction in Southern Italy taking Trani from the control of the Byzantine diocese of Bari. Bari became autonomous and Salerno was raised to the archiepiscopal dignity. In the presence of the emperor, he formally condemned simony at a synod held in St. Peter's in 981, upon having regained the papal throne. He was buried in the Basilica of the Santa Croce in Gerusalemme, one of the seven patriarchal Basilicas in Rome. It is believed that Benedict had gone on pilgrimage to Jerusalem before his election and had returned with a relic of the true Cross.

136. John XIV (983-984)

Born in Pavia and called Peter, John XIV had been archchancellor of Otto II for the kingdom of Italy and Bishop of Pavia when placed on the papal throne by the emperor's initiative. The Roman Church had been vacant for more than six month. It would appear that Otto had had the fourth abbot of Cluny, Mayeul, elected, but he declined. It is unknown whether a regular election took place. Peter changed his name to John to avoid having the name of the apostle Peter. John was totally at sea in Rome. He had the support of no group and depended absolutely on the emperor. The sudden death of Otto from malaria gave the anti-Pope Boniface VII the opportunity to return from Constantinople. The Pope was arrested and shut away in the Castel Sant'Angelo, where he died of hunger or poisoning. Boniface VII ascended the papal throne following the death of John XIV. In 985 he died unexpectedly or he may have been murdered. In the older lists of the Roman Pontiffs, Boniface features as a Pope, and his successor is called Boniface VIII. However, in 1904 he was officially assigned to the list of anti-Popes.

137. John XV (985-996)

Cardinal Priest of San Vitale, John was a man of great culture and a writer. The Crescenzi family procured his election, since John Crescenzio, the head of the family, was governor of Rome and the Papal States, and bore the title of «Roman Patrician». Although the imperial government had no part in his election, the Pope maintained good relations with the empress regent Theophano, who died in 991. In Rome his liberty of action was restricted by his dependence on the Crescenzi family, but he conducted an active political policy with England, Poland (where the duke Miezko placed his territory under Roman jurisdiction), and Germany where he cooperated with the ecclesiastical policies of the imperial government. At a synod held in the Lateran, he formally canonized Ulrich of Augsburg. This was the first such canonization. He intervened in France when a synod, at the will of the France king, Hugh Capet, deposed Arnold, Bishop of Rheims and replaced him with Gilbert d'Aurillac, the future Sylvester II. A long quarrel ensued, during which the Bishops refused papal obedience, which only ended with the deposition of Gilbert. This is regarded as the first manifestation of gallicanism, or the tendency of the Church in France to assert autonomy from the Roman Church. For much of his pontificate, especially from 988 on, power in Rome lay in the hands of Crescenzi II, son of John Crecenzio. He was an utter despot and «troubled and oppressed the Pope» as his legate in Germany, Leo the Abbot, recounts. Manipulated by the Crescenzi and unpopular because of his avarice and nepotism, John was obliged to seek refuge in Sutri, from where he invoked the assistance of Otto III, who had reached majority. Before Otto entered Italy, the Pope had returned to Rome and taken up residence in the Lateran where he died in 996. A delegation of the Roman nobility took news of his death to the emperor at Ravenna, where they also asked him to ratify his successor's election.

138. Gregory V *(996-999)*

The first German to accede to the papal throne, Gregory V or Bruno as he was called before election, was the son of the duke of Carinthia and a cousin of Otto III who had him elected at the age of twenty-four. He was accompanied to Rome by the Archbishop of Mainz and by Hildbald of Worms, the imperial chancellor. He took the name of Gregory in honour of Gregory the Great. Immediately following his enthronement, he crowned Otto II as Holy Roman Emperor, and conferred on him the title of Roman Patrician which had previously been in the possession of the Crescenzi family. Crescenzi II Nomentano, who had been responsable for the vissitudes of John XV, was exiled but pardoned by the Pope in an effort to win the support of the Roman nobility. The new Pope showed himself to be too independent of the emperor's wishes. He sided with Arnold in the controversy surrounding the nomination of an Archbishop of Rheims, rather than Gilbert d'Aurillac. Otto refused to renew the pact made by Otto I with the Holy See and would not restore the Pentapoli, which had been part of the donation of Pepin, to the Papal States. When Otto III left Rome, refusing to defend the Pope, Gregory was obliged to take refuge with the duke of Spoleto, in the wake of a revolt conducted by Crescenzi II. Having failed to take the City by force, the Pope withdrew to Pavia where he convoked a synod in which he excommunicated Crescenzi and reinstituted the norms of Pope Symmachus on papal elections. Simony was also denounced. In Rome, Crescenzi II was preparing to install an anti-Pope in the person of Giovanni Filgato, Bishop of Piacenza, who had been preceptor to Otto. Being Greek, the proposal had the backing of the Byzantine emperor. He took the name of John XVI. Excommunicated by the Western episcopate, the anti-Pope was deposed and imprisoned in 998 when Otto returned to Rome. In prison he was blinded and horribly mutilated. Crescenzi II was decapitated and Gregory V entered the City and took possession of his See. Having accepted the restoration of Arnold to Rheims, the Pope agreed to the nomination of Gilbert d'Aurillac to the see of Ravenna. The Pope also tried to resurrect the See of Meresburg, which had been suppressed by Benedict VII. Gregory died of malaria at thrity-three, although he may have been poisoned. His epitaph praised his ability to preach in Latin, French and German.

139. Sylvester II *(999-1003)*

A close friend and teacher of Otto III, Gerbert d'Aurillac was one of those elevated to the papacy on the advice of Odilo, Abbot of Cluny. He was the first Frenchman to become Pope. As his name suggests, he intended to model his pontificate on that of St. Sylvester and his close cooperation with the emperor. Gilbert was born in Alvernia of a modest family. He was known for his great knowledge of mathematics, astronomy and dialectics. He had been in Rome and Ravenna as part of the court of Otto II, who named him Abbot of Bobbio. Chosen to substitute Arnold as Bishop of Rheims by the French king, he became engulfed in a long controversy between the Pope (John XV and Gregory V), and the French bishops who held that a synod took precedence over a Pope. In 996 he returned to the court of Otto III to defend his position. He became a close friend and counsellor of Otto. In 998 the emperor named him Archbishop of Ravenna. Having become Pope, he took a position of strong defence of the authority of the Roman See which he exercised in an authoritarian manner in various synods and with various metropolitans. He was an enthusiastic reformer, imposing clerical celibacy, and condemning nepotism and simony. In close collaboration with Otto, he floated the idea of a *restauratio imperii*, the reestablishment of the Holy Roman Empire. Otto hastened to restore the Pentapoli to the Papal States in 1001, specifying that his donation was made of his own free will and not because of the terms of the *Donation of Constantine* which he considered false. Together with the emperor, he organized the Church in Poland and Hungry and sent the a crown to Stephen I. In 1001, a revolt broke out over imperial domination in the City. Both Pope and emperor were constrained to withdraw from Rome. Otto III died of malaria before he could return. Sylvester returned to the City, which had come under the control of John II Crescenzi, and continued to exercise the pontifical office until his death in 1003. Notwithstanding his political significance, Sylvester II's reputation rests on his fame as an extraordinarily cultured man. He was an avid collector of Latin codices, he was among the first to use an abacus, to study the terrestrial globe and organ music.

140. John XVII *(May-November 1003)*

John was a Roman called Sicco and was most probably related to the Crescenzi family. He was placed on the papal throne by Giovanni II Crescenzi, «Patrician of the Romans», who effectively held power in Rome from 1003-1012. According to a chronicler, he had sought to establish relations with the emperor Henry II but was forbidden to do so by Giovanni II Crescenzi. It is not known how he died.

141. John XVIII *(1003-1009)*

Phasianus, a Roman and most probably a relative of the Crescenzi family, was Cardinal Priest of St Peter when Giovanni II Crescenzi placed him on the papal throne. He took the name John. He began an energetic ecclesiastical programme: in Germany he succeeded in persuading Henry II to restore the See of Meresburg and to approve the creation of the See of Bamberg while Bavaria was designated as the centre for the missionary efforts among the Slavs. In France he intervened strongly against the Bishops of Sens and Orléans in a controversy relating to the jurisdiction of the abbey of Fleury. He convoked them to Rome and threatened to place the kingdom under interdict were they to disobey him. In 1004, he crowned Henry in Pavia but failed to have him come to Rome because of the opposition of Giovanni II Crescenzi. It is possible that during his pontificate the schism between Rome and Constantinople healed through the influence of the Crescenzi who were very closely allied to the Byzantines. In 1004, he continued the pactice of canonizations by canonizing five martyred Polish hermits. It is possible that he was forced to resign and become a monk at the monastery of St. Paul's Outside the Walls where he died.

142. Sergius IV *(109-1112)*

Peter, the son of a shoemaker, nicknamed *Os porci* or pig's snout, was Bishop of Albano when Giovanni II Crescenzi placed him on the throne in 1009. He took the name of Sergius. He maintained close relations with Henry II, king of Germany, and he sent Legates for the consecration of the cathedral of Bamberg. Henry would not, however, come to Rome because of the opposition of the Crescenzi family. During his pontificate, relations with the Patriarch of Constantinople deteriorated. In 1009, news reached Rome that the Saracens had partly destroyed the Holy Sepulchre in Jerusalem. An encyclical letter, circulated under his name, inviting Christians to send an armed force to liberated it, is almost certainly false. It is certain that he attempted to organise the Italian states to expel the Saracens from Sicily. He died at the same time as Giovanni II Crescenzi. It is possible that both were assassinated. Grave public disorder followed and the election of one of the Counts of Tusculum, the main rivals of the Crescenzi. Sergius was buried in the Lateran Basilica where his epitaph still survives.

143. Benedict VIII *(1012-1024)*

Teofilatto of the Counts of Tusculum, was a lay man at the time of his election, and took the name of Benedict. With his arrival, the counts of Tusculum, descendants of the Teofilatto family returned to Rome and took power from the Crescenzi family, who had attempted to impose a Pope of their own, Gregory. Benedict defeated Gregory in the field. The latter took refuge in Germany where he appealed in vain to the emperor against Benedict. The German king recognised Benedict since he offered better political guarantees than the candidate of the Crescenzi who were traditionally anti-imperial. In 1014 Benedict crowned Henry II as emperor in St. Peter's. The emperor swore to defend the Roman Church and *de facto* renounced his sovereignty over the Papal States. The Pope adopted a policy towards the German Church that was favourable to the emperor, confirming the rights of the episcopal See of Bamberg and granting the pallium to the Archbishop of Mainz. Benedict was a political Pope, a capable administrator, and strong man in arms who succeeded in giving the Papal States a primary role in contemporary politics. Allied with Pisa and Genua, he defeated the Arabs who had attempted to invade Southern Italy. Personally participating in a naval battle, he liberated Sardinia from muslim domination. He reestablished the political authority of Rome in the Campania and in Tuscany, and supported a revolt against the Byzantines in Southern Italy, sending a squadron of Norman horsemen against the Byzantines. In 1019, the Byzantines quelled the rebellion at Canne and began an assault on the Papal States. The Pope went to Germany and requested the emperor's assistance. The Popes' arrival on German soil was an event of major significance. Pope and emperor met at Bamberg where Benedict VII received a renewal of the *Privilegium Othonianum* granted in 962, in addition to the necessary military aid. While the imperial forces failed to defeat those of Byzantium, they did succeed in blocking their advance into central Italy. Encouraged by the emperor, Benedict embarked on a genuine programme of ecclesiastical reform. Immediately following the imperial coronation, he convoked at synod in Ravenna and, in the presence of the emperor, he promulgated a series of norms against simony, and to restore ecclesiastical discipline, including the establishment of a minimum age for the reception of Holy Orders. At a synod at Pavia in 1022, he promulgated a series of strict canons which prohibited the marriage of clerics, including subdeacons. Children of such marriages were to be regarded as servants of the ecclesiastical glebes. Notwithstanding his enthusiasm for reform, especially the cluniac reform, Benedict's principle interest always remained political, which sharply contrasted with the more religious interests of the emperor Henry II. The question of clerical celibacy preoccupied the Pope because of its effects of dispersal of ecclesiastical goods.

144. John XIX *(1024-1032)*

Benedict VIII was succeeded by his younger brother Romanus, a lay man who exercised civil jurisdiction in the City and the offices of *dux, consul et senator*. John succeeded in pacifying the feuding factions of Rome and in establishing civil concord. During his pontificate, the Byzantines continued their efforts to stem the growing influence of Rome in the Southern Italian Church. They attempted to arrive at an understanding with regard to respective spheres of influence, as the chronicler Rudolf recounts. In return for rich gifts, the same chronicler records that the Pope was prepared to recognise the prerogatives of the ecumenical Patriarch of Constantinople. In 1027 John crowned the successor of Henry II in St. Peter's, Conrad II who had already been crowned king of Italy at Pavia. The ceremony took place in the presence of Rudolf of Burgundy and Canute of Denmark and England. The new emperor expected an attitude of submission from the Pope: he refused to renew the *privilegium othonianum*, and constrained him to have Aquileia raised to the rank of an archdiocese, with Grado as a suffragan, and to install his counsellor Poppo as archbishop and metropolitan of all the Italian churches. John XIX encouraged and protected the cluniac reform movement and was closely connected with Odilo, Abbot of Cluny.

145. Benedict IX *(1032-1044; March - May 1045; 1047-1048)*

Teofilatto was the third son of Alberic III, and youngest brother of Benedict VII and John XIX. Head of the family of the dukes of Tusculum, he was a lay man aged about thirty at the time of his election. He is the only Pope to have occupied the papal throne on three separate occasions. He governed well during the first period and provided secure civil government with the assistance of his father's army. He introduced a centralising reform of the Curia in 1037. He was more independent of the emperor than his predecessor: in 1037 he resisted Conrad's request for ratification of the deposition of Heribert of Milan. Only after a year did he agree to excommunicate Heribert and recognise the successor installed by Conrad. He played an important role in supporting the imperial expedition to Southern Italy and used the opportunity to bring the abbey of Monte Cassino under immediate Roman jurisdiction. Initially, he maintained good relations with Henry III, Conrad's successor, and reversing the decision of John XIX, restored the patriarchal dignity to Grado. In 1044, his violent and dissolute life together with the hated government of the Tusculanum family provoked a revolt. In September 1044, Benedict was banished but not formally deposed. He was replaced by Sylvester III, the candidate of the rival Crescenzi family. In March he excommunicated his rival and repossessed, if only for three months, the papal throne. In May 1045, for unknown reasons, he abdicated in favour of his protege John Gratia, who was duly elected as Gregory VI. Having received a very large sum of money from his successor, Benedict retired to his family's estates near Tusculum. In 1046 the emperor Henry III intervened. He had come to Rome for his coronation. He found the City in disarray and three simultaneous Popes. Henry convoked a synod at Sutri and invited all three Popes. Benedict IX did not come and was formally deposed. Sylvester and Gregory were also deposed and a new Pope elected. Sudiger of Bamberg took the name of Clement II. Benedict was re-installed by an enthusiastic crowd, probably corrupted with money from the Tusculum family, in November 1047 following the death of Clement II. In July 1048, the emperor Henry III drove him from the City with the assistance of Boniface of Tuscany. He was replaced by Poppo of Brixen who took the name of Damasus II. Benedict once again withdrew to his estates near Tusculum and continued to regard himself as the lawful Pope. In 1049 a synod held in the Lateran found him guilty of simony and excommunicated him. He died in September 1055 and was buried, probably at Grottaferrata, in January 1056.

146. Sylvester III *(January - March 1045)*

Sylvester II had been Bishop of Sabina when elected Pope, following the flight of Benedict IX in 1044. Displaced after two months by Benedict, he was excommunicated, and returned to his diocese. He had been made Pope against his will and had no wish to occupy the chair of Peter. His condemnation by the synod of Sutri in 1046 did not depose him from his diocese. He died in 1062. There is some doubt as to the legitimacy of his election.

147. Gregory VI *(1045-1046)*

John Gratia had been archpriest of San Giovanni a Porta Latina and was probably connected with the Pierleoni family. He was the god-father of Benedict IX who designated him Pope at his abdication, which was a canonically irregular act. After his election, Gregory gave Benedict a very large sum of money - an act that had overtones of simony. It would appear that his election was formally valid. He was associated with those circles which promoted the reform of the Church, to the extent that St. Peter Damien, a leading reformer, welcomed his election as a heavy blow for simoniacal practises. His chaplain was Hildebrand of Soana, the future Gregory VII. Gregory VI was deposed at the synod of Sutri by the emperor who had arrived in the City with the intention of restoring some order. The same synod declared that Gregory VI had obtained the papacy by simony. Some sources hold that Gregory VI presided at the synod of Sutri and that he freely confessed his simony and resigned the papacy. While this version of events does not correspond to reality, it does serve to avoid the difficulties posed by the actions of the emperor Henry III who, in contravention of the canons, had convoked a synod in which he had judged and condemned the Roman Pontiff. Following his deposition, Gregory was exiled to Germany where he lived under the supervision of the Bishop of Cologne, in the company of Hildebrand of Soana. He died suddenly, shortly after the death of Clement II, which had opened the possibility of his restoration to the Papal throne.

148. Clement II *(1046-1047)*

Sudiger was a Saxon noble, highly esteemed by Henry III, and Bishop of Bamberg at the time of his election. He accompanied Henry to Italy and following the synod of Sutri, he was designated Pope by his sovereign, who was desirous of freeing the administration of the Apostolic See from the control of the feuding Roman families. On the day of enthronement as Bishop of Rome, Clement crowned Henry as emperor and conferred on him the dignity of «Patrician of the Romans», which virtually gave him control of papal elections. Presiding at a synod held in Rome, he condemned simony. Whosoever knowingly had himself ordained by a simoniacal bishop was obliged to do severe penance. He gave unquestioned support to the reform movement of Cluny. St. Peter Damien, however, lamented the slowness with which the movement advanced. In the Summer of 1046, he left Rome with the emperor for the South of Italy, but halted in the Marches, perhaps because of civil disturbances. He died unexpectedly, probably of malaria, at the monastery of St. Thomas near Pesaro. He was buried in the Cathedral of Bamberg. His tomb was opened in 1731 and evidence suggested that he had been tall and blond.

149. Damasus II *(July-August 1048)*

Of Tyrolese origin, Poppo had been Bishop of Brixen. He formed part of Henry III's Italian train and played an important role in the synod in which Clement II condemned simony. Following the death of Clement II, Wazo of Liège sought the restoration of Gregory VI whose deposition he regarded as unlawful. The emperor, however, chose Poppo. With the help of Boniface of Tuscany, Benedict IX had taken possession of the Apostolic See, which obliged Damasus to return to Germany. Only the intervention of Henry III, who threatened Boniface, resolved the situation. Damasus was consecrated and enthroned but died some twenty days later, probably of malaria, at Palestrina.

150. St. Leo IX *(1049-1054)*

Bruno of Egisheim, and Alsatian and a close relative of the emperor, was born on 21 June 1002. He was a great Pope, did much to restore the prestige of the papacy, and set in motion many of the reforms of Gregory VII. He was educated at Toul and became Bishop of that See in 1027. He carried out a thorough reform of the diocese. Without having heard the Roman delegation, Henry III designated him Pope on the death of Damasus II because of his support for the reform movement. It is said that he agreed to a pact in order to gain the support of the Roman clergy and people. He arrived in Rome dressed as a pilgrim. He was immediately acclaimed and enthroned. His name was chosen as a clear reference to St. Leo the Great. In a synod he reiterated the condemnation of simony, removed a great number of simoniacal bishops, and reaffirmed the statute of Clement II requiring penance of those who had had themselves ordained by simoniacal bishops. Leo IX reformed the Curia and brought many from the reform movement into it, including Hildebrand of Soana, the future Gregory

VII, Humber of Moyenmoutier, subsequently Cardinal of Silva Candida, who became his closest advisor. Hugo of Cluny and Peter Damien were among his counsellors. In the synod of Vercelli, he condemned Berengar of Tour's symbolic interpretation of the Eucharist. Without imperial support, in 1053, he led a small contingent against the Normans who threatened the dominions of the Papal States in the South of Italy. He was defeated at Civitate dai Normanni and was confined in Benevento for nine months. In this context, the Patriarch of Constantinople, reacting to what he considered Roman interference in Southern Italy, closed all Latin rite churches in Byzantine territory, violently attacked Western liturgical usage, and condemned the Western use of unleavened bread for the Eucharist. While still in the captivity of the Normans, Leo sent Cardinal Humber of Silva Candida to Constantinople where he proved to be as intransigent as the Patriarch, Michael Cerulario. On 16 July 1054, the Cardinal de Silva Candida deposed the bull excommunicating Cerulario and his supporters on the altar of Santa Sofia. These responded by excommunicating the Pope. This signalled the beginning of the Eastern schism which dates from the reign of Leo IX. By then, however, Leo had died. In 1087, because of the miracles that happened at his tomb, the Blessed Victor III had the body of Leo IX exhumed and placed under an altar in St. Peter's. His feast day is 19 April.

151. Victor II *(1055-1057)*

The Swabian Gebhard, Count of Tollenstein and Hirschberg, born about 1018, was invested with the See of Eichstaett in 1042. He became one of Henry III's principal advisors, and had counselled the emperor against sending the imperial army to assist Leo IX in his campaign against the Normans. His election was imposed by the emperor against the wishes of the Roman delegation which had come to Mainz under Hildebrand, the future Gregory VII, to seek the imperial designation. When the new Pope finally acceded to the throne of Peter, the Roman See had been vacant for almost a year. He took the name Victor II. Following a synod held in Florence at which both Pope and emperor presided, simony was once again condemned along with the marriage and concubinage of the clergy and the alienation of ecclesiastical goods. Similar synods were held in France under the presidency of the Papal legate, Hildebrand. Victor II was an able ruler, capable of addressing the political problems then facing the Apostolic See. In the North, the Papal States were threatened by the expansionist policy of Godfrey of Lorraine who had married the widow of Count Boniface of Tuscany. The emperor marched into Italy, chased off Godfrey and took his wife and daughter, Mathilda, hostages. Henry III reinforced the Papal States by ceding the duchy of Spoleto and the county of Fermo to the Pope. In 1056 Victor II travelled to Germany, like his predecessor, to obtain imperial assistance to curb the Norman expansion in Southern Italy. The Pope was in Germany at the time of Henry III's death and helped to secure the succession of his infant son Henry IV. Victor succeeded in reconciling Godfrey of Lorraine and Balwin of Flanders with the emperor. The Pope died of fever at Arezzo and was buried in Santa Maria Rotonda (the Mausoleum of Theodoric) in Ravenna.

152. Stephen IX or X (1057-1058)

The younger brother of Godfrey of Lorraine, Frederick was born towards the beginning of the eleventh century. He had been educated at Liège, where he was closely associated with the reform circle. Leo IX had brought him to Rome as an advisor. He had also been legate in Constantinople in 1054. During the quarrel between his brother and the emperor, he withdrew to Monte Cassino. Following the reconciliation of his brother with the emperor, Victor II named him abbot of Monte Cassino and Cardinal priest of San Crisogono. He was immediately elected on the death of Leo IX without seeking imperial ratification so as to avoid the possibility of the feuding Roman families usurping the papacy. A papal delegation led by Hildebrand went subsequently to Germany to obtain the imperial *placet*. Stephen IX was a zealous reformer: at Monte Cassino, of which he remained abbot, he attempted to restore the original discipline of poverty. St. Peter Damien became Bishop of Ostia, Humbert of Silva Candida his chancellor and Hildebrand his counsellor. He condemned clerical marriages and made the restrictions on consanguinity more strict. In 1057, he sent Hildebrand to Milan to conduct an investigation on a movement that opposed simony and clerical concubinage. While considering installing Godfrey of Lorraine as emperor and an alliance with the Byzantines so as to expel the Normans from Southern Italy, he died at Florence and was buried in the church of Santa Reparata. Already ill, he had the Roman clergy and people swear that they would not elect a successor until Hildebrand had returned from Germany. A party of nobles, led by the counts of Tusculum, took advantage of the situation and elected Giovanni Mincio who took the name of Benedict X. He, however, was never consecrated and is considered an anti-Pope.

153. Nicholas II *(1058-1061)*

Gerhard, Bishop of Florence, came from Burgundy or Lorraine. He was elected at Siena in December 1058, having been designated by Hildebrand, Godfrey of Lorraine-Tuscany and the imperial court. At Rome, the opponents of ecclesiastical reform elected an anti-Pope, Benedict X. In synod at Sutri, Nicholas excommunicated Benedict and declared him an usurper of the Roman Church. With the assistance of Godfrey's army, he took possession of Rome. In political matters, Nicholas reversed papal policy and made an alliance with the Normans by which Richard of Aversa was enfeoffed with the principality of Capua, and Robert Guiscard with the duchies of Apulia, Calabria and Sicily, in exchange for their oath of fealty. In this manner, much of Southern Italy came under the feudal sovereignty of the papacy. This political move caused great anxiety in Germany, then ruled by the empress-regent, Agnes, mother of the emperor, Henry IV. In religious matters, Nicholas decidedly favoured reform. Hildebrand became archdeacon and many of his advisors were drawn from the ranks of the reform party. Nicholas held an important synod in the Lateran which issued radical norms against clerical marriage and concubinage and prohibited the conferment of ecclesiastical offices by the laity. The same synod, in its struggle against simony, also modified the rules governing the papal election by reserving priority of voting to the Cardinal Bishops. The other Cardinals would then have a vote, and only after that the rest of the clergy. The Roman people were left to acclaim the one elected. Election could take place outside of Rome and a non-Roman cleric could be elected. The synod also reaffirmed, but with various restrictions, the imperial approval. The synod also dealt with a number of doctrinal questions including Berengar of Tour's symbolic interpretation of the Eucharist. It extracted a cleared profession of Eucharistic faith from Berengar. Further synods held during the pontificate of Nicholas II reinforced and extended this policy. Peter Damien and Anselm of Lucca were sent to Milan to make contact with the *Pataria* reform group. They succeeded in having the Archbishop of Milan give his support to the reform movement, especially in counteracting simony and in promoting clerical celibacy. The force of Nicholas' determination to stamp out simony aroused the hostility of the German clergy, where a synod declared his acts null, and broke communion with him. He died in Florence and was buried in Santa Reparata.

154. Alexander II *(1061-1073)*

Anselm of Lucca was born at Baggio, near Milan. He had been a member of the imperial court of Henry III, who named him to the See of Lucca. He was an ardent supporter of the *Pataria* movement. He was designated Pope by Hildebrand but had to be enthroned with the assistance of Norman troops in view of the hostility of the Roman nobility which had been excluded from his election. The imperial court, which had been in serious conflict with Nicholas II, was also excluded from Alexander's election. It convoked a synod in Basil and elected an anti-Pope, the Lombard Kidult, Bishop of Parma, an opponent of the reform movement, who took the name of Honorius II. The anti-Pope took Rome twice by force of arms, not withstanding the fact that the new imperial regent, Anno of Cologne, supported the election of Alexander. At the synod of Mantua, held in 1064, Alexander swore a solemn oath purging himself of an accusation of simony and excommunicated Honorius. The Pope launched an intensive reform which was carried out through numerous synods in France and Spain presided over by Papal legates. Alexander obtained from the king of Aragon the substitution of the Mozarabic rite with that of Rome. In 1066, the Pope supported William the Conqueror against the Saxons and sent him the banner of St. Peter for his successful expedition to England. He also supported the Normans and the French in their efforts against the muslims in Southern Italy. In Germany he severely suppressed simony. Tensions gave rise to open conflict in 1071 when the Guido, the Archbishop of Milan, died. Henry IV imposed his candidate but the supporters of the *Pataria* movement, with the support of the papal legate, elected Atto as Archbishop of Milan. A schism followed which resulted in the excommunication of five of Henry's counsellors who were guilty of simony. Alexander II resumed relations with Constantinople and unsuccessfully attempted to heal the schism of 1054.

155. St. Gregory VII (1073-1085)

Born at Ravacum or Soana in Tuscany of a humble family, Hildebrand was educated in Rome. In 1046 he accompanied Gregory VI into exile in Cologne. He subsequently entered a monastery of the cluniac reform, possibly even that of Cluny itself, until Leo IX recalled him to Rome to assume important offices in 1049. He was one of the most important figures in the reform movement and heavily influenced the policy of Nicholas II and Alexander II. On the death of Alexander II he became Pope by popular acclamation and took the name of Gregory in honour of Gregory the Great. Henry IV was neither consulted nor informed of his election, given the strained relations between the imperial court and the papacy. The reform of the Church was the central objective of the pontificate and closely related to that was the clear affirmation of the sanctity of the Pope and his absolute supremacy over spiritual and temporal authorities. That authority also included the right of nomination and deposition. This was set out in the twenty-seven propositions of the *Dictatus Papae* of 1075. An indispensable prerequisite for the Church's reform was liberation from lay interference. The investiture crisis ensued as a result of the Pope's efforts to exclude the civil power from ecclesiastical nominations. This policy provoked a strong reaction in Germany. In 1076 Henry convoked a synod at Worms and, with the support of the Lombard bishops, had it depose the Pope. Gregory responded by excommunicating the emperor and releasing his subjects from all obedience to him. The excommunication threatened the very crown of Henry which was sought by his rival, Rudolf of Swabia, who had himself crowned king. Henry decided on a policy of submission and presented himself as a pilgrim seeking absolution in Canossa, where Gregory had taken refuge with the countess Mathilda of Tuscany. The conflict reignited in 1080. The Pope excommunicated Henry IV and recognised Rudolf as lawful king of Germany. Henry convoked a synod of the German Bishops in Brixen which deposed the Pope, and named Guidbert of Ravenna as anti-Pope. Guidbert had already been excommunicated in 1076 for his position on investiture. Guidbert took the name of Clement III and was enthroned as Pope. Henry IV was immediately crowned as emperor. When many of Gregory's supporters deserted him, he took refuge in the Castel Sant'Angelo. Liberated by the troops of Robert Guiscard, Gregory had to flee Rome, where a popular revolt had broken out. He took refuge firstly at Monte Cassino, and subsequently at Salerno where he died and was buried. The anti-Pope Clement III re-occupied Rome and continued to usurp the papal office until 1098. While the question of investiture was central to Gregory's pontificate, he remains an important Pope for other reasons: he was particularly concerned for the North European Churches, as his letters demonstrate, and for the Church in Spain where he succeeded in having the Roman rite introduced into the kingdom of Castile. He adopted a more moderate and diplomatic approach to the resistence of the French and English monarchs to his policy on investiture. He tried unsuccessfully to organize a crusade to liberate the Holy Sepulchre in Jerusalem, which he intended to lead himself. He hoped that the crusade would also reestablish communion with the Eastern Church. He is an important Pope in the history of the Church, although his ideals seemed defeated at the time of his death. He was beatified in 1584 and canonized by Paul V in 1606. His feast day is 25 May.

156. **Blessed Victor III** *(1086-1087)*

Victor III was elected almost a year after the death of Gregory VII as a result of the pressure exerted on the Roman Cardinals by the Normans. The new Pope was a decedent of the Lombard dukes of Benevento and was originally called Dauferius. Having spent some years as a hermit, he became a monk and took the name of Desiderius. He became abbot of Monte Cassino in 1058. Named Cardinal of Santa Cecilia and Apostolic Vicar for Southern Italy by Nicholas II, Victor had occupied numerous political offices and had been responsible for the alliance between the papacy and the Normans. He took a mediatory position in the controversy between Gregory VII and Henry IV, which cost him the Pope's favour. When Gregory was forced to flee Rome, Victor received him in Monte Cassino, and was at his bedside when he died in Salerno. While a follower of the Gregorian reform, he espoused its more moderate form. He never enjoyed the support of its more radical adherents. Four days after his election and before he had been consecrated, he was obliged to return to Monte Cassino due the revolt that had broken out in the City. A synod convoked at Capua, dominated by the Pope's major supporter, Jordanus of Capua, confirmed his election, not withstanding the opposition of the radical elements of the reform movement led by Archbishop Hugh of Lyons. In May 1087 he was consecrated in St. Peter's. Part of the City still was in the hands of the anti-Pope Clement III. Henry IV was preparing an expedition into Italy. The Pope was once again obliged to seek refuge in Monte Cassino from where he convoked the synod of Benevento which reiterated the prohibition of lay investiture. Victor died at Monte Cassino of which he had remained abbot during his pontificate. Under his guidance the monastery entered a period of great flowering as can be seen from the codices of its library. A cult grew up after his death. It was confirmed by Leo XIII in 1887. His feast day is 16 September.

157. **Blessed Urban II** *(1088-1099)*

Born Odo de Lagery at Chatillon-sur-Marne of a knightly family, he was abbot of Cluny when called to Rome by Gregory VII, named Cardinal Bishop of Ostia, and given important political office. He was elected by the Gregorian party following the death of Victor III, and took the name of Urban. The papal election was held at Terracina since Rome was still in the hands of the anti-Pope Clement III. A convinced supporter of reform, he took a moderate line until such time as his position was strengthened. While adhering to the principles of the reform, he adopted a moderate position in Germany in his dealings with the emperor, avoiding the use of legates who were unwelcome among the German clergy. The emperor, however, continued to support the anti-Pope and obliged the Pope to seek refuge among the Normans in Southern Italy. The Pope only succeeded in regaining the Lateran in 1094 and the Castel Sant'Angelo in 1098. He began a policy of centralization of the Church, reorganized papal finances and increased the importance of the Sacred College. The term *Curia Romana* appears for the first time in history in a bull issued by Urban II in 1089. He greatly encouraged monasticism, especially the Canons Regular. Many of his decisions made their way into the sources of canon law. His policy of gradual imposition of the Gregorian reform was successful in France but encountered difficulties in England. In Spain he encouraged the Christian reconquest of the country and extended the feudal sovereignty of the Church in

Aragon and Castile. He remained a very close ally of the Normans in Southern Italy. Urban granted widespread power over the Church in Sicily -equal to that of a legate- to Roger of Sicily and his successors. These were only abolished in 1867 by the Blessed Pius IX. From 1095 he relaunched the Gregorian reform with much energy in the South of Italy. The project was linked to his efforts to restore unity with Constantinople. Thanks to the efforts of Anselm of Canterbury, the Greek Bishops who attended the synod of Bari were able to accept the double procession of the Spirit from the Father and the Son of the Latin creed. This had been a traditional subject of controversy between East and West. One of the principal objects of his efforts to reestablish union was the liberation of the Holy Land. In November 1095, at a synod held in Clermont which relaunched the Gregorian reform and imposed a tax on all of Christendom, Urban formally indicted the first crusade to liberate Jerusalem from muslim domination. He died two months after the relief of Jerusalem (29 July 1099) without having received notice of it. Leo XIII confirmed his cult in 1881. His feast day is 28 July.

158. **Paschal II** *(1099-1118)*

Rainerius was born in the Romagna of a humble family. He became a monk and was deeply influenced by the cluniac reform. Under Gregory VII he was named Abbot of San Lorenzo fuori Mura and Cardinal Priest of San Clemente. He succeeded in dislodging the anti-Pope Clement III from Rome, and eventually gained the advantage over three successive anti-Popes elected by the Clementine party (Theodoric, Albert, Sylvester IV). The Pope immediately relaunched the campaign against lay investiture. Relations with Germany deteriorated. He renewed the excommunication of Henry IV and backed the revolt of his son Henry V, king of Germany since 1116. In 1111, Henry V arrived in Italy for his imperial coronation and to resolve the question of investiture. A compromise was reached, the emperor renounced his rights to lay investiture and the Church in Germany renounced the *regalia*, the properties and rights received from the emperor. The agreement was read during the coronation and gave rise to such protest that the ceremony had to be abandoned. Henry V arrested the Pope and all the Cardinals. After two months of imprisonment, and the emperor's threat to recognise the anti-Pope Clement III, the Pope capitulated and the so called privilege of the *Ponte Mammolo* gave formal recognition to his right to investiture. The Pope also agreed not to excommunicate him for any reason. Henry V was crowned emperor in St. Peter's. Humiliated by the experience, the Pope thought of abdicating. In 1112 he convoked a synod in the Lateran and formally annulled the concession of 1111. In a further synod of 1116 he formally reaffirmed the prohibition on lay investiture. Thanks to Hugh of Chartres, a theological distinction was being developed between the spiritual aspects of ecclesiastical office and other temporal functions attached to it. This distinction allowed the French and English monarchs to renounce their investiture rights, in return for the maintenance of the Bishops' feudal oath of fealty to the sovereign. Paschal II zealously supported the crusades. In 1105 he gave his blessing to the expedition of Bohemond II against the Eastern emperor. This further complicated relations with Constantinople. In 1116 a new initiative by the emperor Alexius to restore unity foundered on the preliminary demand that he recognise the primacy of the Roman See. In 1116 the Pope fled Rome and took refuge in Benevento, while Maurice of Braga, taking the name of Gregory VIII, became anti-Pope and crowned Henry V as emperor. Paschal II died in Rome on 21 January 1118.

159. Gelasius II *(1118-1119)*

Born in Gaeta, John, a monk of Monte Cassino, has been named Cardinal Deacon and Chancellor by Urban II. He directed the Papal Chancellery for almost thirty years and profoundly reformed the style of Papal documents. He was a faithful advisor of Paschal II. Elected Pope in Santa Maria in Pallara on the Aventine, he was taken and imprisoned by Cencio Frangipane, head of a Roman faction deeply hostile to Paschal II. When freed by the Prefect of the City, he was obliged to take refuge in Gaeta along with the Cardinals when news of Henry V's impending arrival in Rome became known. He was ordained priest and consecrated Bishop at Gaeta. Having unsuccessfully persuaded him to return to Rome so as to conclude an agreement on the investiture crisis, Henry V had Maurice Burdinus, Archbishop of Braga elected. Braga took the name of Gregory VIII. Gelasius excommunicated the emperor and the imposter. He ensured recognition of this excommunication by having letters sent to all of the major Sees. Gelasius returned to Rome, following Henry's retreat into Germany, but could not take possession of St. Peter's or the Lateran which were in the hands of Braga's supporters. While saying Mass in Santa Pressede, he was again taken by the Frangipani but he was able to make his escape to Genua and thence by sea to Marseilles. He held synod in Vienne in 1119. He authorized the preaching of St. Norbert of Xanten, the founder of the Praemonstatensians. He withdrew to Cluny and died there without having been able to fulfill his ambition to hold a Council so as definitively to resolve the crisis between the papacy and the empire. He was interred in Cluny.

160. Calixtus II *(1119-1124)*

Guido, the son of the Count William of Burgundy, was closely related to the ruling families of France, England and Germany. In 1088 he became Bishop of Vienne and was a strong supporter of the reform movement. He bitterly opposed the capitulation of Paschal II on the question of lay investiture. In 1112 he convoked a synod in his diocese and excommunicated Henry V and condemned lay investiture as heresy. On the death of Gelasius, he was elected and crowned at Vienne by a small group of Cardinals. The other Cardinals and the Roman clergy and people subsequently acclaimed the election. His first attempt, in 1119, to resolve the investiture problem failed. The Pope condemned lay investiture, excommunicated the emperor and set out for the City where he was triumphantly received. Gregory VIII fled to Sutri but was delivered over to the Pope who had him cross the City, through the insults of the multitude, tethered to the back of a camel. Negotiations with the emperor resumed in1122. Three Cardinals were despatched to Worms, among them Lambert of Ostia (the future Honorius II), to approve the concordat of Worms which ended the investiture controversy. The accord was a compromise which safeguarded the Church's liberty by obliging the emperor to renounce investing the Bishops with the ring and crozier, which were signs of spiritual authority, but leaving to him the right to invested those who had been elected for the episcopal office with the temporal prerogatives (the *regalia*), symbolized by the sceptre which represented temporal authority. These concessions were presented as a strategic choice by the Pope rather than a concession of principle. The accord was hailed as a victory for the Church, as can be seen in the frescos painted in the Lateran to commemorate the event. In 1123, the First Lateran Council (ninth ecumenical) solemnly ratified the Concordat of Worms.

161. Honorius II *(1124-1130)*

The election ensuing on the death of Calixtus II was complicated by many unforseen circumstances. The Pierleoni proposed and withdrew their candidate, following which the Cardinal Priest Theobaldo Boccadipecora, who took the name of Celestine II, was unanimously elected. As the new Pope was being enthroned, Robert Frangipane and his troops, with the complicity of Aimerico the Chancellor, interrupted the ceremony and forcefully installed Lambert of Ostia on the throne of Peter. Celestine II, who had been injured, resigned the office. Although lawfully elected, his name does not appear in the list of Popes but in that of the anti-Popes. Following these events, another Pope was regularly elected and he took the name of Honorius II. Lamberto Scannabecchi was born at Imola to a poor family. He had been a trusted advisor of Calixtus II and had played a decisive role in drawing up the stipulations of the concordat of Worms. Some historians see his election not so much as the result of a struggle between the rival Frangipane and Pierleoni families, but of a struggle between older and newer interpretations of the Gregorian reform, the latter concentrating on new aspects of ecclesiastical reform in the wake of the conclusion of the investiture controversy. In 1125, Honorius supported Lothair III in his claim to the German throne and received the unprecedented request to confirm Lothair's election. The Pope had further political successes in England and France. He failed, however, to prevent the formation of a Norman kingdom in Southern Italy, but recognised Roger of Sicily as duke of Apulia in 1128. He approved the order of the Canons of Premontré in 1126, and, in 1129, the statutes drawn up for the Knights Templar by St. Bernard of Clairvaux. When he fell gravely ill in 1130, Aimerico, his chancellor, had him taken to the monastery of San Gregorio al Monte Celio and placed under the protection of the Frangipani. He was buried immediately following his death so as to proceed to the election of a successor. His remains were subsequently transferred to the Lateran.

162. Innocent II *(1130-1143)*

Lorenzo Papareschi was born to a noble Roman family. In 1116, he became Cardinal of Sant'Angelo and exercised many important political offices. On the death of Honorius II, he was elected immediately by a minority of the Cardinals and enthroned by night, unknown to anyone. This irregular election was not recognised by the majority of the Sacred College which met in the Basilica of San Marco and elected Pietro Pierleoni who took the name of Anacletus II. Both were crowned on 23 February. This schism lasted eight years: both had been irregularly elected, both belonged to the reform movement, though to different schools. Anacletus had greater support in Rome. Roger II sustained him, in return for which Anacletus offered him the crown of Sicily, Apulia, and Calabria. The greater part of the reform movement supported Innocent, including St. Bernard of Clairvaux who won the kings of France and England for Innocent, while Norbert of Xanten, Bishop of Magdeburg, secured the support of Lothair for Innocent in exchange for a promise of imperial coronation. Although he had to flee to France, by 1132 he was universally recognised as the lawful Pope, except in Scotland, Aquitaine, and in Southern Italy. Innocent II met with Lothair at Piacenza and proceeded to Rome where he crowned him emperor in the Lateran. The Leonine city and St. Peter's were still in the hands of Anacletus. Lothair used this occasion to attempt reopening the question of investiture and the concordat of Worms. The Pope, however, granted him rights of investiture with regard to the vast dominions in Tuscany that had been left to the papacy by the Countess Mathilda, with the condition that after a certain period of time they would revert to the Roman See. Innocent was unable to hold Rome and was obliged to seek refuge in Pisa. Lothair's death in 1137 further complicated matters. The death of Anacletus in 1138 finally resolved the schism. A new anti-Pope, Victor IV, gave up after some months and Innocent, left without rivals, entered the City. The Second Lateran Council of 1139 (tenth ecumenical Council) resolved the question of the schism, declaring void all the ordinations and dispositions of Anacletus. It also reconfirmed reform measures previously issued. After much hesitation, the Pope sided with St. Bernard in the controversy between him and Abelard, and confirmed the condemnation of the synod of Sens. His final years were marked by a number of setbacks: he was defeated in the field by Roger II in 1139, taken prisoner and forced to recognise him as king of Sicily. A dispute with Louis VII of France led to an interdict. On his death, Rome was left in the grips of serious conflict caused by the constitution of a popular council for the City, which was independent of the papacy and determined to wrest civil power from it.

163. Celestine II *(1143-1144)*

Celestine II, previously called Guido, was born of a noble family in Città di Castello, in Umbria. A favoured pupil of Abelard, he was an intellectual who could also boast the title of «master». Having come to Rome, he was nominated Cardinal Deacon of Santa Maria in Via Lata, and promoted to Cardinal Priest of San Marco by Honorius II. He was a reformer and deeply committed to the party headed by Aimerico, chancellor of Innocent II. On his election, he revoked the interdict pronounced by his predecessor on Louis VII of France. He tried unsuccessfully to withhold his recognition of Roger II as king of Sicily. He bequeathed his personal library, some fifty-six books including two works of Abelard, to the Church of Città di Castello.

164. Lucius II *(1144-1145)*

Gerardo Caccianemici, born in Bologna, was a Canon Regular of St. Freddiano of Lucca. He entered the Curia and was nominated Cardinal Priest of Santa Croce in Gerusalemme under Calixtus II. Important diplomatic missions in Germany and Southern Italy were entrusted to him. He succeeded Aimerico as Chancellor and Librarian in 1141. He was friendly with St. Bernard of Clairvaux and Peter the Venerable, abbot of Cluny. The greatest problem facing his pontificate was the town council which had been constituted in Rome which was not only independent of the Apostolic See but was intent of wresting the civil government of the City from the papacy, which it wished to confine to strictly ecclesiastical matters. Giordano Pierleoni, brother of the anti-Pope Anacletus II, became governor of Rome and took the ancient title of *patricius Romanorum*. Having unsuccessfully pleaded for assistance from Roger II of Sicily, and Conrad III Hohenstaufen, the new German king, Lucius assailed the Campidoglio with whatever of his own forces he could muster in the Campania. Lucius was hit by a stone in the affray and died shortly afterwards in the monastery at San Gregorio.

165. Blessed Eugenius III *(1145-1153)*

Born of a humble family from Pisa, Bernardo Pignatelli was the first Cistercian monk to be elected Pope. Eugenius had been abbot of the monastery of Ss.Vincenzo e Anastasio at Tre Fontane. St. Bernard of Clairvaux became his principal advisor and wrote a tract for him on the duties of the Roman Pontiff, the *De consideratione*. Because of the conflict with the Roman City Council, he was consecrated at Farfa and established his court at Viterbo. He was the last of the reforming Popes and presided at several important synods in France and Germany dealing not only with disciplinary matters but also with doctrinal questions. He examined the visions of Hildegard of Bingen and the teaching of the scholastic philosopher Gilbert of Porretano. Eugenius III began an important series of ecclesiastical reforms in Ireland which included the establishment of four metropolitan Sees. Odessa fell to the Turks in December 1145. Eugenius proclaimed a second crusade and sent St. Bernard to preach it France whither he eventually went to organise it. The crusade, which he hoped would improve relations with the Eastern Church was joined by the king of France and Conrad III of Germany, but ended in failure. When Roger II of Sicily, with the blessing of St. Bernard, attempted to raise a crusade against Byzantium, the Pope refused to recognise it. Eugenius returned to Italy in 1148 and excommunicated Arnulf of Breccia, a lay reformer who played an important role in the Roman Commune. Granted military assistance by Roger II of Sicily, the Pope returned to Rome in 1152, and crowned Conrad III as Holy Roman Emperor, in return for his support against the Roman Commune. This political move collapsed with the unexpected death of the emperor but was resumed under his son and successor, Frederick I Barbarossa. Pope and emperor made an alliance by the terms of the treaty of Constance in 1153. Frederick returned to Italy for his coronation but Eugenius died at Tivoli before the emperor reached the City. He was buried in St. Peter's. Miracles have been attributed to his intercession. The Blessed Pius IX confirmed his cult in 1872. His feast day is 8 July.

166. Anastasius IV *(1153-1154)*

A Roman of humble birth, Anastasius was known as Corrado before his election. Paschal II had named him Cardinal Priest of Santa Pudenziana. Honorius II promoted him to the suburbicarian diocese of Sabina in 1126. He supported Innocent II against the anti-Pope Anacletus II, and acted as his vicar for the City, as in indeed for Eugenius III during his many absences from Rome. He was chosen for his intimate knowledge of the City and because he was known not to entertain hostility to the Roman Commune. The new Pope was consecrated and enthroned in the Lateran. He established his residence in the City and built a new palace near the Pantheon. In ecclesiastical policy he adopted a conciliatory approach where his predecessor had been intransigent. He was buried in the Lateran in the sarcophagus of St. Helena.

167. Adrian IV *(1154-1159)*

Nicholas Breckspear was born in England about the year 1100. He was the only Englishman to be elected Pope. He studied in France and had been a Canon of St. Rufus near Avignon. Eugenius III had sent him as legate to Scandinavia to reform and reorganise the Church. Elected without controversy, he was determined to assert papal supremacy against the Church's enemies and ruled firmly and decisively. He renewed the treaty of Constance and sought the assistance of Frederick I against the Roman Commune and the king of Sicily. He placed Rome under interdict because the City continued to maintain relations with Arnulf of Brescia. Thanks to the emperor's assistance, Arnulf of Brescia was captured and executed. This did not completely rout the Roman Commune which manipulated tensions between the Pope and the emperor in an unsuccessful effort to obtain imperial recognition. Adrian embarked, almost immediately, on a course leading to conflict with Frederick because of the latter's ambitions for an imperial restoration. During his coronation, Frederick appeared visibly uncomfortable with indications of his submission to the Pope, on which Adrian had insisted. The emperor returned to Germany leaving the Pope with no military assistance in Rome. This forced Adrian radically to change his political course and make peace with the king of Sicily: by the treaty of Benevento the Pope recognised his rights in the South of Italy and in Sicily in exchange for the recognition of the Pope's feudal sovereignty. Adrian thus returned to Rome. The treaty of Benevento, however, was contested by elements of the Curia, in addition to arousing the indignation of the emperor. Relations between Pope and emperor deteriorated to breaking point on at least two occasions: at the diet of Besancon (1157) and that of Roncaglia (1158). The Pope retired to Anagni and was preparing to excommunicate the emperor when he died. During his pontificate, the title of *Christi Vicarius* came into common use. The Bull *Laudabiliter*, of disputed authenticity, authorized the king of England to reform ecclesiastical discipline in Ireland.

168. Alexander III *(1159-1181)*

Rolando Baldinelli was born in Siena, and his identification with a similarly named canonist of Bologna does not seem certain. Baldinelli was firstly Cardinal Deacon of Sts. Cosmas and Damien and subsequently Cardinal Priest of San Marco and Chancellor. He was a trusted advisor of Adrian IV and supported his pro-Norman policy against the empire. An number of pro-imperial Cardinals contested his election and proceeded to elect Ottaviano da Monticello as anti-Pope Victor IV. While Alexander was consecrated at Ninfa, Victor IV was consecrated at Farfa. A schism began which lasted until 1178 and which produced two further anti- Popes -Paschal III (elected 1164) and Calixtus III (elected in 1168). The synod of Pavia, convoked by the emperor and attended by the German and Italian bishops recognised the anti-Pope. The clergy and major religious orders met in synod held in Toulouse, with the kings of England and France presiding, and recognised Alexander. The abbey of Cluny, however, sided with the anti-Pope. In 1162, Alexander transferred the Curia to Sens, in France. He returned to Rome in 1165 but Barbarossa's occupation of the City obliged him to seek refuge in Benevento. In an effort to acquire as much recognition as possible, Alexander allied himself with the anti-imperialist Lombard league. The emperor was defeated at the battle of Legnano and, in 1177, concluded the Peace of Venice with Alexander, whom he recognised as legitimate Pope, in return for which his excommunication was lifted. While schism was not the only major issue of Alexander's long pontificate, it greatly conditioned his political programme and obliged him to be cautious in his actions. In the controversy between Thomas à Becket, Archbishop of Canterbury, and Henry II of England, the Pope hesitantly took the part of the Archbishop after whose murder in 1170, he formally imposed severe penalties of the king of England but left open the possibility of reaching a compromise on their execution. In matters of principle Alexander was most rigid. In March 1179 he presided at the Third Lateran Council (the eleventh ecumenical) which formally ended the schism and represented an important stage in the development of papal legislation. New norms governing the election of the Pope were fixed, and stipulated the requirement of at least two thirds of the votes of the Sacred College to secure election -a practice that still obtains. Alexander greatly encouraged the development of the universities and the Cathedral schools. He began the persecution of the Cathar heresy, a form of manichaeism which was widespread in France. Many of his decisions were later incorporated into collections of canon law. The hostility of the Roman Commune once again obliged him to leave the City, and in 1179 the pro-imperial party elected the anti-Pope, Innocent III who lasted no longer than a few months. Alexander died at Civita Castellana. His remains were brought back to Rome and buried in the Lateran, amid the insults of the Romans who had never accepted him.

169. **Lucius III** *(1181-1185)*

Ubaldo Allucingoli was born at Lucca around the 1110. He became a Cistercian monk. Under the pontificate of Innocent II, he became Cardinal Deacon of Sant'Adriano and Cardinal Priest of Santa Prassede. Promoted to the See of Ostia by Alexander III, he took part in the negotiations leading to the Treaty of Benevento and the Peace of Venice. He was a trusted advisor of Alexander III and had the favour of Frederick I Barbarossa. Although elected in Rome, the hostility of the population constrained him to establish his court outside of the City, for the most part at Velletri or Anagni. St. Thomas Beckett regarded him as incorruptible but indecisive. This ensured that Lucius never reached the objectives he set himself: peace with the emperor and another crusade. Negotiations with the emperor began in Verona, but with too many questions left unresolved -such as the legacy of the Countess Mathilda of Tuscany- no agreement could be reached, a situation which was further complicated by the Pope's inability to fulfill the emperor's wishes by crowning his son, Henry, nor by providing his candidate to the Bishopric of Trier. At Verona, new procedures were agreed for the suppression of heresy and incorporated into the important decretal *Ad abolendam*. These provided for the excommunication of heretics, the confiscation of their goods, and their consignment to the civil tribunals for punishment. The Verona negotiations were interrupted by news of the betrothal of the emperor's son, Henry, to Constance, daughter of the King of Sicily, which engendered hostility and anxiety among certain elements of the Curia. The Pope died before the formalisation of an inevitable breakdown in relations between the Papacy and the emperor. He was buried in the Cathedral of Verona.

170. Urban III *(1185-1187)*

Uberto Crivelli, of a noble Milanese family, had been named Cardinal of San Lorenzo in Damaso and Archbishop of Milan in1185 by Luicus III. He was unanimously elected by the Cardinals at Verona, but maintained the See of Milan *in commendam*. Although hostile to the emperor, initially he continued the negotiations, giving assurances to Frederick on those questions which remained unresolved and by sending his legates to the marriage of Henry and Constance which was celebrated in Milan. He refused imperial coronation to Henry and suspended the Patriarch of Aquileia when he usurped the rights of the Archbishop of Milan by crowning Henry king of Italy. Relations with the empire were ruptured in 1186 when Urban refused to nominate the imperial candidate for the diocese of Trier and, instead, consecrate his rival Volmar. The imperial troops, under Henry's command, occupied the Papal States and isolated the Pope and the Curia in Verona. Urban encouraged Cremona to revolt against the emperor, an in retaliation for the emperor's invasion of the Papal States, nominated as his legate in Germany, Philip von Heinsberg, Archbishop of Cologne, and a leading member of the anti-Barbarossa faction in Germany. Having attempted to backdown from this position, the Pope became intransigent and threatened Frederick with excommunication. Driven out of Verona by the city authorities, who were loyal to the emperor, he took refuge in Ferrara, where he died. He was buried in the Cathedral of Ferrara.

171. **Gregory VIII** *(October -December 1187)*

Born in Benevento, Alberto de Morra had been professor of law in Bologna and undertaken important missions for Alexander III. From 1118 he had exercised the office of Chancellor of the Holy Roman Church. A profoundly religious man, Gregory sought to resolve the problem with the emperor and reform ecclesiastical discipline during his brief pontificate. Shortly before his election, news reached Europe that Saladin had taken Jerusalem. Convinced that this was divine retribution for the sins of the world, Gregory immediately proclaimed a crusade and sent legates to preach it throughout Europe. Relations with the emperor had deteriorated to point that the Curia was practically imprisoned by the imperial forces in Verona. Gregory took a more conciliatory line and tried to meet the emperor's wishes. He was freed and escorted to Rome with the Cardinals. In Lucca, he ordered the exhumation of the remains of the anti-Pope Victor IV. He died in Pisa, where he had halted to mediate a peace between Pisa and Genua, since such was a crucial condition for the success of any crusade. He was buried in the Cathedral of Pisa.

172. **Clement III** *(1187-1191)*

Born to an influential Roman family, Paolo Scolari was Cardinal Bishop of Palestrina when elected to the throne of St. Peter. He established his residence in Rome. Clement installed himself in the Lateran and received the fealty of the Roman commune in return for a share in civil administration of the City. He effected a reconciliation with the emperor, mainly by ceding on many important points and leaving the emperor in a position of dominance. The Pact of Strasbourg sealed the accord, and provided for Henry's coronation and the restitution of the Papal States to the papacy (following occupation in 1186), and compromised on the nomination of the See of Trier. Clement's major preoccupation was the crusade proclaimed by his predecessor. Its successful undertaking required concord between Christian princes. He concluded the agreement between Pisa and Genoa, and, through his legates, sought to connect the preaching of the crusade with the need for a general peace among Christians. The death of William II of Sicily in 1189 re-opened the problem of the Sicilian succession, to which Henry entertained pretensions in virtue of his marriage to Constance. An assembly of Sicilian nobles, however, elected Tancred of Lecce, Roger II's nephew, as king with the Pope's consent, though without investiture. Relations with the empire deteriorated and the Pope found himself between two hostile parties. Clement died in 1191, just as Henry was about to descend on Rome for his imperial coronation, on his way to take possession of the Kingdom of Sicily.

173. Celestine III *(1191-1198)*

Giacento Bobone, a member of a Roman aristocratic family which subsequently changed its name to Orsini, was Cardinal Deacon of Santa Maria in Cosmedin when elected Pope at the age of eighty-five. He was a disciple of Abelard and had defended him against St. Bernard of Clairvaux at the council of Sens, at which he participated as a representative of the Curia. Created Cardinal by Celestine II, he had undertaken several important diplomatic missions to the emperor, under Adrian IV and Alexander III. As with Cardinal Allucingoli, Thomas Beckett considered him incorruptible. The first act of his pontificate was the imperial coronation of Henry VI von Hohenstaufen, who was at the gates of Rome, while on his campaign to conquer Sicily. With the failure of that expedition, Henry returned to Germany to face a difficult internal situation. Relations with the papacy deteriorated. Henry arbitrarily nominated a number of bishops, and failed to punish the murder of Albert of Brabant, Bishop of Liège. He also imprisoned Richard the Lionheart of England, notwithstanding the papal protection he enjoyed as a knight returning from the crusade. Although he invested Tancred of Lecce with the kingdom of Sicily, he did not make too forceful an intervention in this dispute, apart from placing the abbey of Monte Cassino under interdict for its pro-imperial tendencies. Celestine gave outright support to the Christian reconquest of Spain. In Rome he proved an able administrator. In 1192, he had his Chamberlain, Cencio (the future Honorius III) compile the *Liber Censuum*, which was a census of all institutions dependent on the Apostolic See and tributaries of it. His principal problem, however, was his relations with the empire. Following the death of Tancred in 1194, Henry VI succeeded in having himself crowned king of Sicily. Henry intended uniting the imperial crown with that of Sicily in an hereditary monarchy, for which he needed the Pope's assistance. To gain his good favour, Henry proposed a crusade. The Pope accepted but maintained a policy of tactical silence with regard to the question of an hereditary monarchy. He eventually rejected a compromise solution put to him by the emperor: the Pope would receive a fixed income taxed on the income of all the German Cathedrals, in return for which he would cede his South Italian territories to the emperor who would incorporate them into the empire. A revolt, encouraged by Celestine, broke out in Sicily. Having suppressed the revolt, Henry died at Messina and was buried in the Cathedral of Palermo. The Pope immediately began a campaign to recover his lost territories and allied himself with Tuscany which was hostile to the emperor. By 1197, Celestine had reached a very great age

83

and asked to be allowed to abdicate, provided he were succeeded by Giovanni di San Paolo, Cardinal of Santa Prisca. The proposition was rejected and Celestine died shortly afterwards.

174. Innocent III *(1198-1216)*

Born at Anagni, Lothair of the Counts of Segni, Cardinal Deacon of SS. Sergio e Bacco, was thirty-seven when elected Pope. He had studied Theology at Paris and Law at Bologna. Highly intelligent, he combined strength with flexibility, and was an able politician. In his theocratic world-view, the Vicar of Christ was placed «mid-way between God and man, below God but above man». The Pope's task was to rule the world, not just the Christian Church. He re-asserted Papal authority in Rome, reorganized the Papal States, and incorporated Spoleto and Ancona into the patrimony of the Apostolic See. Constance, queen of Sicily and widow of Henry VI, paid feudal homage to him and, in 1118, appointed him guardian of her son, Frederick II. Initially, Innocent supported Otto of Saxony for the German crown but was obliged to withdraw such support when the latter invaded Southern Italy and Sicily. The Pope deposed Otto and replaced him with his ward, Frederick, after he had promised that the kingdoms of Germany and Italy would remain perpetually separate. In England, he received the formal submission and homage of king John. The kingdoms of Aragon, Portugal and Poland all became vassals of the Apostolic See. In France, however, his efforts were less successful. Innocent's principal interests were the crusades, reform of the Church, and the suppression of heresy. In the wake of his election, he proclaimed a crusade. Under Venetian leadership, however, the crusade changed course and laid siege to Constantinople in 1218, thereby hastening the collapse of the Eastern Empire. Convinced that the fall of Constantinople would aid Christian unity, Innocent accepted the *fait accompli* and proclaimed another crusade against Islam. In ecclesiastical affairs, he did much to improve ecclesiastical training and discipline. He purged the papal administration and reformed the monastic discipline. Attracted to the ideal of evangelical poverty, he gave his approval to St. Francis and his first followers in the itenerant preachers' movement. Innocent successfully maintained many radical groups within Catholic orthodoxy, especially the *umiliati* in Lombardy. In 1199, St. Dominic de Guzman was charged with preaching against the Cathars in the South of France. In 1208, Innocent launched the Albigensian crusade, the first not to have been directed against the infidel. In 1215, he convoked the Fourth Lateran Council (twelfth ecumenical), attended by twelve hundred bishops, abbots and priors, which would prove to be of crucial significance for the Church. The Council issued seventy decrees, formally defining the Eucharist in terms of transubstantiation; launching a campaign against heresy; establishing the annual duty of confession and Holy Communion at Easter; imposing a distinctive mark on Jews; and proclaiming a general peace among Christian princes for four years so as to prepare for another crusade. Innocent, who was an outstanding canonist, has left about six thousand letters and many decretals which, even in his own time, were already received into Canon Law. In 1210, he ordered the preparation of the *Compilatio tertia* for the use of the university of Bologna. The Chancellery Registers, which are almost uninterrupted, begin with the reign of Innocent III. The Pope died of fever in Perugia and was buried in its Cathedral. In 1892, Leo XIII had the remains of Innocent III transferred to the Lateran, and placed in a tomb by Giuseppe Lucchetti.

175. Honorius III *(1216-1227)*

As Cencio Sevelli, a Roman, Honorius III had been Papal Chamberlain, having been nominated Cardinal Deacon of Santa Lucia in Orthea under Celestine III, and promoted to Cardinal Priest of Ss. Giovanni e Paolo under Innocent III. Honorius had compiled the *Liber Censuum* (1198) of the dependent and tributary institutions of the Apostolic See. His principal preoccupation was the crusade proclaimed by his predecessor, Innocent III, to which he gave much enthusiastic support; intervening as arbiter in a dispute between Aragon and France, and France and England, so as to pacify Christendom in preparation for it. The fifth crusade was a further failure. Honorius II lay the blame for the disaster at the feet of Frederick II who had promised to participate but kept postponing his departure for the Holy Land. In 1225, the Pope threatened to excommunicate him were he not to have departed before 1227. Notwithstanding his promises before the concession of imperial coronation, Frederick II planned the unification of the kingdoms of Germany and Sicily so as to assert imperial authority in Italy and over the Papacy. Honorius III enthusiastically encouraged a mission to convert the Baltic countries, and a crusade against the Moors in Spain. He redoubled his efforts against the Cathars, and entrusted a crusade against them to the not wholly disinterested Louis VII of France. The Pope approved the Dominican Order in 1216 and that of the Franciscans in 1223, and approved a rule for the Carmelite in 1226. He also approved the institution of the third order lay associations attached to the mendicant orders. The *Compilatio quinta*, a collection of decretals of Honorius III, is regarded as the first official Canon Law text.

85

176. Gregory IX *(1227-1241)*

Born at Anagni about 1115, Hugo dei Conti di Segni, a nephew of Innocent III, studied theology at Paris and law at Bologna. He was named Cardinal Deacon in 1198 and Cardinal Bishop of Ostia in 1206. Gregory had been legate in several countries and had conducted a number of important diplomatic missions. Energetic and authoritarian, he was a deeply religious man: he was in close contact with St Dominic and St. Francis. As protector of the Franciscans, he was closely involved in drawing up the *Regula*. He encouraged the development of the Poor Clares. He canonized St. Francis in 1228 and St. Dominic in 1234. The pontificate of Gregory IX was dominated by the constant struggle with the emperor Frederick II, who, in 1227, had arrived in Brindisi to embark on the sixth crusade but had fallen ill. Not convinced that he was ill, Gregory excommunicated him. Two years later, Frederick did eventually embark for the crusade, but instead of taking Jerusalem by arms, he negotiated its surrender at an enormous price. A crusade led by an excommunicated emperor who had bought Jerusalem rather than taken it by arms was too much for the Pope who refused to absolve Frederick. Gregory relieved his Sicilian subjects of their oath of obedience to Frederick and favoured his replacement in Germany. When Frederick returned to Italy, he defeated the Papal army, but refrained from invading the Papal States, preferring instead to reach an agreement with the Pope. Under the terms of the treaty of San Germano, the Pope absolved Frederick of his excommunication. The treaty endured for nine years during which time Pope and emperor cooperated with one another: Gregory mediated between Frederick and the Lombard communes, the emperor came to the Pope's assistance on two occasions (1232 and 1234) when civil disturbance obliged him to flee Rome. In 1234, Gregory published the *Liber extra*, the first complete collection of papal decretals, compiled by Raymond de Penafort, which was one of the principal sources for canon law until the twentieth century. Gregory IX also attempted a reconciliation with the Oriental Church. His most important work however was in the field of suppressing heresy. He instituted the Tribunal of the Inquisition in 1231. Although subject to Papal authority, it was initially entrusted to the Dominicans and subsequently to the Franciscans. Their task was to establish heresy by application of new judicial procedures. These were called inquisitional because they were based on inquisitions or investigations (*inquisitiones*). The punishment of death, to be carried out by the civil arm, was formally prescribed, for the first time, for impenitent heretics. Frederick quickly adopted these new norms and received them into civil law in the *Constitutio* of Malfi of 1231. Gregory's name is also linked to the development of the university of Bologna. In 1231, he ordered the university of Paris to re-open after a closure of two years induced by a conflict with Louis IX. The university of Toulouse was founded during Gregory's reign and played an important part in the suppression of heresy in Southern France. Gregory intervened in the affairs of the university of Paris in favour of permitting the study of Aristotle which had been banned. In 1238 a second crisis erupted with the emperor, following on a series of disputes with Frederick which derived from his ambition to impose imperial authority in the whole of Italy, including Rome. The Pope excommunicated Frederick for a second time. Frederick retaliated by convoking a Council to judge the Pope. Gregory responded by convoking a general Council to depose the emperor, «the blasphemous precursor of the anti-Christ». Frederick surrounded the City and deployed his navy from Elba to intercept and arrest the two non-Italian Cardinals who were on their way to Rome. While the emperor was preparing his assault on the City, Gregory died. Frederick withdrew to Sicily, claiming that his quarrel had been with Gregory and not with the Church.

177. Celestine IV *(October-November 1241)*

At the death of Gregory IX, the Sacred College consisted of twelve Cardinals, two of whom were held captive by Frederick. Those who entered the conclave were deeply divided on the question of the position that had to be taken with regard to Frederick. Matteo Rosso Orsini, the powerful Senator of Rome, compelled them to hold the election by accommodating them in abject conditions in the Settizonio palace on the Palatine. After seventy days of grave hardships, and reduced to nine by death, the Cardinals finally elected Godofredo Castiglioni, a member of an aristocratic Milanese family. According to unsubstantiated accounts, he was a nephew of Urban III and a monk of the Cistercian abbey of Hautcombe in Savoy. Celestine had been Cardinal Priest of St. Mark and Cardinal Bishop of Sabina. He had never given any proof of his abilities in the various curial offices that he had occupied. Old and infirm, Celestine died shortly after election, probably without having been crowned.

178. Innocent IV *(1243-1254)*

The Apostolic See remained vacant for eighteen months following the death of Celestine IV. The Cardinals attempted to have Frederick release the two Cardinals he still held captive. Frederick aimed at the election of a Pope who would be sympathetic to his Italian designs. Eventually, Sinabaldi Fieschi, a canonist who had studied and taught in Bologna, was finally elected Pope at Anagni. He belonged to a Genovese aristocratic family. Nominated judge in the Curia in 1226, his ecclesiastical career prospered under Gregory IX, who nominated him Cardinal Priest of San Lorenzo and Vice-Cancellarius. He had also been governor of Ancona. Innocent IV was one of the greatest ever canonist Popes. In addition to three books of decretals, he published a commentary on Gregory IX, the *Apparatus in quinque libros decratalium*. Innocent was absolutely convinced of papal supremacy and used all available means to assert it. Ecclesiastical donations were used without hesitation. Advantage was taken of the system of papal provision to make nominations to vacant benefices. Nepotism flourished during this pontificate. Frederick initially regarded Innocent as pro-imperial in his leanings. Innocent, however, took conflict with the emperor to it apogee. By 1244 an agreement had been reached whereby the Pope would absolve the emperor's excommunication, in return for the latter's withdrawal from the Papal States and other concessions. Determined to defeat the emperor, Innocent left Rome for Genua and thence to Lyons where he established his residence. Here, in July 1245, free from imperial interference, he held the general Council that had been convoked by his predecessor. This was the first Council of Lyons and the thirtheenth ecumenical Council. Frederick was convoked but did not attend. He sent as his representative Thaddeus da Suessa to defend him against the serious charges of which he had been indicted: perjury, violence against the general peace, sacrilege, and heresy. The Council declared him guilty, deposed him, and released his subjects from their oath of obedience to him. The Pope then invited the German Princes to elect a new German king. Frederick II contested the Pope's right to depose him. Innocent, maintaining that he held supreme spiritual and temporal jurisdiction, organised the mendicants orders to preach a crusade against the emperor. Frederick died in 1250 leaving his son, Conrad IV, as his successor. Innocent returned to Italy. The Inquisition, as a permanent institution, was introduced into Italy in 1252 by the Bull *Ad extirpanda*, which also authorised the use of torture in the inquisitorial process. The Pope also gave his support to the unsuccessful crusade of Louis IX, and sent missionaries to convert the khan of Mongolia. Innocent re-established peace between the Church and the Byzantine emperor. The recently founded Church in Prussia was organised into four diocese. Innocent offered the crown of Sicily to several princes, including Edmond, son of the king of England. After the death of Conrad IV in 1254, he eventually bestowed it on Manfred, Frederick's illegitimate son, whom Conrad IV had named regent of Sicily. In accepting Papal suzerainty, Manfred united the kingdom of Sicily to the Papal States and established his residence in Naples. Manfred soon rebelled and defeated the papal army at Foggia. Innocent received the news on his death-bed in Naples. The epitaph on his tomb in Naples Cathedral states that he «defeated the enemy of Christ, the dragon Frederick».

179. Alexander IV *(1254-1261)*

Alexander IV, elected in Naples, was previously Rainaldo of the Counts of Segni, a nephew of Gregory IX who had named him Cardinal Deacon of Sant' Eustachio and, in 1231, promoted him to the Cardinal Bishopric of Ostia. He had never exercised an important role in the pontifical government, except for that of protector of the Franciscan Order. He had good relations with Frederick, but he was far too indecisive to change the policies of his predecessors. In 1255, he excommunicated Manfred, regent of Sicily, who had taken solid control of Sicily and initiated a military offensive against the Papal States, conquering Spoleto, the Romagna, and Ancona. He imposed his rule over Italy through a league of several cities that supported him. The imperial party - now called the Ghibelines - succeeded in having Manfred elected Senator of Rome. Alexander was reduced to living in Viterbo. A long interregnum ensued in Germany, following Conrad's death, since the Pope could not make up his mind as to which candidate he favoured for election. Politically, Alexander's reign was disastrous. Ecclesiastically, it was better: the Pope checked the system of profiteering from papal provisions; he re-opened negotiations with the Eastern emperor; he tried to organise a crusade against the Mongols; he encouraged the mendicant Orders. Alexander founded the hermits of St. Augustine and canonized St. Clare in 1255. He also gave his support to the Friars at the university of Paris when they wished to promote the study of Aristotle. He did not nominate any Cardinals, and at his death the Sacred College had declined to eight members.

180. Urban IV *(1261-1264)*

Born in Troyes to a humble family, Jacques Pantaléon, was not a Cardinal when elected Pope. The Apostolic See had been vacant for three months prior to his election. He had been on a visit to the Curia when the election took place. As Archdeacon of Liège, he had acted as legate for Innocent IV and occupied the office of Patriarch of Jerusalem. He immediately created fourteen Cardinals, six of whom were French. He was an able diplomat and continued the anti-Ghibelines policy of his predecessors. He managed to recover large tracts of the Papal States, and succeeded in developing a Guelph party in Tuscany where the middle-classes began to assert themselves against the aristocratic Ghibelines party. In Northern Italy, Urban supported the Este and Visconti families, who were natural enemies of the Hohenstaufen. He failed to end the interregnum in Germany. The principal objective of his political programme was to wrest Sicily from Manfred and remove any possibility of its union with the empire. Having resolved the problem of Edmond of England's investiture of Sicily, he offered the crown of Sicily to Charles d'Anjou, with whom he concluded a treaty in 1263. In exchange for investiture, Charles promised to pay a hefty annual tribute, protect the Church and the Papal States, and to respect the borders of the papal domain. Soon, however, the Pope was obliged to seek refuge, firstly in Orvieto and subsequently in Perugia, where he died. In the East, the Latin emperor, Baldwin II, was defeated by Michael II Palaeologus. Urban tried to restore the Latin empire but also dealt with the Byzantines in the hope of restoring Church unity. Urban was the first Pope to establish an universal feast, *Corpus Christi*, which he had instituted in Liège, by extending it to the whole Church with the

Bull *Transiturus* of 1264. The liturgy for the feast was drawn up by St. Thomas Aquinas, probably at the request of Urban IV. The connection of the feast of *Corpus Christi* with the miracle of Bolsena would seem to be a subsequent accretion, given that the miracle occurred in 1263.

181. Clement IV *(1265-1268)*

The Cardinals, after four months of Conclave in Perugia, elected another French Pope, Guy Foucois (or Foulques) who took the named of Clement IV. A jurist by training, Clement had received Holy Orders as a widower and quickly made an ecclesiastical career. In 1261, he was nominated Cardinal Bishop of Sabina. He established his court firstly at Perugia and subsequently at Viterbo since the hostility of the Romans made it impossible for him to return to the City. Charles d'Anjou was invested with the crowns of Sicily and Naples in June 1265. The Pope assisted him in taking possession of his kingdom by arranging financial backing for him among the bankers of Tuscany, while in France a crusade was preached against Manfred. A French army entered Italy and defeated Manfred at Benevento. Conradine, son of Conrad IV, arrived in Italy with an army to claim his imperial heritage. He was triumphantly welcomed in Rome. He was excommunicated by the pope and defeated in battle at Tagliacozzo by Charles d'Anjou, now imperial vicar for Tuscany, who tried him and decapitated him in virtue of powers conferred on him by the Pope. Circumstances had made Charles d'Anjou much more powerful than the Pope had ever planned. In 1267, Clement approved his plan to reconquer the Latin empire of the East, despite the fact that serious negotiations were taking place with the Byzantine emperor, Michael II Palaeologus, to restore Christian unity. In 1265, Clement issued the *Bull Licet Ecclesiarum* by which the conferral of all ecclesiastical benefices was theoretically reserved to the Pope. This was a mile-stone in the centralisation of the Western Church. Clement died in Viterbo and was buried in the Dominican convent of Santa Maria in Gradi.

89

182. Blessed Gregory X *(1271-1276)*

The Conclave following the death of Clement IV was held at Viterbo. It was dominated by disputes and lasted almost three years. In an attempt to have the Cardinals elect a Pope, they were locked into the Papal Palace, which had the roof removed. The electors were threatened with the suspension of food unless they elected a Pope. A commission of Cardinals finally chose Theobald Visconti, archdeacon of Liège, who was on crusade at the time and received news of his election at Acre. Of a noble family from Piacenza, Theobald had studied under St. Thomas Aquinas at Paris. When he returned from the Holy Land, he went straight to Rome and was enthroned. He then convoked an ecumenical Council which had three main questions to examine: the crusade, the unity of the Church, and ecclesiastical reform. Gregory embarked on a policy of pacifying the Guelphs and Ghibelines in the central and south Italian Cities, so as to arrive at a general peace which would allow the crusade to concentrate its efforts in the Holy Land. Part of this policy also included selecting a sovereign in Germany capable of counter balancing the growing power of the Angevin dynasty. With

Papal support, Rudolph von Hapsburg was elected German king in 1273. He was crowned king of the Romans in Aachen. Gregory promised to crown him Holy Roman Emperor provided that he renounced all Italian claims. During this pontificate, an ephemeral unity of the Eastern and Western Churches was concluded. Gregory had hoped for this since his stay in Jerusalem. In 1224, he invited representatives of the Eastern Church to attend the Second Council of Lyons at which they accepted the Roman creed with its double procession of the Holy Spirit from the Father and the Son, and papal primacy. An ecclesiastical tithe was levied on Church income in order to finance the crusade in which England, Aragon, Sicily, France and the Eastern Empire took part. The Second Council of Lyons introduced many ecclesiastical reform measures including a limitation on the accumulation of benefices and norms on provisions to vacant sees. The decree *Ubi periculum* mandated that the Conclave was obliged to meet within ten days of the Pope's death, at the place of his death, in complete isolation, and in deteriorating conditions so as to accelerate the process of election. On his journey from Lyons to Rome, Gregory crowned Rudolf von Hapsburg at Lausanne and fixed the date for his imperial coronation. However, he died at Arezzo of fever. He was buried in the Cathedral and his cult quickly developed. In 1713 his cult was approved and Benedict XIV had his name inserted in the *Martyrologium Romanum*. His feast day is 9 January.

183. **Blessed Innocent V** (1276)

Pierto di Tarantasia, a highly cultured Dominican and able theologian, was elected in Arezzo after a short Conclave. He lacked political astuteness. He had studied at Paris and had been professor of theology there. A friend of St. Bonaventure, he had worked with St. Albert the Great, and St. Thomas Aquinas in developing the *ordo studiorum* for the Dominican Order. He wrote a commentary of the sentences of Pater Lombard. The work had been condemned because of its Aristotelian influence when it first appeared at the beginning of the twelfth century but was rehabilitated in 1215. In 1272, Innocent had been named Bishop of Lyons and Cardinal Bishop of Ostia in 1273. He played an important role at the Second Council of Lyons. He was the first Dominican to become Pope. Innocent supported the house of Anjou and reversed the policy of his predecessor by postponing the date of Rudolph's imperial coronation and by confirming Charles d'Anjou as imperial Vicar for Tuscany and Roman Senator. Innocent revived the plan for a crusade but radically altered its scope by accepting Charles d'Anjou's project of directing it towards the reconquest of Constantinople. The Pope send harsh conditions to the Byzantine emperor, who had already agreed to participate in the crusade. Innocent died shortly afterwards and was buried in the Lateran. Charles d'Anjou donated a porphyry sarcophagus (now lost) for the burial of Innocent V. Leo XIII confirmed his cult in 1898. His feast day is 22 June.

184. **Adrian V** *(July-August 1276)*

The Conclave following the death of Innocent V was held in accordance with the dispositions of *Ubi periculum* of Gregory X and under the strict control of Charles d'Anjou, Senator of Rome. In prison-like conditions, and reduced to hunger, the Cardinals elected the Angevin candidate, Ottobono Fieschi, a noble of Genoa, and a nephew of Innocent IV who had created him Cardinal of Saint'Adriano. He had proved himself as legate in England. Following his election, Adrian moved to suspend the constitution on papal elections. The Pope retired to Viterbo where he became ill and died without having been crowned. Dante accuses him of avarice in the *Purgatorio* (xix, 88-145). He was buried in the church of San Francesco alla Rocca, in an elegant sarcophagus attributed to Arnolfo di Cambio.

185. **John XXI** *(1276-1277)*

When the Conclave met at Viterbo to elect a new Pope, and the mayor attempted to apply the terms of the constitution *Ubi periculum* which had been suspended by Adrian V, riots broke out. When peace was restored the Cardinals elected Pietro di Giuliano, better known as Pietro Ispano. Born in Lisbon, tradition holds that he had a doctorate in literature from the university of Paris. He had been professor of medicine at Siena. He was an important scholar and had published numerous works, including a manual on logic, the *Summulae*, which had had widespread circulation. He had also published a number of commentaries on Aristotles, a tract entitled *De oculis*, and a popular manual in medicine, the *Thesaurus paupurum*. The Blessed Gregory X named him Cardinal and Bishop of Tusculum. The name he took is the result of an error as there had never been a John XX. The new Pope had little experience of politics or of the Curia. He retired to study in a cell that he had constructed within the palace in Viterbo, leaving the government of the Church in the hands of Cardinal Orsini who had proposed his candidature in the conclave. Orsini was a decided opponent of the house of Anjou. John XXI refused to confirm Charles d'Anjou in the office of Senator of Rome and of imperial Vicar for Tuscany. Orsini revived the plan to crown Rudolf von Hapsburg as Holy Roman Emperor. Plans for a crusade were also revived and an anti-muslim alliance was reached with the Tartars. John XXI resumed relations with the Eastern Church and obtained acceptance of all Roman conditions from the Emperor Michael VIII who was preoccupied by the campaign of the house of Anjou against Constantinople. As a result of the Bull *Relatio nimis implacida*, Etienne Tempier, Archbishop of Paris, condemned as Avorreist a series of propositions from St. Thomas Aquinas. John XXI died when the ceiling of his appartment collapsed. Dante numbers him among the theologians in his *Paradiso* (XII, 134-135). A sculpture of John XXI is to be found on his tomb in the cathedral of Viterbo.

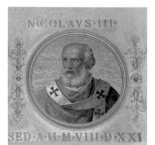

186. Nicholas III *(1277-1280)*

Following the death of John XXI, the conclave lasted six months and finally elected Giovanni Gaetano Orsini, Cardinal Deacon of San Niccolò in Carcere, who had conducted the political policy of the Apostolic See during the reign of the late Pope. Nicholas' principal aim was to counteract the influence of the house of Anjou in Italy. He deprived Charles d'Anjou of the dignity of Senator of Rome, and reserved it to himself, thereby initiating a form of papal lordship of Rome. He resumed negotiations with Rudolf von Hapsburg who renounced all imperial claims to the Romagna in return for imperial coronation. Thus, with the acquisition of the Romagne, the Papal States assumed a territorial extension that they were destined to conserve until 1860. Nicholas arranged a peace between the house of Hapsburg and that of Anjou which was to have been sealed by the marriage of Rudolph's daughter with a nephew of Charles d'Anjou. It would appear that Nicholas intended to divide the empire into four kingdoms, Germany, Burgundy, Lombardy and Tuscany, and to transform the German crown into a hereditary monarchy. He advanced the projected crusade and pacified the Christian princes, and resumed talks with the Byzantines on the unity of the Church, thereby blocking Charles d'Anjou's proposed reconquests of Constantinople. Nicholas, however, imposed stricter terms on the Eastern emperor, including the institution of a permanent legate in Constantinople. He named many worthy Cardinals. As protector of the Franciscans, he encouraged the Order, as well as that of the Dominicans. He intervened on the controversial question of Franciscan poverty and accepted the distinction made by St. Bonaventure between property which could not belong to the order, and the «use» of the goods of the poor which was absolutely necessary for the friars. He rebuilt the *Sanctum Sanctorum* in the Lateran, and was the first Pope to establish his residence in the Vatican Palace which he enlarged and beautified. He died unexpectedly at Soriano al Cimino near Viterbo. A contemporary chronicler noted that «no one on earth equalled him for the favour he showed to his relations». Dante places hin in the *Inferno* (XIX, 69-72). He was buried in the chapel of St. Nicholas which he built in the Vatican Palace.

187. Martin IV *(1281-1285)*

The Conclave was held at Viterbo and lasted six months. The mayor of Viterbo, a supporter of the house of Anjou, expelled Matteo Orsini, the leader of the opponents of the house of Anjou, and imprisoned two Cardinals. Under pressure form the mayor, the Conclave eventually elected Simon de Brie (or Brion). He had been chancellor and keeper of the seals for St. Louis IX, king of France. Urban IV had named him Cardinal of Santa Cecilia. The new Pope chose the name of Martin IV because of a confusion in the lists of Popes which listed Martin I and Martin II as Martin I and Martin III. He was obliged to remain outside of Rome, in consequence of which he was crowned at Orviedo and established his court there for most of his pontificate. Martin was an instrument of Charles d'Anjou and promoted his political programme as much as he possibly could. He immediately conferred on him the title of Senator of Rome *ad vitam*, of which he himself had been invested *qua pontifice*, thereby effectively consigning the political government of the Papal States to him. He accepted the presence of Sicilian troops in the Papal States, and replaced the office of rector of the Romagne with that of a royal official. He maintained good relations with Rudolph von Hapsburg, although he abandoned the idea of an imperial coronation. His most fateful decision was that of agreeing to the Angevin plan of reconquering Constantinople which he proclaimed as a crusade. Despite the Eastern emperor's acceptance of all Latin conditions, Martin excommunicated him as a schismatic, thereby wrecking the proposed union of the Church that had been agreed at the Second Council of Lyons in 1274. The expedition against Constantinople which was planned for 1283 failed to materialise as a result of a successful revolt against the house of Anjou in Sicily, the so-called Sicilian Vespers of March 1282. This did not diminish the Pope's support for the Angevin dynasty: Martin refused to accept direct sovereignty over Sicily offered to him by the insurgents. When Peter III of Aragon accepted the Sicilian crown 1283, he was excommunicated and deposed. Martin's ecclesiastical policies fared no better than his political enterprises. He protected the mendicant orders and granted them wide ranging faculties for preaching and hearing confessions at the expense of the secular clergy. Such was the polemic to which this gave rise among the clergy, that Boniface VIII was obliged to reform the original concession. Martin died at Perugia, shortly after the death of Charles d'Anjou.

188. Honorius IV *(1285-1287)*

Giacomo Sevelli, a Roman aristocrat and Cardinal Deacon of Santa Maria in Cosmedin was elected in a very short Conclave held in Perugia. He was enthusiastically received in Rome where he was crowned. He firstly established his residence at the Vatican and subsequently at a new palace which had been built on the Aventine. He was elected Senator of Rome *ad vitam*. The civil government of the City was entrusted to his brother Pandolfo. Honorius succeed in reasserting his authority in the Papal States, including the Romagne, and in pacifying them. The question of the kingdom of Sicily remained open as Honorius still wished to have it restored to the house of Anjou. Diverting the funds collected by the Blessed Gregory X for the crusade to this objective, Honorius supported the «crusade» of the king of France against Peter of Aragon who had been excommunicated and deposed by Martin IV. Following the death of Peter of Aragon in 1285, Honorius excommunicated his son James, who had been crowned king of Sicily. The Pope refused to accept the resignation of Charles II, heir of Charles d'Anjou, who was held prisoner by the Aragonese. Honorius re-opened negotiations with Rudolph von Hapsburg on the question of an imperial coronation. Honorius was a strong defender of the Franciscans and the Dominicans to whom he entrusted the administration of the Inquisition. He condemned the pauperistic sect know as the «apostolici». He encouraged the study of Oriental languages in the university of Paris.

189. Nicholas IV *(1288-1292)*

The Conclave to elect a successor to Honorius IV lasted for almost a year. The Roman heat caused the deaths of six Cardinals which necessitated suspending the Conclave. When it resumed, the only Cardinal not to have fled the City was elected. Giralomo Masci was the first Franciscan to be elected Pope. He had been born in Ascoli Piceno and had entered the Franciscans at an early age. He succeeded St. Bonaventure as minister general in1274. Nicholas III had named him Cardinal Priest of Santa Pudenziana and had consulted him in preparation for the Bull on poverty. Elected Senator of Roma *ad vitam*, Nicholas was unable to establish his court in Rome because of the continuous feuding among the rival Roman families. He supported the Colonnas. In relation to Sicily, he continued the policy of his predecessors, unsuccessfully attempting to dislodge the Aragonese and re-install the house of Anjou. In 1291, he was obliged to accept the union of the crowns of Sicily and Aragon in the person of James of Aragon. Nicholas was particularly sensitive to the problem of the Holy Land where the last remaining Christian outposts fell to the muslims. After the fall of St. John of Acre in 1291, the Pope, with the support of the khan of Persia who was attempting to combat the muslim advance, Nicholas proclaimed another crusade which proved impossible to organise because of the discord among he Christian princes. Nicholas was the first of the missionary Popes, sending Franciscan missionaries to the khan of China, among them Giovanni da Montecorvino, whom Clement V named first Archbishop of Peking. The Bull *Coelistis altitudo* had important consequences for the reform of the Sacred College of Cardinals and directed half the income of the Apostolic See to this purpose. He restored Santa Maria Maggiore and the Lateran Basilica using the best available artists of the day, including Arnolfo di Cambio, Pietro Cavallini, and Iacopo Torriti. He also built a palace at Santa Maria Maggiore where he established his residence. He was buried in Santa Maria Maggiore. His tomb is marked by a sixteenth century monument by Domenico Fontana.

190. St. Celestine V *(July-December 1294)*

Twenty-two months passed between the death of Nicholas IV and the election of his successor. The twelve Cardinals could not agree on a candidate and the Conclave was twice suspended. In October 1293, the Conclave resumed at Perugia. Charles II d'Anjou arrived in Perugia to exert pressure on the Cardinals in a effort to recover Sicily. Serious riots broke out in Rome and Orvieto. Eventually, the Cardinal Dean, Latino Malabranca, related a prophecy of a pious hermit to the Conclave according to which the vengeance of God would strike the Cardinals were they not to elect a candidate, and ended by suggesting the election of its author, Pietro da Morrone. The son of simple peasants from the Molise, he had entered the Benedictine order at an early age, and retreated to the hermetical life in the mountains of the Abruzzi, firstly in a cave on the Monte Morrone, and subsequently on the heights of the Maiella. Here, he founded the «Celestini». Under his direction they flourished and founded two monasteries. They were eventually incorporated into the Benedictine Order. His fame as a healer, ascetic and as a reformer was widespread in the kingdom of Naples and won for him the protection of Charles I. His election in 1294 was greeted with enthusiasm among the populace and in the more radical of the religious Orders. He was regarded as the «angelic Pope», sent to inaugurate the era of the Holy Spirit, and purify the Church and the world. Astride an ass, he was escorted by Charles II d'Anjou to Aquila where he was consecrated in the Church of Santa Maria di Collemaggio, taking the name of Celestine V. The choice of the Abruzzi, part of the kingdom of Naples, reflected the wishes of Charles II d'Anjou, as did the choice of the Castel Nuovo di Napoli for the Pope's residence. Dominated by Charles II, Celestine nominated seven new French Cardinals and ratified a controversial treaty which restored Sicily to the house of Anjou. Celestine reactivated the norms of Gregory X on the Conclave. Such was the Pope's lack of learning that the consistories had to be conducted in Italian rather than Latin. Confusion began to hamper the papal administration. Celestine protected the spiritualist Franciscans who observed a rule of absolute poverty. Early in his pontificate, the Pope decided to retire into prayer. Having consulted a number of the Cardinals, especially Cardinal Benedetto Caetani, Celestine was assured that abdication was possible. The Pope abdicated in Consistory and resumed the style of «Peter the Monk». His successor, Cardinal Caetani, prohibited him from returning to his hermitage for fear of schism. Having attempted to flee, he was captured and imprisoned in the castle of Fumone where he died. The spiritualist Franciscans propagated the legend that he had been either assassinated or died of maltreatment. Clement V canonised him in 1313. His feast day is 19 May.

191. **Boniface VIII** *(1294-1303)*

Benedetto Caetani was elected according to the norms for the conduct of the Conclave reactivated a few days after the abdication of his predecessor. Born in 1235 at Anagni to a family of petty nobles, Boniface had studied law at Bologna. Having served as a papal notary, he was created Cardinal Deacon of San Nicolò in Carcere by Martin IV and promoted to Cardinal Priest of San Martino ai Monti by Nicholas IV. He had conducted important diplomatic and political missions in France and England. He had advised his predecessor to abdicate, for which he incurred the odium of the Franciscan spirituals whom Celestine V had encouraged. Following his election, Boniface immediately annulled practically all of the provisions of his predecessor, and moved the Papal court from Naples to Rome where he was crowned on 23 January 1295. Not many of his political interventions were successful. Despite his efforts to restore the crown of Sicily to Charles II d'Anjou, the peace of Caltabellotta obliged him to ceded it to Frederick of Aragon. He tried unsuccessfully to pacify the European states in an effort to raise a crusade. The dominant question of this pontificate was Boniface's violent clash with Philip the Fair of France. The problem began in 1296 when the pope prohibited the imposition of taxes on the French clergy without the Pope's consent. The king was obliged to withdraw the tax and change his policy. On this occasion, the Pope canonised Louis IX, king of France and grandfather of Philip the Fair. Boniface then clashed with the Colonna family who represented the opposition to the spiritual Franciscans. Both Colonna Cardinals were deposed and excommunicated. The Colonnas called for the a general Council to judge the accusations made against the Pope that he had had his predecessor murdered. In 1298, Boniface defeated the Colonnas, raised their castles to the ground and confiscated their goods. Both Colonna Cardinals escaped to the French court. Victorious and born up by a wave of popular support, Boniface proclaimed 1300 as a Holy Year and guaranteed a plenary indulgence to whomsoever made the pilgrimage to the tombs of the Apostles. This was the first Holy Year and was Boniface's greatest success. Relations with the king of France deteriorated in 1301 after he had deposed a French Bishop without the Pope's consent. Seeing the incident as a matter of principle, the Pope convoked a synod of the French Bishops in Rome so as to determine the source of authority over the clergy, the Pope or the king. Thirty-nine French Bishops took part in the synod, despite the opposition of the French king. Both in the synod and in the successive Bull, *Unam Sanctam*, the Pope reiterated the supreme authority of the Pope over every secular authority, a doctrine which was not new to the Roman Church, but which was offensive to the idea of monarchical power. Guided by Guillaume de Nogaret, the French king called for a Council to depose the Pope who was accused of illegitimacy, immorality and heresy. The Pope was about to excommunicate the French king, when Sciarra Colonna and a band of French mercenaries attacked the Papal residence at Anagni and forced Boniface to abdicate. The Pope declared that he was ready to die and was imprisoned. This is the famous outrage of Anagni. A popular uprising saved Boniface who was liberated and returned to Rome and to the protection of the Orsini family. He died a month later at the Vatican on 11 October. Boniface's pontificate was an important incident in the Church's history, notwithstanding his arrogance and authoritarian manner which gained him many enemies. He was a great canonist and published in 1298 the *Liber sextus* as a follow up to the *Liber extra* published in 1234 by Gregory IX, which constituted the third part of the *Corpus Iuris Canonici*. Boniface reorganised the administration of the Curia, the Vatican archives and Library. He limited the faculties to preach and hear confessions granted to the mendicants by his predecessors since they had given rise to much tension with the secular clergy. Boniface was a great patron of the arts and employed Giotto and Arnolfo di Cambio. In 1303, he founded the Roman university of the *Sedes Sapientiae*.

192. **Blessed Benedict XI** *(1303-1304)*

Niccolò Boccasini, Cardinal Bishop of Ostia, was unanimously elected in the Conclave following the death of Boniface VIII, from which both Colonna Cardinals were excluded on the basis that they had been excommunicated. Benedict XI was born in Treviso to a humble family. Having entered the Dominican Order he became its Master general in 1296. He had supported Boniface VIII against the Colonnas. Boniface had named him Cardinal and had entrusted many delicate diplomatic missions to him. Benedict was elected with the support of those Cardinals who had sustained Boniface VIII, whose baptismal name the new Pope assumed. Benedict was inclined to accommodation and compromise. However, he incurred the displeasure of the Colonnas because he had lifted the excommunication pronounced against them but refused to restore office or property to them. Riots followed and the Pope was obliged to remove the court to Perugia. Relations with Philip IV remained tense for he still persisted in his plan to have Boniface VIII condemned posthumously by a Council. The Pope took a conciliatory position and lifted all censures under which the king had been placed. On the king's insistence, Benedict entered into a compromise which undid much of the political policy of Boniface VIII, including his prohibition on clerical taxation. All of the French involved in the «outrage of Anagni» were forgiven with the exception of the king's counsellor, Guillaume de Nogaret. The Pope summoned Nogaret and his Italian accomplices before his courts. Benedict, however, died at Perugia. Unlike his predecessor, Benedict had taken frequent counsel of his Cardinals. He named three Dominican Cardinals and annulled the Bull of Boniface VIII which had limited the faculties of mendicants. Benedict was hostile to the spiritual Franciscans and imprisoned Arnaldo di Villanova, the Catalan doctor of Boniface VIII. Miraculous cures were attributed to him at his tomb in the Cathedral of Perugia. Clement XII confirmed his cult in 1736. His feast day is 7 July.

193. Clement V *(1305-1314)*

The Conclave that followed the death of Benedict XI lasted for eleven months. It was divided into two factions, one supporting the French, the other opposing them. Finally, Bertrand de Got, Archbishop of Bordeaux, was elected Pope. He studied in Orléans and Bologna, and had been appointed Bishop of Comminges in 1295. Clement was weak and indecisive. He had been one of the French Bishops who participated at the synod of Rome convoked by Boniface VIII in 1302, but managed to retain the favour of Philip (IV) the Fair. Clement was crowned in Lyons and established his court at Avignon, a territory which belonged not to the king of France, but to the Angevine king of Naples, and therefore a vassal of the Apostolic See. His residence at Avignon was always intended as provisional. He lived in the Dominican Convent, and only partially transferred the archive of the Apostolic See to Avignon. With Clement V, the so called «Babylonian Captivity» of the Roman Church began. It lasted for seventy years. Clement was utterly dependent on Philip the Fair. He did, however, succeed in resisting the king's pressure to have an ecumenical Council convoked so as make a formal condemnation of Boniface VIII, as the king earnestly desired, at the humiliating expense of the Holy See by rehabilitating the Colonnas; absolving Guillaume de Nogaret; a bull approving the actions of Philip in his contest with Boniface; and the canonization of Celestine V as a confessor, rather than a martyr of Boniface VIII. He completely acquiesced on the question of the Templars. The wealth of the Order aroused the envy of Philip the Fair. In 1317 the king arrested the Templars in France. Under torture they admitted to heinous crimes: blasphemous and satanic rites, immorality and heresy. Under pressure from the king, the Council of Vienne, the fifteenth ecumenical Council, was convoked in 1312. Notwithstanding the contrary opinion of the Council's majority, the Pope dissolved the Order and their property was sequestered for the use of the French king until his death, after which it was to be consigned to the Order of the Hospital of St. John of Jerusalem. Clement V made several interventions in international politics: he conducted a successful campaign against Venice to recover papal control of Ferrara; for the imperial succession, he did not support Charles de Valois, Philp's brother, but Henry of Luxembourg who was crowned in the Lateran as Henry VII. Clement also nominated Robert of Naples as imperial vicar for Italy, and with the Bull *Pastoralis Cura* outlined a theocratic political theory, in which the Apostolic See held absolute supremacy over the empire. He intervened in the controversy among the Franciscans on the question of poverty and succeeded only in antagonising both sides of the dispute. Clement instituted chairs of oriental languages in the universities of Paris, Oxford, Bologna and Salamanca. He also founded the universities of Orléans and Perugia. Clement devoted notable energy to centralising the government of the Church, especially by amplifying the range of Papal benefices. He published the *Clementine*, a collection of his own decretals and those of his two immediate predecessors. Clement died at Carpentras and was buried at Uzeste, near his birth place. An unbridled nepotism was practised during this pontificate: Clement named five members of his own family to the Sacred College, and emptied the papal coffers to the benefit of his own family.

97

194. John XXII (1316-1334)

The Apostolic See was vacant for two years subsequent to the death of Clement V. The Conclave met firstly at Carpentras and then at Lyons where Jacques Duèse was elected as a compromise candidate. Born to a middle-class family in Cahors, he studied law at Montpellier and began his career as chancellor of Charles d'Anjou and Robert of Naples, Bishop of Avignon and Cardinal. He was the second of the Avignon Popes, and continued the policy of centralising the ecclesiastical administration of the papacy begun by his predecessors: capitular nominations were excluded from episcopal jurisdiction; the dioceses were re-organised; the fiscal system was reformed so that the income for the first year of all ecclesiastical benefices devolved on the Apostolic See; the Curia was enlarged and rationalised. The pontificate of John XXII was dominated by conflict with the emperor and by the controversy among the Franciscans on the question of poverty. In 1323, the Franciscans formally declared orthodox the doctrine of the poverty of Christ and the Apostles. The Pope quickly condemned the assertion. In doing so, he came into conflict not only with the «spirituals», whom he had persecuted in 1318, but also with more representative figures within the Order, such as the Minister General, Michele da Cesena, and the philosopher William of Ockham. The dissidents were excommunicated and took refuge in Bavaria at the court of the German king, Louis of Bavaria, who had also been excommunicated for his refusal to recognise the Pope's authority in the Italian peninsula and for having advanced his imperial claims. Supported by the political theorist Marsilio da Padova, who maintained that the empire was independent of the papacy, Louis called for a Council to be held, claiming that the Pope's position on Franciscan poverty was heretical. In 1328, Louis marched on Rome, had himself crowned emperor by the Captain of the People, Sciarra Colonna, deposed John XXII and replaced him with an anti-Pope in the person of the «spiritual» Franciscan Pietro Rainalducci who took the name of Nicholas V. The anti-Pope did not last long. Having been initially supported by the enemies of John XXII, he found himself abandoned when Louis returned to Germany. Nicholas abjured and made a formal act of submission. In 1329, John XXII issued the Bull *Quia vir reprobus*, in which he declared that the right to property was antecedent to original sin, and condemned twenty eight propositions deriving form the German mystic, Meister Echart. John XXII was not especially known for his theological prowess and experienced many difficulties in the later stages of his pontificate when he advanced a version of the theology of the beatific vision that won almost universal rejection among the theologians. Louis of Bavaria and William of Ockham used this incident in another attempt to depose him. On his death-bed, John made a partial retraction of his position. While not a gifted theologian, John was brilliant canonist. His decretals, the *Extravagantes*, remains a fundamental canon law text. During his pontificate, missions were established in Asia, and dioceses were founded in Anatolia, Armenia, India and Persia. During the pontificate of John XXII, the Sacred College became increasingly dominated by the French. Many of the Pope's relatives and friends received benefices and offices during his reign.

195. Benedict XII *(1334-1342)*

Jacques Fournier was born of a humble family near Toulouse. He had entered the Cistercians at a very early age, and studied theology in Paris. Nominated Bishop of Pamiers, he was subsequently transferred to Mirepoix. He was an able inquisitor and his registers are an important historical source for the Cathar heresy. In 1337, he was named Cardinal Priest of Santa Prisca and was highly regarded as a theologian at the court of John XXII, whom he succeeded after a very short Conclave, because the favourite, Jean de Comminges, refused to give an undertaking to maintain the papal court in Avignon. It would seem that Benedict XII, at the invitation of the Italian Cardinals, did intend to establish the court temporarily in Bologna. He began the restoration of St. Peter's and of the Lateran but eventually abandoned the idea of leaving Avignon. He transferred all of the papal archive to Avignon and built a new palace in Avignon, the old palace, which resembled a fortress. In the only consistory he held for the creation of cardinals, he nominated five French Cardinals and one Italian. The Pope was more interested in the correction of abuses than in politics. He reformed and regulated the system of ecclesiastical benefices and prohibited the commendation and cumulation of benefices. The obligation of residence was strictly enforced, the Curia was reformed, as were the system of honours and the Sacred Penitentiary. The first sentence of the Roman Rota dates from the pontificate of Benedict XII. The Pope reformed the religious life of the mendicants, the Cistercians, and of the Benedictines. The Bull *Summi magistri*, by which the Benedictine Order was reformed, remained in force up to the Council of Trent. In 1336, he finally decided the question of the degree to which the blessed possess the vision of God, by declaring that they had «an intuitive vision, *facie in faciem*, of the essence of God. In the political arena, Benedict tried to mediate in the controversy between France and England, but failed to prevent the outbreak of the Hundred Years War. In Italy, papal authority was in grave crisis. The Church lost control of the Romagna, Bologna and Ancona. No accord could be made with Louis of Bavaria, above all because of the opposition of France, to whose political programme the Pope was entirely subservient. The second imperial diet of Frankfort issued the constitution *Licet iuris* which clearly stated the independence of the empire from the Apostolic See, and claimed that the emperor's power was divinely conferred without intermediary. Francesco Petrarca described Benedict as incapable and given to wine. He was a rigorist and a legalist completely opposed to any form of nepotism.

196. Clement VI *(1342-1352)*

Pierre Roget was born at the Chateau de Maumont, near Limoges. He joined the Benedictines and graduated in Theology at the University of Paris. From the See of Arras, he was promoted to Rouen, and created Cardinal in 1342. Clement was elected without difficulties in the Conclave of 1342. He immediately received the Roman delegation which pleaded with him to return the papal court to the City and to declare a jubilee every fifty years rather than once a century. He agreed to their second request and declared 1350 a Holy Year, which enabled Rome to recover from the economic collapse it had been suffering. With regard to returning the papal court to Rome, an implicit answer was given to the request when Clement acquired the city of Avignon and the County of Venasque from Johanna I of Naples, thereby rendering it the property of the Apostolic See. The Pope was, however, very attentive to Italian and Roman politics. In Italy, having failed to recover the Romagna, he was obliged to enfeoffs the city of Bologna to Giovanni Visconti, Lord of Milan, for eleven years. He conducted a policy of aggression against the Roman aristocratic families, and initially supported an initiative of popular government under Coal di Rienzo, whom he received in Avignon. However, in view of di Rienzo's anti papal activity, Clement excommunicated him. While his heart favoured the French in the Hundred Years War, Clement played an important mediatory role in the process leading to the treaty of Malestroit, signed in 1343. Allied with Venice, he attempted to raise a crusade but had little success. Clement began talks with the Byzantine emperor and the Armenians with a view to restoring Church unity. He continued the struggle with Louis of Bavaria, whom he deposed and excommunicated. When Louis died in 1347, Clement succeeded in having the electors recognise his candidate, Charles of Bohemia, as German king. Charles had sworn not to interfere in Italian affairs. Charles was crowned at Bonn, while the dissident Franciscans who had enjoyed the protection of Louis of Bavaria were obliged to submit to the Apostolic See. When the black plague devastated Europe in 1348, Clement took a courageous stand in defending, amongst others, the Jews who had been accused of starting the plague. The Pope maintained a splendid court and patronised many artists and intellectuals. He built the magnificent new palace in Avignon, but the expenses involved in its building soon emptied the coffers of the Apostolic See that had been carefully built up by his predecessor. This necessitated increasing the concession of benefices and taxes. The latter provoked a re-action in England and Germany because of the fiscal implications of the outflow of money to the papal coffers. Clement was buried at La Chaise-Dieu. His tomb was desecrated by the Huguenots in 1562.

197. **Innocent VI** *(1352-1362)*

Before electing Innocent VI, the Sacred College attempted to promulgate laws designed to increase its own influence and regulate the creation of new Cardinals. Etienne Aubert, a distinguished canonist and professor at Toulouse was elected, and immediately deemed such legislation invalid since the Conclave had no authority to promulgate law nor to limit papal power. Innocent VI resumed the rigorists policy of Benedict XII. He gave new impetus to ecclesiastical renewal by restoring discipline to the Dominican Order, persecuting the Franciscan spiritualists, a good number of whom were imprisoned or sent to the galleys. St. Bridget of Sweden, who at first supported Innocent VI, subsequently denounced him and described him as the persecutor of the «flock of Christ». The Pope intended to return his court to Rome and did much to pacify the Papal States, then in the grip of feuds and struggles, by sending Gil Albornoz as his legate. The choice of Albornoz was momentous. Not only did he succeed in recovering Bologna from the Visconti family, but he also began the modernisation and centralisation of the States. In an attempt to restore papal authority in Rome, Albornoz supported the second revolt of Cola di Rienzo, by naming him Senator of Rome. The attempt failed when he was killed in a popular commotion. Innocent maintained good relations with Charles of Luxembourg whom the Bishop of Ostia was authorised to crown Holy Roman Emperor in 1355. Charles published the famous Golden Bull in 1356 for the regulation of the imperial election in which no mention was made of the Pope's traditional right to confirm the election. Innocent made no reaction to it. He intervened on several occasions with England and France during the Hundred Years War. Innocent convinced them to accept the terms of the treaty of Brétingy which lasted for a decade. Negotiations with the Byzantines on Church unity came to a standstill. Innocent fortified the city of Avignon to protect it from the ravages of marauding troops disbanded as a result of the treaty of Brétingy who had turned to pillage and plundering the countryside.

198. **Blessed Urban V** *(1362-1370)*

Blessed Urban V returned the Curia to Rome, even if only temporarily. Guillaume Grimoard, born of an aristocratic family from the South of France (Grizac), had studied law in Montpellier and Toulouse before entering the Benedictine Order. He had been papal legate in Italy and had carried out several important diplomatic missions. When elected, he was not a Cardinal and was on a mission in Naples. He was crowned in Avignon. He was a profoundly religious man and retained the Benedictine habit during his pontificate. He continued the reform policy of Innocent VI, reformed the Curia, eliminated waste, abolished the accumulation of benefices, and encouraged the centralisation begun by the previous Avignon Popes. He reserved provision to all major sees and abbeys to the Apostolic See. The major preoccupation of this pontificate was the crusade to the Holy Land and the subsidiary question of Church union. An attempted crusade against the Turks in 1363 and 1365 was all but a failure. The proposal of a crusade required the Pope to return to Rome and Urban was conscious of this fact. That, however, could not come about until Rome and Italy had been secured by the pacification and centralisation of the Papal States, a task which was been pursued by Cardinal Albornoz. In 1364, Urban concluded a peace with the Visconti family with whom he had been in deep conflict on the question of the return of the city of Bologna to the papacy. In 1367, he left Avignon, bringing in his train a reluctant Curia. He disembarked at Corneto near Tarquinia, moved to Rome and took up residence at the Vatican whose restoration he had overseen from Avignon. The Lateran had been destroyed by fire in 1360. Part of the Curia, with responsibility for financial administration, remained in Avignon. Urban received the emperor Charles IV in Rome in 1368, and the Byzantine emperor John V Palaeologos in 1369 who, in an effort to win Western support against the Turks, publicly abjured Orthodoxy before the Pope and embraced Catholicism. Church union, however, did not follow. Rather than convoke an ecumenical Council, as the Byzantines demanded, Urban preferred to institute a Latin Church in the Eastern Empire and was prepared to send missionaries to make converts from orthodoxy. The Italian political situation became critical and the Pope was obliged to consider returning to Avignon. In 1370, Perugia rebelled and was placed under interdict. Rome revolted and the Pope moved the court to Viterbo and eventually to Montefiascone. Mercenaries in the pay of the Visconti threatened the northern borders of the Papal States. In 1369, the Hundred Years War resumed. Urban believed that his peace efforts could better be conducted from Avignon. He believed that as the Holy Spirit had led him to return to Rome, he was again prompting him to retire to Avignon. Amid the supplications of the Romans, the invocations of Petrarch and the dark prophecies of St. Bridget of Sweden, Urban embarked for Marseilles. He died two months after his return to Avignon. He was buried in the Cathedral of Avignon but his remains were subsequently transferred to the abbey of St. Victor in Marseilles where a cult developed around his tomb. The Blessed Pius IX confirmed the cult on 19 December 1870.

199. Gregory XI *(1370-1378)*

Pierre Roger de Beaufort, born of a noble family from Limoges and a nephew of Clement VI, was forty-two when elected Pope after a short Conclave held in Avignon. He had studied law under Baldo deli Ubaldi in Perugia. He had conducted several important missions and was highly regarded by the Cardinals for his erudition and political astuteness. Gregory continued the policies of his predecessors: the crusade, Church union, and the pacification of Europe. He devoted special attention to the suppression of heresy in France, Spain and Germany. He condemned nineteen theses proposed by the English theologian John Wycliffe and insisted on the investigation of his works. He introduced a Cardinal Protector for the Dominican Order. While his ecclesiastical policy required his return to Rome, the unstable Italian political situation made it impossible for him to return to the City. The Visconti continued their expansionism in the north of Italy. In 1373 the Pope constituted a league against the Visconti and placed them under interdict. When on the point of departing Avignon to crush the Visconti, circumstances changed and compelled the Pope to make peace with them. Florence, allied to Bologna, and a good part of the Papal States rose against Gregory. In the face of the Florentine rebellion and that of the Papal States, Gregory sent Cardinal Robert de Genève to reconquer the Papal States [this Cardinal would later become the anti-Pope Clement VII]. Finally, Gregory, besieged by the implorations of St. Catherine of Siena, embarked for Italy and entered Rome on 17 January 1377. Conflict continued to devastate Italy. The Papal Legate, Robert de Genève conducted an appalling massacre in Cesena, negotiations with Florence bore no success, the Romans rebelled and eventually Gregory was obliged to take refuge in Anagni. In 1378, a peace conference opened at Sarzana during which Gregory died in Rome.

200. Urban VI *(1378-1389)*

The first conclave to have been held in Rome since 1303 was conducted in the midst of public disorder. Fearing that a French Pope would return to Avignon, the mob invaded the Vatican palace and demanded the election of a Roman or at least of an Italian. Bartolomeo Prignano, Archbishop of Bari, was elected. He had been an important canonist and had occupied a prominent position in the court of Avignon. In Rome he held responsibility for the Apostolic Chancellery. Urban VI had a strong and obstinate character and immediately fought with the Cardinals. In reply to a French proposal to return to Avignon, he stated that he was prepared to create as many Italian Cardinals as would be necessary to reduce the French to a minority within the Sacred College. The French retired to Anagni. When Urban refused to entertain any form of compromise, the Cardinals in Anagni declared his election invalid since it had not been conducted in freedom but under pressure from the Roman mob. The French Cardinals invited him to abdicate and to communicate his decision to the other sovereigns.

Subsequently, at Fondi, they elected Robert de Genève who took the name of Clement VII, and so began the Western Schism that was destined to last until 1417. St. Catherine of Siena strenuously supported Urban, as did the empire, England, and the central European States. France, Burgundy, Savoy, Naples, Castile and Aragon supported Clement VII. At first, both contenders attempted to settles the question of the legitimacy of their elections by arms. The mercenaries of Urban VI secured Rome for him. There he installed a new Curia and created twenty nine Cardinals. Clement VII retired to Avignon. Urban rejected all proposals put to him to resolve the schism, including that of convoking a general Council. Rather, he was preoccupied with Naples, which he intended giving to one of his nephews. He deposed queen Johanna, who had supported his rival, and replaced her with Carlo di Durazzo, with whom he fought almost immediately. Plots, mysterious disappearances of Cardinals, and Urban's constant flights throughout Italy, inevitably hastened the end of his pontificate. Having bankrupted the Papal States and reduced them to anarchy, he was abandoned by all. Before his death, he declared that the Jubilee Year would be celebrated every thirty-three years, in imitation of the age of Our Lord, and proclaimed 1390 a Holy year. He extended to the entire Church the feast of the Visitation of the Blessed Virgin Mary which had been observed by the Franciscans. The Pope died at Rome, possibly from poisoning in 1389 and was buried in the crypt of St. Peter's.

201. Boniface IX *(1389-1404)*

Pietro Tomacelli, a Neopolitan aristocrat, was elected Pope by a conclave consisting of fourteen Italian cardinals. Created Cardinal by Urban VI, he was much more diplomatic than his predecessor, and rejected any proposal to resolve the schism by convoking a Council. Boniface succeeded in winning many of the Cardinals to himself. He promised Clement VII that were he to abdicate, he would permit him to retain the cardinalatial dignity and depute him legate for France and Spain. When Clement died in 1394, Boniface refused to have anything to do with his successor, Pedro de Luan, who had taken the name of Benedict XIII. The problem with the kingdom of Naples was resolved by Boniface's abandonment of the political policy of his predecessor. He recognised Ladislao, son of Carlo di Durazzo, as legitimate sovereign and crowned him in Gaeta. Under his rule, Naples returned to the obedience of Rome. He strengthened his position in the Papal States by investing two of his brothers with the lordships of Spoleto and Ancona. Boniface adopted a policy of leaving power to local families in return for their oath of fealty and the payment of tribute. The Holy Year of 1390 won him the affection of the Romans, but conflicts broke out again in the City which obliged Boniface to move to Perugia and Assisi. He returned to Rome in 1398, abolished all civic institutions and reserved to himself the right to nominate senators. The Campidoglio was converted into a fortress and Castel Sant' Angelo, which had been ruinous, was rebuilt. Boniface used every available means to obtain revenue for the Apostolic See and increased ecclesiastical taxation. Baldassare Costa was his financial advisor. He subsequently became the anti-Pope John XXIII. Boniface died suddenly while treating with the emessaries of the anti-Pope Benedict XIII. He created six Cardinals and canonised St. Bridget of Sweden.

202. Innocent VII *(1404-1406)*

Cosimo (Cosma) Gentile Miglioati was born to a prosperous family from Sulmona in the Abruzzi. He studied law in Bologna and had taught at Perugia and Padua. He had been a Papal Collector in England for ten years. Nominated to the See of Ravenna, he was translated to that of Bologna. Boniface IX named him Cardinal and legate in Lombardy and Tuscany. He was elected from among the eight Cardinals who participated at the Conclave, despite the supplications of the representatives of Benedict XIII to postpone the Conclave until such time as a means could be found to end the schism. Innocent's relations with Benedict XIII were marked by renewed intransigence. A proposal, advanced by the king of Germany, to convoke a Council was abandoned. He clashed with the Romans who wished to recover the civil liberties that had been abolished by Boniface IX. Innocent was obliged to call on Ladislao of Naples to suppress a revolt in the City. Eventually, he was obligded to acquiesce to the demands of the Romans after further armed conflict erupted during which one of his nephews slew eleven representatives of the Roman municipality. The Pope was obliged to move to Viterbo, and Ladislao occupied the Castel Sant'Angelo. Innocent returned to Rome in 1406 after Ladislao had restored order. In recognition of his services, Ladislao was proclaimed defender and *gonfaloniere* of the Church. Although ineffective in his political policies, Innocent took important cultural initiatives in Rome, including a reorganisation of the Roman university where he founded the faculties of medicine, philosophy, logic and rhetoric, and Greek.

104

203. Gregory XII *(1406-1415)*

Schism dominated the conclave that followed the death of Innocent VII. The only means of resolving the problem was the *via concessionis*, the contemporaneous abdication of Pope and anti-Pope and the election of a new Pontiff. The fourteen cardinals who entered the Conclave swore solemnly that he would abdicate, were the anti-Pope to likewise or die; that he would not nominate Cardinals except to maintain an equal number with those in Avignon; and that within three months he would have initiated negotiations with the anti-Pope. The Latin Patriarch of Constantinople and Cardinal Priest of San Marco, Angelo Correr, of a Venetian noble family, was elected. He was already eighty years old, indecisive and much preoccupied with resolving the schism. The meeting with Benedict XIII was to be held at Savona, then under the obedience of Avignon. Gregory's policy changed and he began to prevaricate. Both rivals communicated with each other without meeting: Gregory from Lucca and Benedict from Portovenere. Gregory became increasingly worried that were he to resign, Benedict would be left to take his place. When Gregory broke his election promise and nominated nine new Cardinals, including two of his nephews, the majority of the Cardinals deserted him and made for Pisa. In 1409, the Cardinals, who had been joined by four Cardinals from Avignon, decided to meet in Council. Both Gregory and Benedict refused to participate, and each called his own Council. The Council of Pisa accused both Popes of bad faith, and deposed them as schismatics, obdurate heretics, and perjurers. The Council declared the Apostolic See vacant. The Cardinals then elected another Pope, Peter Philgaro, a Greek from Crete, who took the name of Alexander V. Not only had the Council of Pisa failed to resolve the schism, but now found itself with three Popes rather than two. Gregory XII attempted to hold his Council at Cividale, near Aquileia, but dissolved it after a few sessions and fled to Gaeta and the protection of king Ladislaus of Naples who, with the German king, continued to support him. With the death of Alexander V, a successor, Baldassare Costa from Naples, was named and he took the name of John XXIII. Both John XXIII and Alexander V have been regarded as anti-Popes, even if some historians refer to them as the «conciliar Popes». At the instigation of Sigismund, the German king, John XXIII convoked the Council of Constance in 1414 to end the schism. While John XXIII seemed likely to retain the tiara, he was eventually forced to abdicate. He took flight, however, in an attempt to avoid abdication but was declared deposed by the Council. Gregory XII abdicated in 1415. The two colleges of Cardinals united, and having deemed Gregory XII ineligible, they conferred on him a dignity immediately below the Pope. He died in 1417 at Recanati shortly before the election of his successor.

204. **Martin V** *(1417-1431)*

The new Pope was elected in Constance by twenty two Cardinals and five national representatives. Odo Colonna was born at Genazzano. Created Cardinal by Innocent VII, he was among those who had organised the Council of Pisa. He supported John XXIII at the Council of Constance until his flight deprived him of any possibility of acquiring the tiara. Martin V's election brought the Western schism to a close, although Benedict XIII and his successor Clement VIII, both anti-Popes, continued to claim the papacy until 1429. The reform of the Church now began *in capite et membris*. Martin intended to reduce abuses, to reinforce Papal authority, and repudiate the conciliarist thesis - that a Council had authority over the Pope. He also had to face the problem of declined income since the Church had lost many of her rights and privileges during the schism. A series of concordats enabled him to reach agreement in the field of ecclesiastical taxation, especially in France. In April 1418, Martin closed the Council and issued a Bull which was not published because in it he had prohibited recourse to a general Council against the Pope. He transferred his residence to Rome in September 1420 and began the task of recovering the Papal States which had been reduced to chaos by the schism. Martin dislodged the Neopolitan garrison from Rome and defeated the condottiere Braccio da Mentone who had taken over central Italy. In 1429 a revolt was suppressed in Bologna and in Northern Italy. Martin also made large concessions to his nephews. The Pope supported numerous peace initiatives, especially in England and France which were still engaged in the Hundred Years War. He made an unsuccessful attempt to convoke an ecumenical Council in Constantinople to restore the unity of the Church. His crusade against the Hussites in Bohemia was no more successful. Martin was moderate with regard to the Jews, and approved the devotion to the most holy name of Jesus, popularised by St. Bernardino of Siena. The Pope began a vast programme of urban renewal in Rome and employed the best available artists on the project. Contrary to his own position on conciliarism, he executed the terms of the conciliar decree *Frequens*, which required a Council to be held every five years, by convoking the Council of Pavia. The council was to have been held but had to be transferred to Siena because of an outbreak of plague. The Pope dissolved the Council in Siena and convoked another to be held in Basel in 1431. Meanwhile, he published a reforming constitution containing strict norms for the lifestyle of the Curia and enjoined residence on diocesan bishops. He died suddenly in 1431, having named Cardinal Giulanio Cesarini his legate for the Council of Basel.

205. Eugenius IV *(1431-1447)*

Prior to the conclave held to elect a successor for Martin V, each of the Cardinals swore that, in the event of election, he would accept the involvement of the College of Cardinals in the government of the Church. Gabriele Condulmer, a Venetian Canon of St. Augustine, was elected. A relative of Gregory XII, he had been nominated Bishop of Siena and Cardinal of San Clemente by him. He had participated at the Council of Constance. During the pontificate of Martin V, he had been governor of Ancona and Bologna. The main difficulty facing Eugenius IV was the Council of Basel which had been convoked by his predecessor. The Council had been dissolved by Eugenius who promised to convoke another one within eighteen months. The Council refused to dissolve and issued a declaration claiming that the authority of the Council was superior to that of the Pope, following the conciliarist teaching of the Council of Constance. Only six Cardinals sided with Eugenius. Sigismund, the German king, intervened to prevent yet another schism. The Pope was forced to recognise the legitimacy and continuity of the Council. The Bull of dissolution had to be withdrawn. Eugenius crowned Sigismund as Holy Roman Emperor in Rome in 1433. In 1434, public disorder, fomented by the Colonnas who had become enemies of Eugenius since they had been obliged to restore much territory ceded to them by Martin V, broke out in the City, and the condottiere Francesco Sforza occupied the Papal States. Eugenius fled the City for Florence where he established his residence. A further controversy arose when the Council of Basel abolished the annates and other ecclesiastical taxes. Eugenius formally opposed this move. The Pope transferred the Council to Ferrara in 1437. A number of the council Fathers decided to remain in Basel. At Basel, they firstly suspended and then deposed Eugenius IV and formally elected Amadeus VIII of Savoy as Pope, who took the name Felix V. He was destined to be the last anti-Pope in the history of the Church. France and Germany declared neutrality. France, however, manipulated the situation to promulgate the *Pragmatic sanction* of Bourges, which effectively declared the French Church independent of the Pope in administrative matters, and in those relating to the conferral of benefices. France accepted many of the decisions of the Council of Basel. On 8 January 1438, the Papal Legate, Cardinal Nicolò Albergati, formally opened the Council of Ferrara and immediately initiated negotiations with the Greek delegates on the question of Church unity. In 1439, the Council was moved to Florence because of the plague in Ferrara, and was recognised as the seventeenth ecumenical council. On 6 July 1439, the Council promulgated the Bull *Laetentur Coeli* which formally restored Church unity. The Bull was accepted by the Byzantine emperor who was seeking allies in his efforts to repel the imminent advance of the Turks. The union did not last long but it was significant in that the Greeks accepted papal primacy, the Catholic formulation of the doctrines of Purgatory, the Eucharist, and the double procession of the Holy Spirit from the Father and the Son, the so called *Filioque* clause. The act of unity strengthened the Pope's prestige enormously: the main advisor of the anti-Pope Felix V, Enea Silvio Piccolomini, changed sides and supported Eugenius. The main states also gave their support to Eugenius: Germany recognised him and stipulated the need for a Concordat to regulate ecclesiastical affairs in the country; France also recognised him but retained its *Pragmatic sanction*, in the face of papal opposition. Eugenius IV finally defeated any attempt to have the government of the Pope shadowed by a Council. This victory was due, perhaps, to force of circumstances rather than to the Pope's capacity for effective government.

206. Nicholas V *(1447- 1455)*

Tommaso Parentucelli, a doctor's son from Sarzana near La Spezia, was elected as a compromise candidate. He had studied theology in Bologna and entered the service of Cardinal Niccolò Albergati, and followed him into the service of the Curia. As Bishop of Bologna, he was papal delegate to the Diet of Frankfort where he played an important role in winning German recognition of Eugenius IV. In recompense, he was given the red hat. When he was elected, he took the name of his patron, Niccolò Albergati. Nicholas V was politically astute and immediately ratified a accord with Frederick III in which he had obtained broad ecclesiastical concession in Germany. He was successful in bringing peace to the Church: through the mediation of Charles VIII of France, the anti-Pope, Felix V, abdicated in 1449, and, in exchange, received the red hat and nomination as papal vicar and legate in Savoy. The Council of Basel, which had been transferred to Lausanne, according to the terms of the agreement made between the Pope and the German king, dissolved, having elected «Tommaso di Sarzana» as Pope. Many of the Cardinals of Felix V were admitted to the Sacred College. The year 1450 was declared a Holy Year. Thousands of pilgrims came to Rome, alleviating the papal coffers and restoring the prestige of the Papacy. During the Holy Year of 1450, the Pope solemnly canonized St. Bernardino of Siena. Nicholas V also succeeded in establishing his authority in the Papal States. He was the first of the humanist Popes. His cultural interests were highly significant for the evolution of the renaissance. Nicholas was indeed the true founder of the Vatican Library, to which he left one thousand two hundred Greek and Latin manuscripts. He began the reconstruction of Rome and changed its aspect completely by restoring churches and palaces in the new renaissance style. His idea was to transform the City into a centre from which spread a culture that was at once Christian and humanist. In 1452, he crowned Frederick III as Holy Roman Emperor in St. Peter's. The discovery of a plot against Nicholas V led by the republican Stefano Porcari was a severe blow to his image of triumphant reconciliation. News of the fall of Constantinople to the Turks filled Christendom with foreboding. The Pope tried unsuccessfully to launch a crusade. He did, however, succeed in obtaining the peace of Lodi which ensured a peace of twenty years among the Italian States, including Genua. While Nicholas did not favour nepotism, he did not undertake the kind of reform of which the Church had need.

207. Calixtus III *(1455-1458)*

Alfonso de Borja (or Borgia), a brilliant canonist, had been secretary to king Alfonso V of Aragon. He persuaded the king not to support the Council of Basel, for which he was rewarded by nomination as Cardinal Priest of Ss. Quattro Incoronati. He was an austere and reserved man. He was elected as a compromise between the favourites in the election: the candidate of the Colonna family, and the Greek Cardinal Bessarion. Calixtus spent his entire pontificate absorbed with the organisation of a crusade to recover Constantinople from the Turks. He suspended Nicholas V's plans for the rebuilding of Rome, imposed taxes, encouraged indulgences, and gathered funds wherever possible. His financial plans (called the Turkish tithe) were bitterly resented both in France, where the University of Paris called for a Council, and in Germany where a compromise was arranged through the diplomatic skills of Enea Silvio Piccolomini. In Italy, the Pope fought with the king of Naples, Alfonso V of Aragon, who had diverted a fleet intended for the crusade and attacked Genua. The crusade did not accomplish much, except for an important defeat of the Turks near Belgrade (1456), which was much celebrated throughout Christendom. Calixtus re-opened the process on Joan of Arc who had been burned at Rouen in 1431 as a witch and a heretic. He declared her innocence in 1456, following a meticulous process which established her innocence. He issued restrictions against the Jews. Calixtus was inclined to nepotism and nominated two of his nephews Cardinals, one of them being Rodrigo Borgia (the future Alexander VI). He filled the Curia with Spaniards, thereby arousing the hostility of the Italian clergy and the citizens of Rome. Following his death, great violence was practised on the «Catalans».

208. **Pius II** *(1458-1464)*

Enea Silvio Piccolomini was born to an impoverished noble family at Corsignano, near Siena, which was subsequently renamed Pienza. He studied humanities at Siena and Florence. He had been secretary to several Cardinals, including Cardinal Albergati, and had taken part in many diplomatic missions. As an official of the Council of Basel, he had supported the anti-Pope Felix V, whose secretary he had also been, before transferring to the service of Frederick III in Germany where he became a close friend of the German chancellor Kaspar Schlick. As a highly cultivated humanist, he had composed several short stories and risqués comedies. In 1445, following a serious illness, he underwent a profound conversion which changed his life. He was ordained a priest and adopted a more orderly lifestyle, while continuing to write and study the classics. He eventually abandoned the anti-Pope and entered the service of Eugenius IV. Pius convinced the Pope to recognise Frederick III and the German electoral princes. Named Bishop of Triest, he was transferred to Siena and created Cardinal by Calixtus III. In the Curia, he was an anomaly, but in 1458 he was elected Pope and took the name of Pius as a explicit reference to the *pius Aenea* of Virgil. His entire pontificate was spent planning a crusade that never happened. While conscious of the need for reform, his pre-occupation with the crusade prevented his addressing the reform question. He proclaimed a crusade immediately after his election and called a congress of Christian princes at Mantua to plan it. He clashed with the French who were irritated that he had chosen Ferrante d'Aragona for the throne of Naples rather than one of the Angevin princes. The question of ecclesiastical privileges in France also gave rise to tension with the French monarch. In Germany he became involved in several controversies and may have aggravated anti papal sentiment there. He fought with Jiri Podiebrad, the king of Bohemia, on the question of a reconciliation with the moderate Hussites, favoured by the king. Podiebrad offered to lead the crusade. When the opposition began to mute the idea that the council had authority over the Pope, a position which Pius had held in his youth, he excommunicated them with the Bull *Execrabilis*. In 1461, with no support for the crusade, he wrote a letter to the Sultan Mahomet II, which was never despatched, in which he disproved the Koran and invited him to convert to Christianity and accept the crown of the Eastern empire. With the support of Venice and Hungary, he proclaimed a new crusade whose departure was set for Ancona in 1464. Pius intended to lead it himself. When he arrived at Ancona he found few troops. By the time the Venetian galleys put in at Ancona, Pius had taken ill and was at the point of death. His heart was buried in Ancona and his body transferred to Rome. Criticised for his frequent changes of position (justified by the Bull of retraction of 1463 in which he exhorted his critics to reject Aeneas and give ear to Pius), Pius did have an original concept of a Christian Europe.

209. Paul II *(1446-1471)*

Pietro Barbo was born to a Venetian merchant family and was a nephew of Eugenius IV. Created Cardinal Deacon at the age of twenty three, Nicholas V promoted him to Cardinal Priest of San Marco. He was elected in the first ballot. Before voting in the Conclave, the Cardinals bound themselves observe new dispositions governing the relationship between the Pope and the Sacred College, and to convoke a General Council every three years. Paul II immediately revoked these norms and abandoned any effort at reform. He resisted all pressure to call a general Council, especially from France and Germany. He continued plans for a crusade against the Turks, but encountered the same difficulties as his predecessor. Having failed to reach an agreement with the king of Bohemia, as his predecessor had failed, Paul excommunicated him in 1466 for his encouragement of the Hussites and threatened to proclaim a crusade against him. An accord was reached between the Apostolic See and the Persians against the Turks. Paul also attempted a reconciliation with the Russian Church. With the fall of Negroponte to the Turks in 1471, the last Venetian outpost in Greece disappeared. Paul convoked the Christian princes to Rome and proclaimed a new crusade, which also failed. He continued to use the revenues from the recently discovered aluminium mines in Tolfa which had been set aside to finance the crusade. Paul fixed the Jubilee Year at every twenty-fifth year and proclaimed a Holy Year for 1475. He encouraged spectacular popular festivals in Rome and included the banners of the Roman Jews in the carnival of 1466. He built the Palazzo San Marco, the present Palazzo Venezia, which became his principal Roman residence. Influenced by the climate of classical studies, he restored many of the antiquities of the City, surrounded himself with scholars and installed the first printing press in Rome. In the Curia he never enjoyed much popularity, as can be judged from the biography written by the humanist scholar Bartolomeo Platina. Paul II abolished the college of the *abbreviatori*, which consisted of many of the leading Italian humanists. In 1468 he abolished the *Accadmia Romana di Pomponio Leto* for its pagan ethos. Many of the leading humanists belonged to it, including Platina.

210. Sixtus IV *(1471-1478)*

Franca della Rovere was born in Savona. He had entered the Franciscans, and had studied at Bologna and Padova. He was a notable preacher and an accomplished theologian who was much admired by the humanist Cardinal Bessarion. He became Minister General of the Franciscans in 1464. In 1467 he was named Cardinal of San Pietro in Vincoli. His election in 1471 came as a surprise and was due, not only to his fame as a preacher and theologian, but also to the astute series of promises made by his nephew, Pietro Riario, assistant of the Conclave, to several Cardinals and princes. Sixtus continued his predecessors' policy and resumed efforts to raise a crusade, but with little success. In 1480, Otranto, in Apulia, fell to the Turks, and was only liberated in 1482 thanks to the death of Mahomet II. He continued negotiations with Ivan III of Russia not only on the question of the reconciliation of the Russian Church, but also to obtain Russian support against the Turks. Sixtus IV continued his conflict with the French king on the question of the *pragmatic sanction* and the prerogatives of the French Church. In 1478, he acceded to the request of the Spanish monarchs to have the Spanish Inquisition erected. This decision he soon regretted and there began a long political and jurisdictional conflict with that institution. His relations with the reform party which called for a Council were dire. He annulled the decrees of the Council of Constance in 1478. Faced with a challenge from the Croat Archbishop, Andrea Zamometic, to revive the Council of Basel, Sixtus renewed the prohibition of taking recourse against the Pope at a general Council. He encouraged the mendicant orders and canonised St. Bonaventure in 1482. He approved the feast of the Immaculate Conception and assigned a proper office for it. He greatly favoured his own family, advancing six of his nephews to the Cardinalate, among them Pietro and Girolamo Riario, the nemesis of his pontificate - the latter masterminded the de' Pazzi plot against the Medicis, which succeeded in assassinating Giuliano de' Medici in 1487. He declared war on Ferrara and Venice in an attempt to provide his nephews with States. Despite the increased income of the Apostolic See, Sixtus left enormous debts. The Pope was a true renaissance prince. He patronised artists and men of letters. He transformed the face of Rome, erecting important masterpieces such as the Ponte Sisto, Santa Maria del Popolo, Santa Maria della Pace, the Sixtine Chapel. He also restored the Hospice of the Santo Spirito, founded the Sixtine choir, reorganised the Vatican Library, entrusting its administration to the humanist, Bartolomeo Platina. He was buried in the crypt of St. Peter's. His splendid funerary monument, cast in bronze, is the work of Antonio Pollaiolo.

211. Innocent VIII *(1484-1492)*

Giovanni Battista Cybo, son of a Roman Senator, was born in Genua. He had studied at Padua and Rome. Sixtus IV had named him Cardinal. He owed his election to his incompetence and weakness, since he was the ideal candidate for Cardinal Giuliano della Rovere while awaiting his own election. He was easily influenced and had little interest in reforming the Curia. Innocent continued to run the papal court as a princely court despite the enormous deficit he had inherited from Sixtus IV. Offices had to be created and sold. His children were married to the Italian princely families. He supported the revolt of the Neapolitan Barons against Ferrante of Aragon, whom he deposed and excommunicated. This move brought disaster to the Papal States, and the loss of Aquila. Innocent named Giovanni Medici, the thirteen year old son of Lorenzo Medici, a Cardinal. He reached an agreement with the Turkish sultan Bayezid II according to the terms of which he agreed to hold Djem, the sultan's younger brother, prisoner at his own court. Djem was delivered to the Pope by the Knights of Jerusalem and Rhodes. In return, the sultan paid an annual pension to the knights and he later gave the Pope the precious Byzantine relic of the lance of Longinus, which traditionally was believed to have pierced the side of Christ on the Cross. Innocent also proposed a crusade but found little response from the European princes. In 1484, Innocent published the Bull *Summis desiderantes affectibus* which began a persecution of witchcraft in Europe, especially in Germany. The Pope also banned and prohibited discussion of the various theories advanced by the Florentine humanist, Pico della Mirandola. The last significant act of his reign was the granting of the title «Most Catholic» to Ferdinand and Isabella or Aragon and Castile following their conquest the kingdom of Granada, the last muslim stronghold in Spain. Innocent died leaving Rome and the Papal States in anarchy and disorder.

212. **Alexander VI** *(1492-1503)*

Rodrigo de Borja was born at Jativa, near Valencia, in 1431. His uncle, Calixtus III, had named him a Cardinal. He became Camerlengo of the Holy Roman Church and had used the office to accumulate enormous wealth. Alexander was highly intelligent and able, but has left a very negative image of himself to posterity. This was in measure due to a lifestyle not easily reconciled with the priestly office, and to the tirades preached against him by Girolamo Savonarola, the Dominican preacher and reformer who dominated the government of Florence between 1494 and 1498. Savonarola was excommunicated and burned at the stake. Many historians believe that Savonarola, had he had support, could have succeeded in his reform efforts and thereby been able to obviate the impending schism in the Church created by the protestant reformers. He lacked the support of Alexander VI who was worldly, corrupt and willing to sacrifice religion for the sake of political power. Alexander was dominated by a lust for power and wealth for himself and for his children, whom he publicly recognised and installed at the papal court. His favourite child was Cesare Borja for whom he intended an ecclesiastical career, naming him a Cardinal, which he subsequently had him renounce so as to marry a French princess. Alexander supported his conquest of the Romagne and his projects to turn the Papal States, in whole or part, into a hereditary State ruled by the Borja. The Pope's European and Italian political policy was dominated by this family concern. In the light of this objective, it becomes possible to understand his numerous and volatile agreements with Charles VIII of France, the king of Naples, Louis XII of France and even with the Turkish sultan Bayezid II. Alexander promoted his political objective through a series of marriages of his children, Lucretia, John duke of Gandia, and Cesare. Revenues from indulgences were used to finance the military campaings of Cesare Borgia. When rumour began to suggest that Cesare had murdered his brother John, the Pope continued to support him. From the point of view of ecclesiastical administration, the pontificate of Alexander VI was not worse than that of his immediate predecessors. The Holy Year of 1500 was celebrated with great solemnity, attention was paid to monastic reform, and of the orders providing missionaries for the newly discovered continent of America. Alexander called Penturicchio to fresco the Borgia apartments in the Vatican palace, and appointed Michelangelo to draw up a plan for the new Basilica of St. Peter. In 1493, at the request of queen Isabella, he drew the famous *raya* delineating the spheres of Spanish and Portugese influence in the New World. During this pontificate, simony reached unprecedented levels. It had been said that his interest in the Church was second to that of earthly interest. But such had been true of several of the renaissance Popes. Alexander was unfortunate to have had a very bad contemporary press. He died of malaria in 1503, after he and Cesare had been taken suddenly ill. At the time, many spoke of poison. Cesare survived his father, but his house of cards collapsed soon after the Pope's death.

213. Pius III *(September- October 1503)*

Born in Siena in1439, Francesco Todeschini Piccolomini was a nephew of Pius II, who gave him the surname of Piccolomini and reared him in his own household. He had been created Cardinal at the age of twenty-one. He was influential in the Curia and had conducted several important diplomatic missions under Pius II, Paul II and Alexander VI, during whose pontificate he had maintained a low profile. He was a man of culture, rigorist and sincere. He founded the Bibliotheca Piccolominiana in Siena Cathedral which was decorated by Penturicchio. He was already gravely ill at the time of his election, which was not an unimportant element in his being chosen to be Pope. He died ten days after his coronation. Contemporaries believed that had he lived he would have convoked a Council and begun the work of reforming the Church.

214. Julius II *(1503-1513)*

A nephew of Pope Sixtus IV, Guilano della Rovere was born at Albisola, near Savona, in 1443 and entered the Franciscan Order. He achieved the highest honours and dignities during the reign of Sixtus IV (Bishop, Cardinal Priest and Cardinal Bishop). Between 1480 and 1482 he had acted as legate in several countries. He played a preeminent role in ecclesiastical affairs during the reign of Innocent VIII, whose election was in large part due to the exertions of Cardinal Guilano della Rovere. Julius was hostile to Alexander VI which obliged him to seek asylum at the court of Charles VIII of France in order to avoid assassination. He accompanied Charles to Italy and tried to persuade him to convoke a council to depose Alexander VI on the grounds of simony. Following the death of Alexander VI, the Conclave favoured the election of a more neutral candidate, but had no hesitation in electing Giuliano della Rovere after the death of Pius III. Julius' entire pontificate was dominated by military and political questions. His first challenge was to restore the Papal States which had been dismembered by the Borja. Piece by piece, he reconquered the territory of the Papal States, taking the Romagne, Bologna and Perugia, which had been abandoned to local tyrants, and finally Rimini and Faenza, which had been lost to the Venetians, were retaken during the war of Cambrai. His decision to support Ferdinand of Aragon's struggle to claim the throne of Naples cost him the friendship of Louis XII of France, successor of his former patron

Charles VIII. In 1511, the French king convoked a council at Pisa to depose Julius. The Pope reacted by convoking a council in Rome in 1512. The «Holy League», consisting of the Pope, England, Venice and Spain, defeated the French and drove them from Italy. By this time, the Papal States also included Parma, Piacenza and Reggio Emilia. It was Julius' boast that he had re-founded the Papal States. Julius was a warrior and bellicose Pope who personally led his armies into battle. Guicciardini wrote of him that there was nothing priestly about him except for his habit and his name. Erasmus, in *In Praise of Folly*, derides his warring zeal. Julius, however, was not just a Pope who succeeded in reestablishing the Papal States and in raising them to a position of primary importance in international politics. He also succeeded in ridding Italy of foreign domination. His ecclesiastical achievements were less striking: the Fifth Lateran Council accomplished little by way of reform. Julius founded the first diocese in America. He was a gifted administrator and left the coffers of the Apostolic See in a very health condition, having found them empty at the time of his election. Julius eschewed any form of nepotism and issued severe laws to curb simony, especially in the election of a Pope. He was obstinate and lived life after the fashion of his contemporaries. He was known as Julius «the terrible». He was an extraordinary patron of the arts and patronised Michelangelo, Bramante, and Raphael. In 1506, he laid the foundation stone for the new basilica of St. Peter and, in a fateful act, assigned revenues deriving from indulgences for its construction.

215. Leo X *(1513-1521)*

Giovanni dei Medici, the son of Lorenzo the Magnificent, was elected Pope at the age of thirty seven without opposition and simony. He was born in Florence in 1475 and had been given a careful classical education. He entered the Sacred College at the age of thirteen. He had shared the exile of the Medicis, firstly in Germany and France and subsequently in Holland where he met Erasmus. He returned to Rome in 1500, but remained outside of political life, devoting his attention instead to music, theatre and the arts. He received his first curial appointment after the death of Alexander VI. He was named legate in Bologna in 1511. With the return of the Medicis in 1512, Leo became *de facto* ruler of Florence and continued to exercise this function even after his election. He was a true renaissance prince. Through nepotism, he attempted to maintain the Papal States and the prestige of the Medicis. He conducted a disastrous war against Urbino in an effort to replace Francesco della Rovere with his nephew, Lorenzo de' Medici. He lost Parma and Piacenza but managed to hold on to Florence. In 1517, the Sacred College mounted a conspiracy against him. He executed one of its members and created thirty one new cardinals to reduce the influence of those involved in the conspiracy. He participated actively in the political life of his times which were dominated by war between France and Spain for control of Italy, and by internecine war between the Italian states, which took the side of one or other of main powers. Leo X firstly sided with the league against France. Following the victory of Francis I at Marignano, he entered into a concordat with France which abrogated the *Pragmatic sanction*, and was destined to remain in force until the French revolution. On the complex question of the imperial succession, at first Leo was inclined to support the candidature of Frederick the Wise of Saxony, Luther's patron, but eventually he accepted the election of Charles V. While he encouraged the work of the Fifth Lateran Council, he was never committed to ecclesiastical reform. The council closed with the proclamation of another crusade against the Turks. He was a prodigious patron of the arts and always short of funds. He carried on the building of St. Peter's, assigning money derived from indulgences for the project. The protestant reformation began in 1517 when Luther nailed his ninety-five theses to the door of the church in Wittenberg. Leo, who was absorbed in political matters, minimalised the affair and failed to grasp the gravity of the situation. In 1520, Leo condemned the positions held by Luther in the Bull *Exsurge Domine*, and excommunicated him in 1521. He granted the title of *Defensor fidei* to Henry VIII of England for his *Defensio septem sacramentorum*. Leo died of malaria, leaving Italy in chaos, the papal coffers empty, and lutheranism rampant in Germany.

216. Adrian VI *(1522-1523)*

The Conclave following the death of Leo X was deeply divided. Unexpectedly, it elected a Flemming, Adrian Florensz, Cardinal of Utrecht. Born to a humble family in 1459, he had been schooled by the Brothers of the Common Life, a lay religious movement that had also exerted an enormous influence on Erasmus. Later, he studied at the university of Louvain, where he subsequently taught law. In 1507, he was appointed preceptor to the young Charles von Hapsburg, and exercised the office of regent of Spain together with the great humanist Cardinal, Francisco Ximénez de Cisneros during Charles' minority. As Bishop of Tortosa, inquisitor of Aragon and Castile, and Cardinal of Utrecht, he ruled Spain between 1520 and 1522 during the king's absence in Germany for his coronation. The new Pope kept his baptismal name, contrary to the custom that had obtained for several centuries. He was an upright, religious and exacting man. He saw his task as one of counteracting lutheranism in Germany and the waging of war on the Turks who had taken Belgrade in 1521, and were then threatening Hungary and Rhodes. He was received in Rome with hostility: he was a Flemming and a foreigner to its renaissance culture, and, more importantly, he was determined to embark on a policy of fiscal rectitude to revive the papal finances. While personally favourable to the condemnation and prosecution of Luther, he was conscious of Rome's responsibilities. In 1522 at the diet of Nuremberg, his legate, Francesco Chieregati, had instructions to assert the responsibilities of the Roman Church. Adrian's strict neutrality between the powers cost him the friendship of his closet ally, the Holy Roman Emperor Charles V. In the wake of the fall of Rhodes to the Turks, he attempted to impose a peace on Christian princes which caused a rupture in relations with France. When Adrian died in 1523, Francis I was preparing to invade Lombardy.

217. Clement VII *(1523-1534)*

Giulio de' Medici was born in Florence in 1479, the natural son of Giuliano de' Medici, nephew of Lorenzo the Magnificent. Leo X named him Archbishop of Florence and Cardinal. Clement VII had played an important role in the political affairs of the papacy under Leo X. He had been responsible for the measures taken against Luther and for the alliance with Charles V in 1521. He remained influential during the pontificate of Adrian VI. His election was difficult but it enjoyed the support of Charles V and was greeted joyfully in Rome. As Pope, however, Clement was indecisive and limited. His primary interest was Florence rather than the Papal States. His political programme with Spain and France was determined by that concern. A succession of alliances with Charles V was succeeded by another series with Francis I. In 1526, he joined the league of Cognac against Charles V, which led to the consequent siege of Rome by the imperial troops in Italy, and to its sacking in 1527, when the *Landesknechten* pillaged the churches of the city destroying many works of art and taking many Cardinals and priests captive. Great hardships were inflicted on the population. Clement VII took refuge in the Castel Sant'Angelo and was prisoner of the imperial troops for six months. He was liberated after payment of a heavy ransom and retired to Viterbo and Orvieto. Eventually, he was reconciled with Charles V whom he crowned Holy Roman Emperor in Bologna in 1530. This was the last imperial coronation. The peace of Bologna restored Florence to the Medicis and left Italy in the hands of Spain, thereby ending its political autonomy. Clement VII obstinately refused to accede to the emperor's demands for a Council to resolve the question of reform. The Church in England became schismatic under this pontificate. The question of the validity of Henry VIII's marriage to Catherine of Aragon was hesitantly and ambiguously approached by Clement. In 1533, under imperial influence from Charles V, a nephew of Catherine of Aragon, he excommunicated Henry. He tried unsuccessfully to counter the growth of protstantism in Switzerland and in Northern Europe. He constituted the diocese of Mexico and encouraged the Catholic mission in America. Clement VII continued the tradition of the renaissance prince, commissioning Michelangelo to paint the Last Judgement in the Sixtine Chapel, and the Medici tombs in the sacristy of San Lorenzo in Florence.

218. **Paul III** *(1534-1549)*

Alessandro Farnese was born in 1468 at Canino to a family of condottieri which held land at Bolsena and Viterbo. He had had a classical education and was named Cardinal Deacon under Alexander VI. Having been invested with many benefices, he was ordained priest in 1519. Prior to his ordination, he had three sons and a daughter. His life after ordination, however, was beyond reproach. He had come to be the leading exponent of reform. Although already old, the Cardinal Dean of the College was elected without difficulty in the Conclave of 1534. As a renaissance prince, he patronised artists and writers, he devoted much attention to the re-building of St. Peter's, he enriched the Vatican Library and began the building of the Palazzo Farnese. Paul named two of nephews Cardinals and conditioned much of his Italian political programme by his family interests. This was the Pope who placed the reform of the Church at the centre of his pontificate by convoking and opening the Council of Trent. In 1536, he set p a commission to examine the question of the reform of the Church. It reported to him in 1537 in a document entitled *Consilium de emendanda ecclesia*, which was destined to remain the basis for the reform. He brought many of the leading exponents of reform into the Sacred College: Reginald Pole, Gaspare Contarini, Gian Pietro Carafa (the future Pius IV). In 1537, he convoked the Council of Mantua, which had to be suspended because of the opposition of Charles V and Francis I. A second attempt to hold the Council in Vicenza in 1538 also failed. With the peace of Crépy and the ending of hostilities between the empire and France in 1544, it became possible to hold the Council. It had to be held in a city acceptable to Charles V, and hence it came to Trent, an imperial city, technically in Germany. In the presence of three legates, the Council, destined to change the face of the Church, opened in Trent on 13 December 1545. The protestants refused to come. Paul III insisted that the Council should not only concern itself with disciplinary reform but also with the doctrinal questions which lay at the heart of the problem with Luther. The decrees emanating from the Council up to 1548 reflect this approach. For various reasons, and in the face of imperial opposition, the Pope suspended the Council and transferred it to Bologna in 1548. Paul III strongly encouraged the new religious orders founded during his pontificate: the Theatines, the Barnabites, the Somasci, and the Ursulines. In 1540, he approved the rule of the Company of Jesus, which had been founded by St. Ignatius Loyola. In order to counter the spread of Lutheranism, he reconstituted the Inquisition, centralising it in the Sacred Congregation of the Holy Office. Politically, the Pope tried to remain neutral in the disputes involving the European powers. He supported the Holy Roman Emperor against the Smalcaldic league. He died in 1549, as the question of the succession to the duchy of Parma and Piacenza, which he had given to the Farnese, complicated his relations with Charles V. Titian's famous portrait of 1543 depicts Paul III at the age of seventy-five.

219. Julius III *(1550-1555)*

The Conclave following the death of Paul III was protracted and contested. Eventually, Giovanni Maria Ciocchi del Monte, a Roman, was elected as a result of a compromise between the French Cardinals and the Farnese. He was completely dominated by Charles V. Only a single vote precluded the election of Reginald Pole, the English reforming Cardinal. Julius III was born in 1487. He was a notable canonist and had been governor of Rome under Clement VII. Paul III had named him vicelegate of Bologna and Cardinal Bishop. He presided at the Council of Trent when it was transferred to Bologna, which incurred the wrath of Charles V. He was another example of a renaissance Pope, a patron of the arts, weak and indolent. Julius, however, could not oppose the spirit of reform which pervaded the Church and the pressure to resume the Council of Trent. The Council indeed resumed in Trent in 1551. For a while a number of protestant theologians participated. The French bishops were absent for Henry II prohibited their attendance. The outbreak of war between France and the Empire, and a revolt in Germany, led to the suspension of the Council in 1552. The Pope tried unsuccessfully to restore peace between France and the Empire. During the suspension of the Council, Julius activated some of the disciplinary reforms. He confirmed the Constitutions of the Jesuits and opened the Germanicum. Julius deployed many efforts to promote the Catholic religion in India, the Far East, and in America. Following the succession of Mary Tudor to the throne of England, the country returned to the Church. Cardinal Pole, a cousin of the Tudors, was sent to England as Legate. Julius built the Villa Giulia outside of the Porta del Popolo and spent much time there. He appointed Michelangelo first architect of St. Peter's, Pierluigi da Palestrina director of the Sixtine Choir, and Marcello Cervini Vatican Librarian. He died of the gout shortly after having sent Cardinal Morone to the Diet of Augsburg, in the hope of restoring Catholicism in Germany.

220. Marcellus II *(April-May 1555)*

Marcello Cervini was the candidate favoured by the reform party among the Cardinals and was elected after a short but controversial Conclave. He retained his own name as Pope. He was born at Montefano, near Macerata, in 1501. He was a gifted and erudite humanist. He had been a Greek translator and was expert in chronology. He was called to the Curia during the reign of Paul III, and had been a tutor to Cardinal Alessandro Farnese, the Pope's nephew. Named Bishop and Cardinal, he assumed an increasingly important role within the Curia, and had been sent on many diplomatic missions, without, however, neglecting the Sees entrusted to his pastoral care. His dioceses were characterized by the results of his reforming zeal. He had also been Legate to Charles V, and had been one of the presidents of the Council of Trent. In 1548, he completely re-organised the Vatican Library. Disapproving of the worldliness of Julius III, he retired to Gubbio. His election was a source of great hope for the reform party. He forbade his relations' moving to Rome, and began a programme to reduce the expenses of the papal court. While preparing a much wider reform, he died of an apoplectic fit after a pontificate of three months. In memory of this reforming Pope, Pierluigi da Palestrina composed the famous *Missa Papae Marcelli*.

221. Paul IV *(1555-1559)*

Gian Pietro Carafa was born at Capriglia, near Avellino, to a Neopolitan noble family in 1476. He had had an excellent classical education which included Hebrew in addition to Greek and Latin. His had been a rapid ecclesiastical career. From the See of Chieti, he was promoted to Archbishop of Brindisi, legate to England, and Nuncio in Flanders and Spain. He was a correspondent of Erasmus. Along with others, Paul took an active interest in the reform of the Oratory of the Divino Amore. Many of his associates were deeply committed to the Catholic reform movement: Giovanni Morone, Reginald Pole, Jacopo Sadoleto. Paul had shared many of the reform ideas of Adrian VI. He renounced his diocese and, together with St. Gaetano Thiene, founded the Theatine Order, which was dedicated to poverty and the reform of the Church. He was created Cardinal in 1536. By then he had abandoned his classical sympathies and given his reform efforts a more pronounced anti-protestant stamp. He was elected at the age of seventy-nine, when he occupied the offices of Inquisitor, Archbishop of Naples and Dean of the Sacred College. His election was hailed as a victory for the reform movement but was roundly opposed by Charles V. The new Pope quickly embarked on an anti-Spanish political programme which eventually led to his siding with France in war against Spain. Spanish troops invaded the Papal States and the Pope was eventually obliged to accept the terms of the Peace of Cave in 1557. His international political decisions were quite rigid: in Germany, he condemned the conciliatory terms of the peace of Augsburg, his efforts in England ensured the return of England to Protestantism after the death of Mary. In his medieval view of the papacy, he refused to recognise the abdication of Charles V and the imperial election of Ferdinand I which had taken place without his authorisation. Paul proved very energetic in the field of reform, though he did not reconvene the Council of Trent which had been in suspense since 1552. In his view, the reform of the Church was to derive solely from the Pope. In 1556, he constituted a commission to advise him on the programme of reform. He was a zealous reformer of ecclesiastical discipline, imposed the obligation of residence on bishops, and was scrupulous in his choice of Cardinals. He appointed a commission for the reform of the Roman Missal and the Breviary. His reform efforts, however, tended increasingly towards the repression of all opposition. Paul was particularly concerned for the operation of the Inquisition and placed Cardinal Michele Ghislieri (the future St. Pius V) at its head. The Pope attended the meetings of the Inquisition regularly. He arrested and tried Cardinal Morone for heresy. Morone had been one of the principal protagonists at the Council of Trent. He also persecuted Cardinal Pole, then legate in England, on the basis of heresy. In 1559, he published the index of prohibited books, which had severe effects on writers and publishers. One of the first acts of his pontificate was the enclosure of the Jewish ghetto in Rome. The measure was intended to encourage their conversion. He issued severe norms against monks who had abandoned their monasteries. Despite this reforming zeal, he was given to nepotism and was much influenced by his nephew Carlo whom he named Cardinal and his counsellor. His harshness induced the odium of the Romans. When he died, a mob attacked and demolished his statue on the Campidoglio, stormed the prison of the Inquisition and released its prisoners, and made armed attacks on a number of religious houses.

222. Pius IV (1559-1565)

Giovanni Angelo Medici was elected after a Conclave of four months which saw the French and Spanish locked in a constant battle. He was considered an able canonist, but was not regarded as a supporter of the Catholic reform movement. He was born in Milan in 1499 to a family unrelated to the Medicis of Florence. He had studied at Bologna, taking doctorates in medicine and jurisprudence. Under Paul III, he had been governor in various cities of the Papal States and eventually vicelegate of Bologna. He had had three natural children. In 1545 he was named Archbishop of Ragusa and Cardinal in 1549. Under Julius III he had been head of the *Segnatura di grazia*, but had left Rome during the pontificate of Paul IV, with whose ideas he disagreed. He was an able politician, given to toleration and conciliation. He immediately rescinded many of the provisions of his predecessor. He rehabilitated Cardinal Morone, reduced the power of the Inquisition, and abolished the laws against vagrant monks. He abandoned the anti-imperial political policies of his predecessor, normalised relations with Spain and reopened the vacant legations in Vienna, Florence and Venice. In 1562, two of Paul IV most hated nephews, Cardinal Carlo Carafa and his brother Giovanni, duke of Paliano, were arrested and executed. He nominated his twenty-two year old nephew, Carlo Borremeo, Archbishop of Milan and Cardinal. Much of his reform policy was due to the influence of his nephew who was his principal advisor in the Curia. The Council of Trent was re-convoked and brought to a conclusion during his pontificate. The Council reconvened at Trent in 1562 and, under the able guidance of Cardinal Morone, its business was quickly conducted. The Council was closed on 4 December 1563 and its decrees were approved in 1564. Pius immediately began the work of applying them in Italy, where the obligation of residence was imposed on bishops, and a new index of prohibited books published which was less restrictive than the index of 1559. The application of the conciliar decrees in other countries was more cautious because of the opposition which they encountered. In an attempt to stem the spread of protestantism, Pius permitted the use of the chalice for the communion of the faithful in Germany, Austria, Hungary, and elsewhere, but postponed any decision in relation to the marriage of the clergy. Hoping that the Church in England might still be reconciled with the Apostolic See, he refrained from excommunicating Elizabeth I of England. In France, he subvented the wars against the Huguenots. In 1564, he obliged the bishops and the higher clergy to make and subscribe to a profession of faith which incorporated the doctrinal decisions of the Council of Trent. Between 1561 and 1562, with the assistance of St. Carlo Borromeo, Pius reformed the Tribunal of the Holy Roman Rota, the Sacred Penitentiary, the Apostolic Chancellery, and the Camera Apostolica. He continued the Council's work of compiling a catechism, and the reform of the Roman Missal and Breviary. Pius resumed the renaissance tradition of patronising artists and writers which had been discontinued by his predecessors. Pius built the Porta Pia, Santa Maria deli Angeli, the Belvedere and the Casina in the Vatican gardens which bears his name to-day.

223. **St. Pius V** *(1566-1572)*

In the conclave following the death of Pius IV, Micele Ghislieri emerged unexpectedly as the candidate of the reform movement which was then led by St. Carlo Borromeo. He was born in 1504 at Bosco, near Alessandria, to a poor family and entered the Dominican Order at an early age. He had studied at Bologna and taught at Pavia. Pius had been Inquisitor of Como and Bergamo, where his zeal brought him to the attention of Cardinal Carafa (subsequently Paul IV), who had him nominated commissar general of the Roman inquisition. His career blossomed under Paul IV who named him bishop, Cardinal and Grand Inquisitor. Pius IV did not like him and marginalised him. The central concern of Pius' pontificate was the application of the decrees of the Council of Trent and the eradication of heresy. Pius was observant and ascetical. Even as Pope he continued to wear a hair shirt. He would have liked to have transformed Rome and the papal court into a monastery. He suppressed immorality, extravagance, feasts, blasphemy and magical practices. He began a rigorous reform of ecclesiastical life, imposing the obligation of residence on the clergy, reforming the religious orders, exercising great care in the nomination of bishops, and choosing the Cardinals with much discrimination. He personally visitated the Roman basilicas, organised periodic visitations of the Roman parishes, and systematically sent apostolic visitators to all parts of the Papal States and to the kingdom of Naples. He prohibited the alienation of ecclesiastical fiefs and reorganised the penal system. Incurring Spanish displeasure, he rehabilitated the members of the Carafa family who had been executed by his predecessor. He stridently opposed nepotism, though he nominated his nephew Michele Bonelli a Cardinal. Between 1566 and 1570, Pius published the Roman Catechism, the Roman Missal, and the Breviary. He instituted a commission to begin the work of revising the Vulgate. Pius was a truly inquisitorial Pope. He greatly favoured the Inquisition and extended its powers, and its work of repressing heresy. He succeeded in preventing the spread of protestantism in Italy. He founded the Congregation of the Index which began the task of supervising writers and publishers. He condemned the theses on grace advanced by Michael Belius, a Flemish precursor of the jansenists. He declared St. Thomas Aquinas a doctor of the Church. Politically, the pontificate of Pius V was characterised by deteriorating relations with the

119

European courts. He excommunicated Elizabeth I of England. He was in constant conflict with Philip II, Catherine de' Medici, Regent of France, and with Maximilian I. He absolutely opposed any form of state control of the Church, republishing in clearer terms the traditional Bull *In Coena Domini*, read every Holy Thursady, and listing all censures reserved to the Pope. With Spain and Venice he constituted a Holy league against the Turks. On 7 October 1571 the fleet of the Holy League defeated the Turks at Lepanto, thereby destroying their maritime supremacy in the Mediterranean. In celebration of this victory, ascribed to the intercession of Our Lady, Pius instituted the feast of Our Lady of Victory, which Gregory XIII transformed into the feast of Our Lady of the Holy Rosary. Pius V was beatified by Clement X in 1672, and canonised by Clement XI in 1712. His feast day is 30 April.

224. Gregory XIII *(1572-1585)*

Ugo Boncompani was born in Bologna in 1502 to a family of merchant origin. He held a doctorate in law and taught the subject at the university of Bologna. He was ordained a priest in Rome at about the age of forty, having lived rakishly and fathered a son, who would later become governor of the Castel Sant'Angelo. Under Paul II he held a number of important juridical offices in the Curia, and was sent on several diplomatic missions by Paul IV who named him a bishop. He attended the Council of Trent as a *peritus* in canon law and was closely involved in drawing up several of its decrees. Created Cardinal by Pius IV, he was sent as legate to Spain where he gained the confidence of Philip II, which was decisive for the Conclave that elected him. He was profoundly influenced by St. Carlo Borromeo and was deeply committed to the reform movement and the implementation of the decrees of the Council of Trent, though without the rigour of his predecessors. His counsellor, Cardinal Galli, exercised the offices that would subsequently devolve on the Secretary of State. The application of the decrees of Trent was overseen by a commission established by the Pope, and by the Apostolic Nunciatures which he re-founded in Cologne, Graz, and Luzern. He fail, however, to overcome French opposition to the publication of the decrees of the Council of Trent. In an effort to counter the spread of protestantism, he devoted much attention to the education of the clergy. In Rome he founded several colleges, designed for the training of the clergy from different countries, which were entrusted to the care of the Jesuits. He reformed the Roman College, in operation since 1551, which was now called the Gregorian in his honour. He founded the Greek, English, Hungarian (subsequently united with the Germanicum) and Maronite colleges. Throughout Europe, Gregory conducted an aggressive anti-protestant policy. He played an active role in the struggle between the Catholic and protestant powers, strongly supporting the Catholic League in France. In 1572, he welcomed the news of the St. Bartholomew massacre with the *Te Deum*. Gregory gave outright support to Spain in its conflict with Elizabeth I of England, and even favoured a plot to assassinate her. A special commission of the Cardinals was constituted to counter the spread of protestantism in Germany and to restore Catholicism elsewhere. This commission had some success in Germany and Poland, but little in Sweden where the king demanded communion under both species and a married clergy as a precondition to any reunification with Rome. Gregory supported the missionary endeavours of the Jesuits in Asia and in America. He approved the Congregation of the Oratory of St. Philip Neri, and the reform of the Carmelites conducted by St. Theresa of Avila. Gregory's name is for ever linked to the reform of the Julian calendar (called after Julius Caesar) which cancelled ten days from the year 1582 (5-14 October), and introduced new rules for the calculation of leap years. The Catholic nations immediately adopted the new calendar while the protestant countries only adopted it more than a century later. Gregory completed the building of the *Gesù* and began the construction of the Palazzo del Quirinale which was to become the summer palace of the Popes. These enterprises emptied the papal coffers. Discontent among the minor nobility which had been dispossessed in the Roman campagna gave rise to a banditry which made life and limb far from safe not only in the Roman countryside, but even in the City itself.

225. Sixtus V *(1585-1590)*

Born at Grotammare near Ancona in 1520, Felice Peretti entered the Franciscans in 1532. He was ordained at Siena and acquired a doctorate in theology in Femo. In Rome he earned reputation as a great preacher. Paul IV named him Inquisitor of Venice. During the reign of Pius V, he was named Bishop, Vicar General of the Franciscans and finally Cardinal. He was overlooked during the pontificate of Gregory XIII, with whom he had differences. On his election, he took the name of Sixtus in memory of his Franciscan predecessor, Sixtus IV. He immediately undertook a campaign to suppress banditry in the Papal States. Simultaneously, measures were set in motion to improve the social and economic conditions of the Papal States. He began draining the Pontine marches, encouraged agriculture, the woolen and silk manufactuaries, and established fixed prices for basic food stuffs. These, and other measures, such as increased taxation and public borrowing, filled the state coffers, making the Papal States one of the richest principalities in Europe. He re-organised the central administration of the Church, fixing the number of Cardinals in the Sacred College at Seventy. He completely re-organised the Curia, creating fifteen permanent Cardinalatial Congregations, nine of which oversaw ecclesiastical affairs, and six for temporal administration. This structure remained in place until the nineteenth century. He continued the work of revising the *Vulgate*, begun by Pius V. A version was published in 1590 but was withdrawn after his death because of its many errors. He declared St. Bonaventure a doctor of the Church. He continued an active international political policy, after the manner of his predecessors, and excommunicated Henri de Navarre who was later destined to succeed to the throne of France as Henri IV. Towards the end of his reign, he began to consider the possibility of a conversion on Henri's part, thereby incurring the hostility of Philip II of Spain, the great opponent of the Huguenot sovereign. Sixtus gave particular importance to the promotion of the missions in the East and in America. The Pope gave the city of Rome a new baroque stamp, opening up new prospects, erecting obelisks, and building many new palaces. He completed the building of St. Peter's and rebuilt the Lateran palace. Sixtus also re-housed the Vatican Library and the Vatican printing press. The Romans detested him, despite the fact that he was not only a great Pope but also a ruler concerned for the well-being of his subjects.

226. Urban VII *(September 1590)*

Giambattista Castagna, although of Genoese origin, was born in Rome in 1521. He had studied law and had held high office in the Segnatura Apostolica, the Church's supreme court of justice. He was named a bishop under Paul IV and had been governor of the Papal States for a brief period. He had also taken part in the final phase of the Council of Trent. Under Pius IV he had been Nuncio in Spain and in Venice, and had also been governor of Bologna. Gregory XIII had named him Cardinal and consultor of the Holy Office. His election was largely due to Spanish influence. He was struck by malaria and died without having been crowned.

227. Gregory XIV *(1590-1591)*

The Conclave following the death of Urban VII lasted two months. It was a deeply contested conclave and characterised by much Spanish interference. It eventually elected Niccolò Sfondrati from Somma, near Milan. He had been born in 1535. He was a jurist and closely linked to St. Charles Borromeo. At twenty-five, he had been named Bishop of Cremona by Pius IV. Having participated at the

final session of the Council of Trent, he devoted his attention to his diocese where he zealously applied the decrees of the Council. Gregory XIII named him Cardinal and brought him into the Curia where he was known for his reforming activities and his close links to St. Philip Neri and the Oratory. He was a deeply religious man but had absolutely no political experience. He named one of his nephews, Paolo Emilio Sfondrati, as head of the papal secretariat. He succeeded in alienating much of the Curia and of the Sacred College. Gregory XIV was closely linked to the Spanish and actively supported the efforts of the Holy League against the new French king, Henri IV, a Huguenot, whose excommunication he renewed, declaring his succession in France impossible. His pontificate was overshadowed by famine, plague, banditry, and inefficient governmental administration. He continued the work of ecclesiastical reform with zeal and ensured the application of the decrees of the Council of Trent.

228. Innocent IX *(October -December 1591)*

Giovanni Antonio Facchinetti was born in Bologna in 1514. He had been a jurist in the service of Cardinal Alessandro Farnese who had sent him to Avignon for some years. Named Bishop by Pius IV, he had participated in the final session of the Council of Trent. As Nuncio in Venice, he had made an important contribution to the formation of the Holy League that eventually resulted in the victory of Lepanto. Under Gregory XIII hae had played a prominent part in the Curia and in the Inquisition. He was created Cardinal in 1583. Old and infirm at the time of his election, which was promoted by the Spanish, it had not been contested by the French party in the

Sacred College. He continue the policy of his predecessor in relation to France. He divided the papal Secretariat into three sections: one for France and Poland, another for Italy and Spain, and a third for Germany. He took measures to curb banditry. He died after a pontificate of two months duration.

229. Clement VIII *(1592-1605)*

Ippolito Aldobrandini, a Florentine, was born in Fano in 1536, after his family had been obliged to leave Florence because of the hostility of the Medicis. Cardinal Farnese arranged for him to study law. He entered into the Curia under Pius IV, patronised by his family. He became a consistorial advocate and a judge of the Holy Roman Rota under Pius V. He accompanied Michele Bonelli to France and Spain. He did not enjoy the favour of Gregory XIII, but under Sixtus V, his career flourished, becoming datarius, Cardinal, Major Penitentiary, and discharging several diplomatic missions. Having been given serious consideration in the previous Conclaves, he was elected with Spanish assistance following the death of Innocent IX. He was a deeply religious man, if somewhat indecisive. He continued the work of applying the decrees of the Council of Trent. He promoted the reforms of the Council in the various religious orders, and published a corrected version of the Vulgate in 1592 - the so-called Pio-Clementine edition which remained in use until the nineteenth century. He published revised editions of the Missal, Breviary and Pontifical. A revised index of prohibited books appeared in 1596 which was stricter than that of Pius IV and included books in Hebrew. Many heretics were burned during the pontificate, including Giordano Bruno. Between 1595 and 1605, he examined the dispute between the Jesuits and the Dominicans on the writings of Luis de Molina on grace, free will, and divine foreknowledge, without ever arriving at a decision on the question. He was closely associated with St. Philip Neri, while the Oratorian historian Ceasre Baronio acted as his confessor. He named Robert Bellarmine Cardinal. Inclined to nepotism, he named both of his nephews, Cinzio and Pietro Aldobrandini, Cardinals in 1593. He left the administration of many ecclesiastical affairs in their hands or in those of other members of his family. In the political arena, he took the important decision to recognise Henri IV as king of France, after his conversion, and he lifted the excommunications that had been pronounced against him. Without great enthusiasm, he was obliged to accept the edict of Nantes of 1598 granting religious liberty to the Huguenots. This decision raised the hostility of Spain and the emperor but had the effect of freeing him of Spanish interference which was then at its most intrusive. Through his nominations to the Sacred College, he succeeded in reducing the influence of the Spanish on an eventual papal election. Following the extinction of the house Este, he succeeded in reincorporating Ferrara into the Papal States. During the pontificate, the Orthodox Poles returned to the Roman obedience and were allowed to retain their own liturgical rite. Clement promoted the counter reform in Switzerland where he nominated St. Francis de Sales to the see of Geneva. His efforts to restore Catholicism in England and Sweden were unsuccessful, as were his attempts to form a coalition against the Turks who were then threatening Austria and Hungary. Clement indicted a Holy Year in 1600 which brought millions of pilgrims to the City. The event represented the climax of his pontificate and of the renewed prestige of the Roman Church.

123

230. Leo XI *(April 1605)*

Alessandro Ottaviano de' Medici was born in Florence in 1535 of a collateral branch of the ruling family. He was a maternal nephew of Leo X, whose name he took. He came to Rome as Ambassador of the Granduke of Florence and quickly became a favourite disciple of St. Philip Neri. In 1583, Gregory XIII created him Cardinal. Having been one of those who succeeded in convincing the Pope to lift the excommunication of Henri IV, he was legate in France from 1596 to 1598. He did much to restore ecclesiastical discipline in France, although he failed to obtain the publication of the decrees of the Council of Trent. In 1598, he conducted the negotiations that led to the peace of Vervins and to peace between France and Spain. Created Cardinal in 1600, he was elected with French support, despite fierce Spanish opposition. He became ill while taking possession of the Lateran and died shortly afterwards.

231. Paul V *(1605-1621)*

Camillo Borgese was born in Rome in 1552 of a family of jurists that originally came from Siena. He held a doctorate in jurisprudence. His had been a brilliant carrier in the Curia. Created Cardinal in 1596, he was named Vicar of Rome and Inquisitor in 1603. Paul V was elected as a compromise candidate between the rival factions within the Conclave. Convinced of the supremacy of the Papacy over all States, he embarked on a collision course with the Italian and European princes. His pontificate was marked by a protracted and bitter struggle with the Republic of Venice which began in 1606 when two priests were tried by the civil courts in Venice. In the ensuing controversy, which quickly escalated into a battle of principle, Venice had the support of the notable theologian Fra Paolo Sarpi, who upheld the autonomy of the State. The Pope placed the city of Venice under interdict but the Venetian clergy ignored it. The Jesuits, who upheld papal supremacy, were expelled from the Republic, and an assassination attempt was made on Sarpi. The interdict was lifted in 1607 after a compromise which became necessary in view of a fear that Venice might have embraced protestantism, and the outbreak of war. Rome emerged badly from the conflict. Venice refused to back down and the weapon of interdict proved futile. Other controversies emerged in Europe. Paul V prohibited English Catholics from swearing oaths of allegiance, as required by parliament, which entailed rejection of the Pope's right to depose sovereigns. In France, Paul condemned Gallicanism and fought with the Estates General which had been convoked in 1614 and proclaimed the direct divine origin of royal authority, and refused to publish the decrees of the Council of Trent. Paul continued the reform of the Church, publishing the *Rituale Romanum*, and approving the foundation of the Congregation of the Oratory of St. Philip Neri in 1612, as well as the Oratory founded in France by the Cardinal Pierre de Bérulle. He canonised St. Carlo Borromeo and Santa Francesca Romana, and beatified St. Ignatius Loyola, St. Theresa of Avila, St. Francis Xavier, and St. Philip Neri. He deferred a decision on the Molinist question. He approved the Holy Office's condemnation of the Copernican system and prohibited the works of Galileo Galilei until they had been corrected. Galilei was prohibited from teaching or propagating the Copernican system. Paul V completed the facade and atrium of St. Peter's, restored the Trajan aqueduct, renamed the *Aqua Paulina*, which was used to feed many of the City's fountains. He constituted the *Arcivio Segreto Vaticano*. Paul also promoted his family interests and built the sumptuous Villa Borgese. In 1618, the thirty years war began in Germany. Initially, he adopted a cautious approach to the war, but later began a policy that was intended to involve the Papal States more closely in the war effort. He died suddenly in 1621 while conducting a procession in the City in thanksgiving for the victory won by the Hapsburgs at the Battle of the White Mountain.

232. Gregory XV *(1621-1623)*

Alessandro Ludovisi was born in Bologna in 1654. He had been educated by the Jesuits at the Collegio Romano, and achieved a doctorate in law at the university of Bologna. He had been involved in many diplomatic missions and had been made a Cardinal in 1621. He was the first Pope to have been educated by the Jesuits. Already old at the time of his election, he chose his twenty-five year old nephew, Cardinal Ludovico Ludovisi, as his secretary. Cardinal Ludovisi quickly came to determine political policy. Gregory XV achieved two major ecclesiastical accomplishments during his pontificate: in 1622 he founded the Congregation of the *Propaganda Fide*, which was placed in the charge of thirteen Cardinals and had full responsibility for Church's missionary activities. On 12 March 1622, he reformed the norms for the papal election, in the hope of excluding external political interference. The reform established a long and detailed series of rules for the Concalve including absolute segregation of the Cardinals, and the secret ballot. He intervened in the thirty years war, calling on the king of Spain to abandon his treaty with the United Provinces, and gave his full support to the Hapsburg efforts to re-establish Catholicism in Germany. His Nuncio in Germany, Carlo Carafa, succeeded in returning Bohemia to Catholicism and in obtaining the electoral dignity for the duke of Bavaria. In gratitude, Maximilian of Bavaria gave the Pope the library of Hidelberg which brought the important Palatine manuscripts into the Vatican Library. On 16 March 1622 Gregory canonised Theresa of Avila, Ignatius Loyola, Philip Neri and Francis Xavier, the great missionary, beatified by his predecessor.

233. Urban VIII *(1623-1644)*

Born in Florence, Maffeo Barbarini came from a family of wealthy merchants. Educated by the Jesuits, he had taken a doctorate in law and entered the service of the Curia, where he had a brilliant career, becoming Nuncio in France (1604), Cardinal (1606), legate in Bologna (1611) and prefect of the Sengatura (1617). A cultivated authoritarian man, the new Pope governed personally and rarely consulted the Sacred College on anything. Closely allied to France, he sought to maintain a kind of neutrality in the thirty years war which was devastating Europe and coming closer to engulfing France, which eventually happened in 1635. Urban abandoned the political policy of his predecessor who had supported the Catholic powers led by the Hapsburgs. This spelled the end of any possible re-catholicisation of Germany. Urban was also committed to the reform of the Church, revising the Breviary, and introducing new rules for beatifications and canonisations. He also revised the Bull *In Coena Domini*, traditionally read on Holy Thursday. The Pope encouraged the Church's missionary efforts. Urban approved the Order of the Visitation and the Congregation of the Mission, founded by St. Vincent de Paul. He strictly imposed the obligation of residence on Bishops and Cardinals. Although he had patronised and protected Galileo Galilei, in 1633 he authorised the Holy Office to prosecute and condemn him. Urban also condemned the doctrines of the Flemish bishop, Cornelius Jansen, in the Bull *In eminenti* of 1642. He advanced his own family, raising several of them to the dignity of Cardinal. He was a munificent Pope who did much to embellish the City, and restore the Castel Sant'Angelo. In 1626, he consecrated the new St. Peter's basilica. Urban demolished many of the classical monuments of the City and used the bronze from the Pantheon for St. Peter's. He incorporated Urbino into the Papal States. He devastated and impoverished the Papal States in the final years of his reign protracting a war against France, Tuscany and Venice, the object of which was to have his nephew installed in the duchy of Castro. This expedition aroused much resentment among the Romans who greeted his death with joy.

234. Innocent X *(1644-1655)*

Giovanni Battista Pamphili was born in Rome in 1574. He had studied at the Collegio Romano, specialising in jurisprudence. He had been a judge of the Holy Roman Rota, Nuncio in Naples, and a member of Cardinal Barbarini's court in France. Nominated Nuncio in Spain in 1626, he was created Cardinal in 1627. In the Conclave which elected him and which lasted for almost a month, he represented a reaction to the pro-French policies of Urban VIII. The veto of Cardinal Giulio Mazarin, prime minister of France, reached Rome too late to prevent his election. Mazarin's protection prevent him from prosecuting the Barbarinis and confiscating their property, as he had attempted shortly after his election. He was not immune to nepotism. The most influential figure at his court was Olympia Maidalchini, whom the Pope consulted on everything. His secretary of state, however, was not his nephew, Olympia's son, Cardinal Camillo Pamphili, but Cardinal Giovanni Giacomo Panciroli, the first formal appointment to this office (1644), and subsequently Cardinal Fabio Chigi (1651), who would succeed as Alexander VII. Innocent X favoured Spain in his political policy. In the war between France and Spain, the Pope maintained a position of formal neutrality. In 1647, when Naples rebelled against Spain, despite the urging of the French ambassador to have him use the opportunity to incorporate Naples into the Papal States, Innocent preferred to do nothing and to allow the Spanish to re-assert their authority in the kingdom. He sent Cardinal Chigi to the peace of Muenster with instructions to oppose the peace of Westphalia (1648). Innocent declared the peace null and void by the Breve *Zelus domus Dei*, whose publication he delayed for political reasons. His most important act was the condemnation of the jansenists. He instituted a commission, at which he personally presided, to examine five propositions extracted from the *Augustinus* (1640) of Jansen. These were condemned as heretical. A long controversy began on the question of grace and predestination, which created much theological division. He also gave decisions in matters relating to the Chinese Rite, and condemned the Jesuits who had introduced Chinese rituals into Catholic worship. Innocent was less munificent than his predecessors, but he built the Villa Pamphili and gave the Piazza Navona its present aspect, ornamenting it with fountains. His portrait by Diego Velazquez is conserved in the Galleria Doria Pamphili in Rome.

235. Alexander VII *(1655-1667)*

Fabio Chigi was born in Siena in 1599. He had studied philosophy, law and theology in Siena. Having come to Rome, he came into contact with intellectual circles and entered the service of the Curia. He was Nuncio in Cologne between 1639 and 1651, and represented the Pope in the negotiations leading to the peace of Westphalia, taking an intransigent position. He was named Secretary of State and Cardinal in 1651. The Conclave following the death of Innocent X lasted almost three months. Alexander's candidature was greatly resisted by the French. He had very poor relations with most of the European monarchs. Relations with France, which had for long been tense, deteriorated under Louis XIV, who expelled the Nuncio from Paris and recalled his ambassador from Rome. Louis occupied Avignon and threatened to invade the Papal States. Alexander was obliged to cede not only on the question of French episcopal nominations but also had to agree to the unheard of humiliation of sending his own nephew, Cardinal Flavio Chigi, to Paris to present his formal excuses to Louis XIV. Alexander reiterated the condemnation of the jansenists and obliged all clergy to sign an anti-jansenist declaration, a measure greatly appreciated in France where Louis XIV was struggling with the jansenists. The Pope normalised relations with Venice, where the Jesuits were re-admitted for the first time since the reign of Paul V. Relations with Spain deteriorated to the extent that the Spanish king refused to receive the Nuncio. Those with John IV of Portugal were not much better. Matters were further complicated by the Portugese king's insistence on appropriating the income of vacant dioceses. He threatened to constituted a national Church. The most significant event of Alexander's pontificate was the conversion of queen Christina of Sweden, who abdicated the throne and moved to Rome where she was received in triumph. Christina proved an embarrassment and the expense of maintaining her court was burdensome on papal finances. Her personal conduct was not regarded as totally edifying. Alexander supported the position of the Jesuits on the question of the Chinese rites, and exempted the Chinese clergy from the use of Latin in the Liturgy. He intervened in the dispute on probabilism, a theological system developed by the Dominicans but appropriated by the Jesuits, condemming many of its tenets as laxist. The Pope beatified (1661) and canonised (1665) St. Francis de Sales whose spirituality had much influenced him. Alexander was a great patron of the arts and entrusted Gian Lorenzo Bernini with the construction of the colonnade of St. Peter's.

236. Clement IX *(1667-1669)*

Giulio Rospigliosi was born to a noble family of Pistoia in 1600. He studied liberal arts with the Jesuits in Rome and jurisprudence in Pisa. He was interested in literature and music and closely involved with a group of musicians that developed the genre of melodrama. Rosipgliosi composed several libretti. Between 1644 and 1653 he was Nuncio in Spain. At the time of the death of Innocent X, he was governor of Rome. Alexander VII named him Cardinal and Secretary of State in 1655. Both Spain and France welcomed his election, having always maintained good relations with both courts. He was not given to nepotism and excluded his family from the political business of the Church. As his name indicates, he was a peacemaker. He resolved the problem with the Portugese crown and normalised relations with France. Ceding to Louis XIV's pressure, he allowed widespread liberty to the France king in the nomination of bishops in France. With regard to the jansenists, Clement accepted a compromise worked out by his Nuncio in France Niccolò Bargellini and the French exterior minister, Huges de Lionne, which was supported by the king. The «Pax Clementina» of 1688 ended the persecution of the jansenists but clearly indicated the extent of the Holy See's subservience to the French crown. In response to renewed hostilities from the Turks, he organised a number of expeditions, composed of French, Spanish and Imperial forces, to assist Venice defend the island of Crete. News of its having been taken by the Turks after a struggle of more than twenty years hastened Clement's death.

237. Clement X *(1670-1676)*

The Conclave following the death of Clement IX was difficult and lasted more than five months. Emilio Altieri, a Cardinal created a month before Clement's death, was elected and took the name of Clement X. He had been born in Rome in 1590. Educated at the Collegio Romano, he took a doctorate in jurisprudence. Having spent some years in the service of the Curia, he took up residence in the diocese of Camerino in 1627 and remained there until he was recalled to Rome by Alexander VII in 1654. As his closest advisor, Clement chose Cardinal Paluzzo Paluzzi Altieri. This was an unfortunate choice not only because the Cardinal was extremely generous with his relatives, but also because he was politically inept and improvident. Clement began his pontificate by addressing the Turkish threat to Poland. In this he had the support of Jan Sobieski, king of Poland since 1674, who had defeated the Turks at Chotin in 1673. Under Clement, relations with France deteriorated once more. The Pope was obliged to cede to Louis XIV when he introduced the principle of the *regalia* to France, which gave him the right to appropriate the income of vacant sees. He canonised St. Gaetano Thiene, St. Francis Borgia, and St. Rose of Lima, the first South American saint. He beatified Pope Pius V, the Spanish mystic John of the Cross, and the martyrs of Gorkum, Dutch Catholics massacred by the Calvinists in 1572.

238. Blessed Innocent XI *(1676-1689)*

After a conclave of two months duration, Benedetto Odescalchi was elected unanimously in 1676. Born to a family of rich merchants in Como in 1611, he had been educated by the Jesuits. After a brief period in commerce, he took a doctorate in jurisprudence and entered the service of the Curia. He was named Cardinal by Innocent X. Nominated Bishop of Novara, he distinguished himself by the rigour of his administration, his piety and his charity to the poor. He showed the same rigour when elected Pope, eliminating abuses, and restoring the papal finances through drastic economic measures. He was concerned for the promotion of the religious life and the training of the clergy. He promoted frequent holy communion and suppressed the Roman carnival. He completely eschewed every form of nepotism. Without directly criticising the Jesuits, he condemned as laxist seventy-five propositions connected with probabilism.

In 1680, he approved the doctrine of probabiliorism which, in doubtful moral cases, advanced the obligation of doing that which was more probably right instead of favouring one's own interest. His hostility to the Jesuits, and his own personal rigorous lifestyle created the impression that he favoured the Jansenists. On the other hand, he permitted the Holy Office to condemn the works of Miguel Molinos, strongly opposed by the Jesuits, and the spiritual teaching of quietism which minimalised human responsibility and activity. Innocent's relations with France were strained. He opposed the *regalia*, which had been tacitly accepted by his predecessor. Louis XIV reacted by publishing the Gallican articles of 1682 which asserted that the papacy had no rights over the temporal affairs of the French Church, and that a council was superior to the Pope. The articles, the work of Jacques-Bénigne Bossuet, Bishop of Meaux, were imposed on the French clergy. The French crisis became more acute when the Pope not only rejected the Gallican articles, but also refused to ratify any episcopal nomination in France, thereby leaving thirty-nine sees vacant. Not even the revocation of the Edict of Nantes, which was welcomed in Rome, succeeded in softening the Pope's attitude to the Gallicanism of Louis XIV. The accession of the Catholic James II to the throne of England was not particularly warmly viewed in Rome, given that the new English monarch was totally dependant on the support of Louis XIV. By 1687 the arrogance of the French ambassador was such that the Pope refused to receive him. Innocent abolished the right of sanctuary enjoyed by embassies. In 1688, Louis XIV was privately informed of his excommunication, in reaction to which he occupied Avignon. The Pope wrongly suspected that Louis XIV lay behind the accession of the protestant William of Orange to the throne of England. In addition to his problems with the French court, Innocent had to address the Turkish problem. As a result of papal policy, Jan III Sobieski, king of Poland, allied with the emperor, defeated the Turks at Vienna in 1683. Immediately following the relief of Vienna, the Pope formed a Holy League consisting of the Holy Roman Empire, Poland, Venice and Russia. In 1686, after more than a century and a half of Turkish dominion, Hungary was liberated of the Turkish yoke, and Belgrade re-taken. These events definitively ended the Turkish advance in danubian Europe. Innocent's severity of life did not endear him to the Romans. He enjoyed a reputation for sanctity after his death. In 1714, Clement XI began the process for his canonisation. In 1744, French opposition blocked the advance of the process. The cause was re-introduced by Pius XII who beatified Innocent in 1956. His feast day is 12 August.

239. Alexander VIII *(1689-1691)*

Pietro Ottoboni, born in 1610 to a recently ennobled family from Padua, had studied jurisprudence and entered the service of the Curia. As a judge of the Holy Roman Rota (1643-1652) he acquired a reputation for the quality of the jurisprudence exhibited in his sentences. Nominated Cardinal and Bishop of Brescia, he resided in his diocese between 1654 and 1664, when he was recalled to the Curia where he was nominated Inquisitor general and Secretary of the Holy Office. In the Conclave that elected him, principally for his learning and exceptional qualities, France and the Holy Roman Empire were represented by two ambassadors extraordinary. At first, the French opposed his election. When he gave an undertaking to improve relations between the Holy See and the French court, the French no longer opposed his election, and restored Avignon to the papacy. The controversy with the French was rekindled, however, on the question of the Gallican Articles, on which the Pope would make no concessions. Alexander condemned them with the Apostolic constitution *Inter multiplies* of 1690. Alexander's relations with the Holy Roman Empire were very strained. He refused the purple to the imperial candidates, and reduced the subventions made to the emperor to defray the costs of the war against the Turks, while simultaneously increasing those given to Venice. The Pope took a rigorous position against the laxism of the Jesuits, the thirty-nine articles of the Jansenists and imprisoned the followers of Molinos. He was munificent and openly nepoistic, naming hie nephew Giovanni Battista Rubini his Secretary of State. He also named his grand nephew, Pietro Ottoboni, a Cardinal. Alexander VIII enjoyed enormous popularity among his subjects. He lowered taxes and increased the importation of cheap food stuffs. He acquired a collection of important manuscripts from the collection of queen Christina of Sweden for the Vatican Library.

240. Innocent XII *(1691-1700)*

Antonio Pignatelli was a member of a distinguished Neopolitan noble family. Born at Spinazzola, in Apulia, in 1615, he had been educated by the Jesuits in Rome, where he began his service in the Curia under Urban VIII. He had been governor of Viterbo, Nuncio in Tuscany, Poland and Vienna. His election came after a long controversial Conclave. Clement X had marginalised him and sent him back to his diocese in Lecce. Recalled to the Curia, he was named Cardinal in 1681, legate to Bologna, and Archbishop of Naples in 1687. Modelling himself on the example of Blessed Innocent XI, he began a rigorous reform of the Curia, commencing with a prohibition on the sale of ecclesiastical offices. In order to obviate the financial consequences of this policy, he reduced the expenses of the Papal court to a minimum, and increased commerce in the ports of Civitavecchia and Nettuno. Innocent was especially interested in the plight of the poor and founded the Hospice of San Michele in Rome for needy young people. He enforced ecclesiastical discipline. Despite the opposition of the Sacred College, Alexander addressed the universally accepted practice of nepotism in a radical manner, issuing the Bull *Romanum decet pontificem* which prohibited the conferral of offices or incomes on the relatives of Popes. He only raised one of his relatives to the dignity of Cardinal. Innocent XII succeeded in improving relations with France. This was rendered easier by the difficulties France encountered in its war against the League of Augsburg. The accord which he made obliged the French bishops to remove their signatures form the Gallican Articles, in exchange for the ratification of episcopal nominations and the normalisation of relations with the French court. Louis XIV revoked his decrees of 1682. The agreement did not, however, end the gallican political policy of the French monarchy, which soon resumed and was destined to continue throughout the entire eighteenth century. The agreement with France complicated relations between Rome and Vienna. Although Innocent XII had played an important mediating role in ending the war which had dissipated the European powers, he was not represented at the Congress that led to the peace of Rijswijck in 1697 which ended French hegemony in Europe. The problem of the Spanish succession emerged at this time: Charles II of Spain, who had no heirs, consulted the Pope on the problem of the Spanish succession. Innocent favoured the French candidate, Philip, duke of Anjou, rather than the emperor's candidate, the archduke Karl. Innocent died a month before Charles II in 1700.

241. Clement XI (1700-1721)

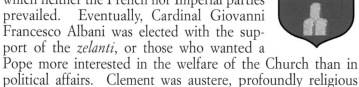

The Conclave lasted forty-six days during which neither the French nor Imperial parties prevailed. Eventually, Cardinal Giovanni Francesco Albani was elected with the support of the *zelanti*, or those who wanted a Pope more interested in the welfare of the Church than in political affairs. Clement was austere, profoundly religious and devoid of all political capacity. Clement was born in Urbino in 1649. He had been given a fine classical education and had attended the classical academy of queen Christina of Sweden. He had studied law and entered the service of the Curia, beginning his career as governor of the Papal States. He was created Cardinal in 1690. He played a decisive role in the government of Alexander VII and Innocent XII. He had drawn up the Bull against nepotism. Clement was ordained a priest only in 1700. Europe was once again at war as his pontificate began. The war of the Spanish succession would have a direct effect on the Papal States. In an attempt to dislodge the Pope from his pro-French position, Imperial troops invaded Naples and parts of the Papal States, and began to move on Rome. The Pope was obliged to sue for peace on very disadvantageous terms which included recognition of the imperial candidate as legitimate king of Spain. Finding himself on the losing side of the war, the Pope played little role in drawing up the peace of Utrecht which made provisions for Sardinia, Parma and Piacenza, and Sicily without taking any account of the Pope's traditional feudal rights. Despite Papal protests, Sicily was given to Victor Amadeus II of Savoy. Clement XI made an unsuccsessful attempt to organise an alliance to liberate the Peloponese from Turkish dominion. In 1713, the Bull *Unigenitus Dei filius* formally condemned jansenism, on the basis of an examination of the works of Pascal Quesnel. The Bull provoked a sharp division among the French clergy, some of whom accepted it, while others rejected it and called for the convocation of a general council. The excommunication of the supporters of jansenism had little effect and demonstrated how the weapon of excommunication had become redundant. Clement was particularly interested in the missions and intervened in the question of Chinese rites which was a source of contention between Jesuit and Dominican missionaries. He condemned the Jesuit position and prohibited the use of Chinese rites, especially those deriving from Confucinism, in Christian worship. The prohibition caused the closure of the mission in China and the persecution of Chinese Christians. It was only revoked two centuries later by Pius XII. In 1708, Clement extended the feast of the Immaculate Conception to the entire Church. He created some seventy Cardinals during his long pontificate. The Pope was a committed patron of the arts and literature. He was especially interested in archeology and collected numerous Oriental manuscripts for the Vatican Library.

242. Innocent XIII *(1721-1724)*

The Conclave following on the death of Clement XI was long and controversial. The Imperial veto excluded the favoured candidate, Cardinal Fabrizio Paolucci, Secretary of State to Clement XI. Finally, Michelangelo Conti was elected. Born to a noble family at Palestrina, in 1655, he had been educated by the Jesuits. Having entered the service of the Curia, he had been governor of the Papal States and Nuncio in Switzerland, and in Portugal (1698-1709). He was created Cardinal in1706 by Clement XI, and named Bishop of Osimo and Viterbo. Innocent was unsuccessfully involved in the resolution of those questions still left open after the war of the Spanish succession. He assigned the kingdoms of Naples and Sicily to the Holy Roman Emperor, Charles VI, but failed to prevent him exercising his authority over the Church in Sicily. He supported the exiled James III, but failed to have the emperor restore Comacchio. Innocent was deeply hostile to the Jesuits, and was at the point of dissolving the order when he came to learn of their opposition to his predecessor's decision with regard to the Chinese rites. He prohibited the reception of novices into the Jesuits. The Jansenists hoped that Innocent would revoke the condemnation issued against them. Innocent, however, maintained and applied the positions taken by his predecessor against the Jansenist. He named his brother Bernardo Cardinal without, however, enriching him, thereby observing the norms issued in 1692 against nepotism. He promoted the economic and social development of the Papal States.

243. Benedict XIII *(1724-1730)*

Pierfrancesco Orsini was a member of a noble family that had given the Church two Popes in the middle ages: Celestine III and Nicholas III. Born in 1649 at Gravina, in Apulia, he entered the Dominican Order at the age of twenty in the face of his family's opposition. He took the names Vincenzo Maria in religion. He taught philosophy at Brescia. In 1672 he was named Cardinal by Clement X, to whom he was related. Benedict had been successively Bishop of Manfredonia, Cesena and Archbishop of Benevento. As bishop, he had zealously devoted himself to the pastoral ministry and published several manuals of pastoral and ascetical theology. In relation to his immediate predecessors, Benedict's career had been something of an anomaly. His election was due in good measure to his lack of political experience which brought the contending parties in a difficult Conclave to agree on Benedict. Continuing the monastic life to which he had been accustomed, he did not want to take up residence in the Vatican palace. Retaining the pastoral government of Benevento, the Pope embarked on an intensive pastoral programme in the diocese of Rome. He imposed a rigid discipline on the Cardinals, and abolished the public lottery which was an unpopular move and deprive the State of significant income. Benedict, who was utterly absorbed with the spiritual life, had complete confidence in the unscrupulous Niccolò Coscia, whom he named Cardinal in 1725. Coscia systematically enriched himself and his supporters by selling ecclesiastical offices and concessions. The state finances collapsed and the prestige of the Holy See continued to decline. Leaving relations with princes to persons such as Niccolò Maria Lercari, Benedict renounced many of the territorial pretensions of the Papacy, recognising Victor Amadeus II of Savoy as king of Sardinia and granting him full control of the Sardinian dioceses. He also conceded control of ecclesiastical affairs in Sicily to the Holy Roman Emperor. The Jansenists had hoped that a Dominican Pope would repeal the anti-Jansenist positions of his predecessors. They attempted to demonstrate how the Bull *Unigenitus Dei Filius* was incompatible with the doctrine of grace and predestination taught by St. Augustine and St. Thomas. Benedict, however, roundly denied any connection between Thomism and Jansenism and reiterated the obligation on the Jansenists of submitting to the terms of the Bull *Unigenitus Dei Filius*. The Pope canonised many Saints including St. John of the Cross, and St. Luigi Gonzaga. His extension of the feast of St. Gregory the Great to the entire Church provoked tension with many of the European courts because of the theocratic content of the texts chosen for the liturgical offices of the feast. He was unpopular among the Romans because of his poor public administration and the collapse of public finances.

244. Clement XII *(1730-1740)*

Lorenzo Corsini, a member of a Florentine noble family with extensive commercial interests, was elected Pope in 1730 following a long and difficult Conclave. Born in 1652, he had studied with the Jesuits in Rome, and had taken a doctorate in law at Pisa. He entered the service of the Curia in 1685. Alexander VII named him Nuncio in Vienna in 1691 but he could not take up office because of a break in

diplomatic relations with the Holy Roman Empire. This had obliged him to remain in Rome where he filled the office of treasurer of the Camera Apostolica. Clement XI named him Cardinal in 1706 and he established his residence in the palazzo Pamphili in the piazza Navona, surrounding himself with artists and men of culture. Although considered a possible candidate in previous Conclaves, he was not elected until 1730, by which time he was aged and almost blind. He named his nephew, Neri Corsini, Cardinal. One of his first acts was the prosecution of Cardinal Coscia who was sentenced to a long period of confinement in the Castel Sant'Angelo, and the payment of hefty fines. He tried unsuccessfully to solve the problem of the exhausted public finances, reintroducing the public lottery, circulating paper money, taxing imports, limiting the exportation of valuables, and by encouraging industry and commerce in Ancona. Public debt, however, had increased by the time of his death in 1740, a factor exacerbated by declined income from Catholic countries. The papacy entered a phase of noticeable international decline during the reign of Clement XII. The Catholic powers no longer referred anything to the Pope, and indeed some even ignored him. In 1731, the Holy Roman Emperor, in virtue of his feudal claims, assigned the duchy of Parma and Piacenza to the Bourbons, despite the fact that the territory had for long been part of the papal dominions. Neither was Clement consulted about the Polish succession which had major territorial and dynastic implications for Italy. Tensions with Spain led to the collapse of diplomatic relations with the Spanish court the kingdom of Naples in 1736. The solution to this problem obliged the Pope to make major concessions including investiture of Charles de Bourbon as king of the Two Sicilies. Initially, Clement restricted the creation of Cardinals to Italians, but was obliged to modify this policy in view of the pressure exerted on him by the Catholic courts. He was the first Pope to condemn masonry and religious indifferentism in the Bull *In emenenti* of 1738. He encouraged the missions, especially in the Orient, and reiterated the prohibition on

Chinese rites, although he had the question reexamined. He sent the distinguished oriental scholar, Cardinal Giuseppe Simonio Assemani, as legate to the Lebanon to a synod
which reformed the Maronite liturgy. Clement canonised St. Vincent de Paul, one of the
strongest opponents of Jansenism. The Pope also carried out a programme of embellish-
ments to the City which included the construction of the principal facade of the Lateran
Basilica and the famous Trevi fountain.

245. Benedict XIV *(1740-1758)*

Born to an impoverished noble family in
Bologna in 1675, Prospero Lorenzo Lamberti-
ni studied at the Collegium Clementinum in
Rome and acquired doctorates in theology and
law. His was brilliant and rapid curial career.
Named Secretary of the Congregation for the Council in 1720,
he subsequently took charge of the various canonisation
processes then in motion. He wrote a classic work on this sub-
ject entitled *De Servorum Dei beatificatione et beatorum canonisatione*. He was an important advisor to Benedict XIII who named him Cardinal. Appointed Archbishop of
Bologna in 1731, he transferred his residence to that city where he was held in high esteem
by the people. At this point, Benedict published several important works, including his
De Synodo Dioecesana. The Conclave following the death of Clement XII lasted six
months - the longest in modern times. Benedict was a born conciliator and quickly concluded a series of concordats with the European powers that contained several important
concessions. The concordat with Spain ceded all episcopal nominations to the Spanish
crown. He restored diplomatic relations with Portugal which had lapsed under Benedict
XIII, and granted the title of "fidelissimus" to the Portugese king. Benedict also took a
conciliatory position with protestant sovereigns, conscious of the difficulties experienced
by their Catholic subjects in the context of the rise of the absolutist states. Benedict maintained good relations with Frederick II and succeeded in retaining control of the Catholic
Church in Prussia. He lacked political wisdom in siding with the enemies of Maria Theresa in the war of the Austrian succession. This occasioned the loss of his ecclesiastical
benefices in Austria, and invasion of the Papal States by the Imperial troops. Benedict
was completely excluded from the Peace of Aachen which brought the war to a close. The
Pope was concerned for the welfare of his subjects and encouraged agriculture and free
trade. While he lowered taxes, he did not introduce the radical economic reforms which
were necessary. His principal concerns always lay in ecclesiastical matters where he acted
with reforming zeal. He introduced norms for marriages between Catholics and protestants in Holland and Belgium which exempted them from the decrees of Trent. He personally worked on a reform of the Breviary which remained unfinished at the time of his
death. He reduced the number of holidays in Italy and in other countries. He ruled definitively against the Chinese rites, and the Malabar rites in India, though in a more attenuated form. He reiterated the condemnation of masonry as well as many works published
by the followers of the enlightenment, among them Montesquieu's *L'esprit des Lois*. He
republished the index of prohibited books. A month before his death, he ordered the
Patriarch of Lisbon to initiate an inquiry into the accusations made against the Jesuits in
Portugal. Benedict was a man of great culture, an accomplished ecclesiastical historian,
and interested in cultural matters. He also won the esteem of protestants and of some
enlightenment circles. With no small embarrassment to Catholics, Voltaire dedicated his
tragedy *Mahomet* to Benedict XIV. The Pope was a devout man, and aware of the prob-

lems of his times. Horace Walpole, the English politician, described him as "a priest without insolence or interests, a prince without favourites, a Pope without nephews".

246. Clement XIII *(1758-1769)*

Born in 1693 to a wealthy and recently ennobled mercantile family in Venice, Carlo Rezzonico, had studied under the Jesuits in Bologna, taken a doctorate in Padua, and had entered the Academy of Noble Ecclesiastics in Rome, destined for a career in the diplomatic service of the Church. Called to the service of the Curia in 1716, he soon occupied a series of important positions, including Venetian Auditor of the Holy Roman Rota. His sentences, in three volumes, were published in 1769. Named Cardinal by Clement XII in 1737, he was soon promoted to the See of Padua where he proved to be a model bishop, in the mould of San Carlo Borromeo. He rebuilt the seminary at his own expense and was particularly concerned for the welfare of the poor. His election was welcomed in Venice, which soon revoked its anti-papal legislation, introduced during the reign of Benedict XIV. His entire pontificate was dominated by the question of the Jesuits, whom the Pope defended with the support of his Secretary of State, the pro-Jesuit Luigi Torrigiani, to the annoyance of many of the Catholic courts of Europe. The controversy began in Portugal where the authoritarian and reform minded prime minister, the Marquis de Pombal, banished the Jesuits from the State, having accused them of illicit involvement in commerce, inciting rebellion among the natives in Paraguay, and of having been party to a plot to assassinate the king. The Pope's protests were futile and eventually led to a breaking off of diplomatic relations. The Portugese example was followed by the Bourbon courts. In 1764, the Company of Jesus was abolished by royal decree in France. In 1767, the Jesuits were expelled from the kingdoms of Spain, Naples and Sicily. At this point, the Pope attempted to use force and issued the *monotorio di Parma* against all jurisdictional provisions in the Bourbon duchy of Parma which had subjected the Church to the state. The monitum annulled all provisions and excommunicated their authors and promoters in the duchy on the basis of the Bull *In coena Domini*. Parma replied by expelling the Jesuits in 1768 and the conjoined Bourbon courts demanded the revocation to Clement's Parma provision. In the face of Papal opposition, the French occupied Avignon, while the king of Naples occupied Benevento and Pontecorvo. The Bourbon courts conjointly demanded the dissolution of the Jesuits. Deciding to resist, the Pope convoked a Consistory for 3 February 1769, but died the night before it was due to have been held. Apart from the Jesuit question, Clement also dealt with the problem of Febronianism which attempted to curb Papal influence in Germany. The theory took its name from the pseudonym used by its greatest promoter, Johann Niklaus von Hontheim, Bishop of Trier. On this issue, Clement moved cautiously since Febronianism enjoyed much support among the German hierarchy. He condemned the enlightenment: the *Encycolopédie* was placed on the index, together with Rousseau's *Emile*, and Helvétius' *De l'ésprit*. In 1766, Clement reiterated the Church's opposition to the writings of the enlightenment in the encyclical letter *Chritianae reipublicae salus*. The Pope held six canonisations, among them Jeanne de Chantal. He approved the Jesuit inspired devotion to the Sacred Heart. During his pontificate, nude statues and paintings in the Roman churches, including the Sixtine Chapel, were covered.

247. Clement XIV *(1769-1744)*

The Conclave was dominated by the Jesuit question. The Bourbon courts expected the election of a Pope who would side with them against the Jesuits, having suffered Clement XIII's unqualified support for the Jesuits. The favourite was Giovanni Vincenzo Ganganelli. Discussion centred on his giving an undertaking to suppress the Company of Jesus. Cardinal Ganganelli had been known to say that such a move would be canonically possible and perhaps advantageous for the Church. The new Pope, son of a country doctor, was born in Sant'Angelo, near Rimini, in 1705. He entered the Franciscans and took the name of Lorenzo. He acquired a doctorate in theology and became rector of the College of St. Boniface in Rome. During this period, he dedicated one of his many works to St. Ignatius Loyola. H was named a consultor of the Holy Office. Refusing the office of Minister General of the Franciscans, he was named Cardinal by Clement XIII in 1759. During the years of conflict with the Bourbon courts, he maintained a neutral position with regard to the Jesuits. Shortly after his election, he opened negotiations with the Bourbon courts to resolve the question and nominated Cardinal Lazzaro Opizio Pallavicini as Secretary of State. Cardinal Pallavicini was known to have close contacts with the court of Spain. Diplomatic relations with Portugal were resumed. Clement confirmed royal appointments to the Portugese dioceses and raised a brother of the Marquis de Pombal to the dignity of Cardinal. The Pope omitted proning the Bull *In Ceona Domini* on Holy Thursday, 1770, since it was a source of his predecessor's difficulties with the Bourbons. Clement postponed the suppression of the Jesuits, hoping that it would be sufficient to prohibit their accepting new recruits which would have led to their slow extinction. When the empress Maria Theresia joined the anti-Jesuit camp in 1773 and Clement faced the possibility of breaking relations with all of the European States, he was obliged to accede to the suppression of the Company of Jesus. In consultation with the court of Spain, the brief *Dominus ac redemptor noster* dissolving the Jesuits was drawn up. It mentioned a need to restore peace in the Church and ordered the complete dissolution of the Order since, at that moment, it was no longer able to achieve the objectives for which it had been founded. This document was hailed as a triumph for the enlightenment and was published throughout Europe, except in Russia and Prussia. The suppression of the Jesuits also included the suppression of their schools and colleges. This had momentous consequences for education and educational policies. The suppression of the Jesuits also had devastating effects on the missions. Immediately following the promulgation of the Brief, France withdrew from Avignon. Benevento and Pontecorvo were not restored to the Pope for some considerable time, and then only at heavy expense. The international prestige of the papacy made no recovery during this pontificate. The protests of the Holy See at the proposed partition of Poland remained unheeded. Clement XIV resumed partial relations with England, and withdrew support from the Stuarts. He was pleased to receive members of the ruling English house in Rome - which was to some advantage to Catholics in England. He tried in vain to restore public finances. The Pope began the building of the Clementine museum (later the Pio-Clementine museum). His final years were spend under the shadow of a morbid fear of assassination. At the time of his death, rumours circulated that he had been poisoned - which were disproved by an autopsy performed on his body. The panegyric read at his obsequies made no reference to the suppression of the Company of Jesus.

136

248. Pius VI (1775-1799)

Angelo Braschi, son of an impoverished noble family, was born at Cesena in the Romagna in 1717. He took a doctorate in jurisprudence and entered the service of Cardinal Antonio Ruffo, before being appointed private secretary to Benedict XIV. Named Bishop by Clement XIII, he moved to the office of the treasurer of the Camera Apostolica. Clement XIV named him Cardinal. The Conclave following the death of Clement XIV was long and arduous. Upon election, Pius VI had to face the problem of increasing State control of the Church. Relations with the king of Naples and the emperor Joseph II immediately deteriorated. Inspired by the enlightenment and Febronianism, the emperor had begun a policy of radical ecclesiastical reforms. Josephinism claimed total state control of the Church, whose influence was strictly limited to the realm of the spiritual, and promoted religious tolerance. In the wake of the suppression of numerous religious orders and similar provisions in the ecclesiastical sphere, Pius VI went as an "apostolic pilgrim" to Vienna in 1782 in an effort to convince the emperor to abandon his ecclesiastical policies. Under the Granduke Pietro Leopoldo of Tuscany, a brother of the emperor, Josephinism began to spread to Italy, and ended in an attempt to establish a national Church in Tuscany that was completely independent of Rome. The Synod of Pistoia of 1786 saw the Jansenist Bishop, Scipione de' Ricci, adopt the gallican articles and absolve the bishops of their obedience to Rome. The Pope condemned this position in 1794. In an attempt to placate the Bourbon courts, with whom Pius had maintained good relations, he sought to persuade Russia and Prussia to suppress the Jesuits. Catherine II resisted all attempts to suppress the Company of Jesus and opened a novitiate for the Order in Russia. In these circumstances, Pius had little option but to give secret approval to the survival of the Jesuits in Russia. His policies emptied the coffers of the papacy. Pius built the Palazzo Braschi, which he gave to his nephew Luigi, the sacristy of St. Peter's, and concluded the building of the Pio-Clementine museum. He tried, with little success, to drain the pontine marches. Most of the reclaimed land was given to his nephews. With the outbreak of the French revolution, the situation changed radically. In 1790, the constituent assembly approved the civil constitution of the clergy which radically altered the structure of the Church and transformed the clergy into civil servants dependant on the State. Bishops and parish priests were appointed by election. The bishops who participated in the assembly appealed the matter to the Pope. Up to that point, they had defended the gallican articles and the prerogatives of the French Church against Rome. Pius was initially cautious on the subject of the civil constitution of the clergy. After eight months, however, he condemned it together with the principles of liberty, equality and fraternity contained in the declaration of the rights of man. Meanwhile, the French clergy were obliged to take a constitutional oath. The clergy split into two groups; the sermentés and the réfractaires. By apostolic Brief of 13 April 1793, Pius suspended all priests who had taken the oath. The revolutionary government applied the traditional response and invaded Avignon. An unbreacheable and bloody chasm opened up between the Church and the revolutionary government which unleashed a bitter and bloody persecution of the clergy and of Catholics. The Pope opened the doors of the Papal States to the exiled French clergy, and joined a coalition of Italian States which was preparing to defend Italy against a French invasion led by Napoleon Bonaparte. It was easily defeated. The Pope was obliged to accept the onerous terms of the peace of Bologna in 1796 and those of the peace of Tolentino in 1797 which ceded Avignon to the French, together with the Legations of Bologna, Ferrara and Ravenna. Rome was also constrained to pay sub-

137

stantial tribute to the revolutionary government, and cede many of its works of arts, archives and libraries. In the apostolic Brief *Pastoralis sollecitudo* Pius was constrained to remind French Catholics of the obligation of obedience to the constituted civil authority. The Brief was not an abandonment of his condemnation of the civil constitution of the clergy nor of the constitutional oath. Pius made a solemn reaffirmation of his apostolic mandate and refused to annul his previous condemnations, notwithstanding the threat of military invasion made by Bonaparte. In 1798, a anti-Jacobin plot gave the Directory its opportunity to invade Rome and declare the Roman Republic. The Pope announced his intention of remaining in Rome. He was expelled and obliged to seek refuge in Tuscany, firstly in Siena and subsequently at the Charterhouse of Florence. He was closely guarded and accompanied by a much reduced court, and a few advisors. Some of the Cardinals remained in Rome while others took refuge in the Austrian States. When war broke out in Italy in 1799, Pius, who was already old and infirm, was bundled into a carriage and transported to France. He was taken to Briancon and then to Valence, where he died a prisoner in the fortress, concluding one of the longest pontificates in history. In 1802, his remains were returned to Rome and buried in St. Peter's. Before he died, he left instructions that the Conclave was to assemble in Venice under Austrian protection.

249. Pius VII *(1800-1823)*

The Conclave assembled in Venice under Austrian protection and elected a compromise candidate, Luigi Barnaba Chiaramonti. He had been born at Cesena in the Romagna in 1742. He had entered the Benedictines, taking the name of Gregory. Having studied in Padua and Rome, he taught theology at Parma and Sant'Anselmo in Rome. Nominated Bishop of Tivoli in 1782, he was promoted to the prestigious See of Imola and named Cardinal in 1785. Pius was open to modern ideas. He created much surprise in 1797 when he declared in a sermon that Catholicism was not necessarily incompatible with democracy. Having being elected Pope, he refused to remain in Venice under Austrian protection and set out for Rome. He named Ercole Consalvi his Secretary of State. He was a diplomat of exceptional ability. Consalvi succeeded in convincing the Austrians, Neapolitans, and even the French, to withdraw from the parts of the Papal States then occupied by them, thus allowing him to reconstitute the Papal States in some form. Pius VII radically changed the policy of his predecessor and attempted to make peace with the French. In 1801, a concordat was signed between the Holy See and Napoleon, the first Consul, which restored Catholicism in France and recognised it as the religion of the vast majority of the French. The concordat brought advantages and disadvantages for the Church. Most of the advantages were contained in the Organic Articles which Napoleon added to the concordat in 1802. These articles increased state interference in the affairs of the Church. A similar, though more advantageous concordat was agreed with the Italian republic in 1803. No agreement could be reached with Germany which had secularised all ecclesiastical property. In a good will gesture, and against the advice of the Curia, Pius went to Paris in 1804 for the coronation of Napoleon. With the outbreak of war between France and most of Europe, relations between Napoleon and the Pope deteriorated. Napoleon had Cardinal Consalvi removed from office but he failed to obtain Pius' approval of the continental blockade of England. Napoleon invaded the rump of the Papal States. The Pope was arrested and transported to Savona and finally to

Fontainebleau. Under great pressure, he signed another concordat in 1813 in which he implicitly renounced the Papal States. Shortly afterwards, he withdrew his signature. Napoleon, in increasing difficulties, freed him. Pius returned to Rome. During the Hundred Days he took precautionary refuge in Genua. The Pope made his entry into Rome on 7 June 1815. The prestige of the papacy after Pius' long years of imprisonment was at a new height. Consalvi was restored as Secretary of State. Pius sent him to the Congress of Vienna where he negotiated the restoration of all papal territories, except Avignon. The most urgent problem facing Pius was the reorganisation of the Church following the revolutionary and Napoleonic period. While Pius supported the idea of the union of throne and altar, at least in Catholic countries, he did not join the Holy Alliance as he had some reservations about its interconfessional character. Consalvi's political programme was intelligent and subtle. It sought to integrate reforms within the old structures of the Papal States. It pleased neither liberals nor conservatives. Pius VII concluded a concordat with protestant Prussia and Orthodox Russia. In France, the concordat of 1801 was confirmed. In the face of opposition from the European States, he reconstituted the Jesuits in 1814. He adopted a neutral position with regard to the revolution against Spain that broke out in South America. He condemned protestant biblical societies, the religious indifferentism of the enlightenment, and masonry. He attempted to restore something of the artistic and cultural prestige of Rome by encouraging artists such as Antonio Canova and by reopening the colleges that had been closed by Napoleon. At the time of his death, after a long pontificate, the papacy enjoyed respect and prestige.

250. Leo XII (1823-1829)

The Conclave following the death of Pius VII was highly contested. Eventually, Annibale della Genga Sermattei was elected. He was the candidate of the *zelanti* who took a hard line in relations to the moderate policies of Cardinal Consalvi, and wanted a Pope who was prepared to devote his energies to more religious matters than the political concerns of the Papal States. Leo XII was born of a noble family at Fabriano in 1760. He had studied in Rome and had been Nuncio in Cologne (1794-1801) and Bavaria (1806-1808). In the period after 1808, he had carried out various diplomatic missions, including an unsuccessful one to Paris. On a number of occasions, he withdrew to a hermitage at the abbey of Monticelli, near Fabriano. His return to Paris in 1814 was marred by a dispute with Cardinal Consalvi who accused him of having prejudiced the interests of the Church. Named a Cardinal in 1816 by Pius VII, he succeeded to the diocese of Senigallia. He became Vicar of Rome in 1820. Immediately following his election, he appointed Cardinal Giulio Maria della Somaglia as Secretary of State, thereby relieving Consalvi of the position, and giving a clear indication of the direction which ecclesiastical and political policy would take during his pontificate. Leo reactivated the Holy Office and the Index, and encouraged the Jesuits. Defiant of the opposition of the Catholic courts of Europe, which feared the spread of liberalism, the Pope indicted a Jubilee Year in 1825. It would be the only Holy Year of the nineteenth century. It was regarded as a return to a mediaeval form of religious practice. The process of modernisation, begun by Pius VI and Pius VII, was arrested. The political and judicial systems ante-dating the French revolution were restored, and the aristocracy resumed a major role in government. University education was strictly controlled and the police presence in general society increased. The Jews, whose position had deteriorated after 1814, were enclosed in the ghetto and subjected to discriminatory laws. The French priest, Félicité-Robert de Lamanais, then in his absolutist theocratic phase, enjoyed considerable influence in Rome at this time, while his principal Italian disciple, Padre Gioacchino Ventura, taught at the *Sapienza* and edited the *Giornale ecclesiastico*. Under Leo XII, the Church made a partial return to the past. In his relations with the European States, Leo initially attempted to reassert the supremacy of the Holy See, but soon resorted to a policy of concordats for which he availed himself of the services of Cardinal Consalvi whom he had named Prefect of the Congregation of the Propaganda Fide. In an important move, he reserved to the Holy See all episcopal nomination in the new South American republics, thereby implicitly recognising their independence from the Spanish and Portugese crowns. He strongly advocated the movement for Catholic emancipation in Ireland, which also brought beneficial consequences for Catholics in England. While Leo XII was a typical representative of the restoration era, he also illustrates the objective shortcomings of this policy in that it was clearly impossible for him (and the other European powers) to return to the political situation obtaining prior to 1789. By the time of his death in 1829, he had grown unpopular among his subjects.

140

251. **Pius VIII** *(1829-1830)*

The moderate Francesco Saverio Castiglioni was elected to succeed Leo XII in a Conclave that lasted five weeks. Born to a noble family at Cingoli, in Marche, in 1761, he had studied law at Bologna and Rome. While Bishop of Montalto he had been imprisoned (1806-1814) by the French for refusing an oath of allegiance to the Napoleonic regime. He had been highly esteemed by Pius VII who named him Cardinal and promoted him to the See of Cesena. In 1821 he was called to the service the Holy See as *Penitenziere Maggiore*. His only encyclical, *Traditi humilitati nostrae* reiterated his predecessors' condemnation of the modern world. While traditionalist, Pius was more flexible than his predecessor in political policy. He reduced the police presence instituted by Leo XII and introduced moderate social and economic reforms. The Pope had difficulties with the Prussian government on the laws governing marriages between protestants and Catholics. Cardinal Giuseppe Albani, his Secretary of State, was closely allied with Austria. His policies were invariably hostile to the liberal movements of the 1830s in Ireland, Belgium and Poland. He condemned the alliance between Catholics and liberals in Belgium and French. Against the advice of the Curia and his Nuncio in Paris, Pius supported the French revolution of 1830. Bishops and priests who supported the legitimist cause in France were denied refuge in the Papal States, and ordered to obey their new sovereign, Louis Philippe, since he had promised to uphold the concordat of 1801. He also conceded the title of "Most Christian King" to Louis Philippe. Pius VIII saw the passing of the Catholic Emancipation Act in Ireland and England which his predecessor had encouraged. The Pope obtained religious liberty for Armenian Christians from the Sultan and erected an Armenian rite archdiocese in Constantinople. The first provincial Synod of the American bishops was held at Baltimore in 1830. The Pope approved its statutes and laid the foundations for close ties between the Holy See and the Church in America.

252. Gregory XVI *(1831-1846)*

The conclave lasted fifty days and eventually elected Bartolemeo Alberto Cappellari. He enjoyed the support of the *zelanti* and the Austrian prime minister, Klemens von Metternich, who wanted a Pope clearly hostile to the revolutionary spirit of the age. A Camondelese monk, Gregory, or Mauro as was known in religion, was born to an aristocratic family in Belluno in 1765. He had taught science and philosophy. He came to Rome in 1795. During the imprisonment of Pius VI, in 1799, he had published a pamphlet on papal infallibility and the temporal sovereignty of the Papal States. Gregory had been Abbot of San Gregorio al Celio and procurator general for the Order. With the arrest of Pius VII, he was obliged to leave Rome, and take refuge in Milan and Padua where he resumed teaching. He returned to Rome in 1814 as Vicar General of the Order. Soon after, he was named Cardinal and Prefect of Propaganda Fide. Such was his opposition to modernity that he prohibited the introduction of railways in the Papal States. He was known to refer to them as the *chemins d'enfer*. Gregory was also hostile to the growing *risorgimento* movement in Italy. His Secretaries of State, Tomasso Bernetti and Luigi Lambruschini, were notable reactionaries. Because of civil disturbances in the Rome, the Pope was obliged to call on Austria to assist in their suppression in 1831. The Austrian government exerted pressure on Gregory to introduce political reforms in the Papal States but Gregory resisted and eventually refused to actuate any reforms. Successive outbreaks necessitated renewed Austrian intervention. France occupied Ancona. For a period of seven years, the Papal States remained under martial law. Liberal Catholicism, espoused by Lamanais and inculcating freedom of conscience, freedom of the press and separation of Church and state, was condemned in the encyclical *Mirari vos* (1832). In 1844, Gregory published *Inter praecipuas machinationes* condemning religious indifferentism and protestant bible societies. While Gregory always defended the rights of the Church, at the same time, when Catholics found themselves in conflict with the civil powers, his conservative instinct prevailed. Thus he condemned the Polish revolt against the Orthodox Czar, and exhorted the Irish bishops to avoid conflict with the British government. On the question of mixed marriages in Prussia, which had led to difficulties between Pius VII and the Prussian government, Gregory adopted an intransigent position, which eventually succeeded. He reorganised the hierarchy, founded new orders and reformed the older ones. Although he strongly promoted the Immaculate Conception of the Blessed Virgin Mary, he did not define the doctrine. During this pontificate, there was a remarkable revival of missionary activity which led to the foundation of seventy new dioceses and vicariates apostolic and the nomination of over two hundred bishops in the missionary territories. Gregory also resolved the question of episcopal nominations in South America without provoking problems with the Spanish and Portugese courts. He condemned slavery in the Brief *In supremo* of 1839. Gregory also encouraged the recruiting and formation of native clergy in the missionary territories. He reorganised the Canadian and American dioceses. The Etruscan and Egyptian museums in the Vatican, and the museum of Christian antiquities in the Lateran, were founded during this pontificate. Gregory's strong opposition to the modern world weighed heavily on his successor's pontificate.

253. Blessed Pius IX *(1846-1878)*

The Conclave following the death of Gregory XVI lasted two days and elected Giovanni Mastai Ferretti, 54, who was known to harbour liberal views. The former Pope's Secretary of State, Cardinal Lambruschini, was the main contender at the Conclave but was not elected because of his known reactionary positions. Pius IX was born to a noble family in the Marche, at Senigallia, in 1792. As a child he had suffered from epilepsy. He had studied at Viterbo and Rome. Ordained in 1819, he had participated in a diplomatic mission to Chile (1823-1825). Subsequently, he became rector of the Istituto San Michele in Rome, Bishop of Spoleto (1827), and Archbishop of Imola (1832). He was named Cardinal in 1840. In the early years of his pontificate, Pius initiated a series of liberal reforms in the Papal States, beginning with an amnesty for political crimes. He liberalised the press, instituted a civic guard, and established consultative bodies composed of the laity to assist in the government of the States. Rome also joined an Italian customs' union. His immediate reaction to the Austrian invasion of Ferrara, which was seen as a attempt to intimidate him, aroused many hopes that he would lead Italian aspirations to national independence. The revolutionary movements of 1848 also spread to Rome and obliged a reluctant Pope to grant a constitution. He participated in the first Italian war of independence, but, in a famous allocution given on 29 April, he declared that the Pope's universal mission precluded his continued involvement in the war. On 15 November, Count Pellegrino Rossi, his able and intelligent prime minister, was assassinated. Shortly after, the Pope was obliged to seek refuge in Gaeta, and the City was declared the Roman Republic. Following the defeat of the Roman Republic by the French, Pius returned to the City in 1850, chose Cardinal Giacomo Antonelli as his Secretary of State, and instituted a form of government that was both autocratic and paternalistic. In 1860, all of the Papal States, except for Rome and Latium, were annexed by the new Italian State, of which Rome was declared capital by Count Cavour in 1861. Under French protection since 1849, the Pope continued to govern Rome and Latium. Following the French withdrawal in 1870, Rome was occupied by Italian troops and declared capital of the kingdom of Italy. Thus ended the temporal power of the Pope. Under the terms of the *leggi di guarentigie*, the new Italian State recognised the inviolability of the person of the Roman Pontiff, and the extraterritorial nature of the Vatican and Lateran Palaces, and of the papal Villa at Castelgandolfo. These laws were the result of a decision of the Italian parliament and not of an accord between the Pope and the new State. They were rejected by Pius with the encyclical letter *Ubi nos*, although these proposals were regarded by some as reasonable and not prejudicial to the interests of the Church and the Apostolic See. The Pope retired to the Vatican palace and considered himself a prisoner. Thus, the "Roman Question" began. In 1871, the Penitenzieria Apostolica declared a *non expedit* which rendered the participation of Catholics in the political life of the new Italian State inopportune. This decision was given popular expression in the famous phrase *né eletti né elettori*. From a political perspective, Pius' long pontificate had negative effects both for the Holy See, in that the Pope had lost temporal power, and for the Italian State which became increasingly anticlerical and anti-Church. From a religious perspective, the pontificate represented a period of major transformation. The loss of temporal power created new challenges for the Church. The papacy responded substantially to those needs, while continuing to treat the Italian State as an usurper. The Church's central government became more pronounced. Deprived of political power, the Bishops became more dependant on Rome. The last traces of State control of the Church were consequently eliminated. Pius created over two hundred new dioceses and Vicariates in Europe and in the United States. The Catholic hierarchy was reconstituted in England and in the Netherlands, the Latin patriarchate of Jerusalem was revived, concordats were concluded with Russia, Spain, Austria and the new Latin American republics. The pontificate of Pius IX is marked by three major events: the first, the proclamation of the doctrine of the Immaculate Conception on 8 December 1854, which declared the Blessed Virgin Mary free of original sin from the moment of her conception. This gave enormous impulse to Marian devotion. The second was the publication of *Quanta cura* and the *Syllabus errorum* of 1864 in which the Pope condemned much of modern thought as erroneous. The condemnation included liberal Catholicism, the notion of progress, democracy and freedom of conscience. The third, and most important event of the pontificate, was the convocation of the First Vatican Council in 1869, just as Rome was about to be invaded. On the 18 July 1870, the constitution *Pastor aeternus* proclaimed the doctrine of papal infallibility which taught that decisions in matters of faith and morals, proclaimed solemnly (*ex cathedra*) by the Pope are infallible. The doctrine cause many reactions throughout the Church: in Holland and Germany several Catholics left the Church, the Austrian government annulled the concordat, the German chancellor, Otto von Bismarck, began a harsh persecution of the Church in Germany and fomented a propaganda campaign against Catholics (*Kulturkampf*). Pius beatified and canonised a large number of Saints and strongly encouraged devotion to the Sacred Heart. Pius was deeply revered, as can be seen from the number of people who came to Rome to celebrate the jubilees of his priestly ordination, his episcopal consecration and his election. In 1881, the funeral procession taking the remains of Pius IX from his provisional burial place in St. Peter's to San Lorenzo fuori le Mura, where he was eventually buried, was attacked by an anti-clerical mob which attempted to throw his body into the Tiber. The pontificate of Pius IX was the longest in history. Pius was beatified by John Paul II in 2000. His feast day is 7 February.

143

254. Leo XIII *(1878-1903)*

After three scrutinies, the Conclave of 1878, the first held after the loss of temporal power, elected Vincenzo Gioacchino Pecci who was considered a moderate. The coronation took place in the Sixtine Chapel. The Italian government feared riots were the new Pope to impart his blessing from the loggia of St. Peter's. Leo XIII was born in 1810 to a family of minor nobility at Carpineto, in Southern Latium. He had studied at Viterbo, the Collegio Romano and at the Accademia dei Nobili Ecclesiastici. Ordained in1837, he entered the service of the Curia and was named governor of Benevento and Perugia. In 1843, he became Nuncio in Belgium. Named Bishop of Perugia in 1846, he was created Cardinal in 1853. Because of Cardinal Antonelli's hostility to him, Leo had been kept away from Rome. Following the Secretary of State's death in 1877, Leo was recalled to the Curia and named Camerlengo. Leo's principal concern was to arrive at a reconciliation between the Church and the modern world, without, however, abandoning the principles underlying the work of his predecessor. Leo adopted a position similar to that of Pius IX on the Roman question. Indeed, he was utterly intransigent on the question of relations with the new Italian State. The *non expedit* was reinforced with a series of directives to Catholics advising them to abstain from the political life of the Italian State, and never abandoned the prospect of recovering temporal sovereignty for the papacy. Some contacts were made with the Italian government but these proved fruitless because of the unbending attitude of Francesco Crispi, the Italian prime minister. During Leo's long pontificate, the Roman question began to become increasingly marginal among the emerging Catholics political movements. The pontificate of Leo XIII proved innovative in the field of social policy. Concern for social inequality began with Leo XIII, probably because of the time he had spent in Belgium, where he had come into contact with the altogether new social reality of a proletarian workforce and the hardships caused by economic progress. In 1891, Leo published the encyclical *Rerum novarum*. It was the fruit of an intense debate among Catholics and was enthusiastically received because it committed the Church to a more humane concept of work, to the defense of the proletariat, and to a form of social progress governed by the laws of religion and morality. The encyclical was a watershed in social thought and was quickly followed up by the emergence of many Catholic movements determined on creating a proper social context. Although dominated by the laity, these movements were closely associated with the parishes and dioceses. These movements broke the hegemony of socialists in matters relating to social questions not only in Italy but throughout the Western world. Leo XIII was an able diplomat and had several political successes at international level, the most important of which was in Germany where Bismarck abandoned his *Kulturkampf*. He failed, however, to carve out a significant role for papal diplomacy, as had been his desire and that of his able Secretary of State, Cardinal Mariano Rampolla. Efforts to reconcile French Catholics with the new republican government proved futile. In ecclesiastical affairs, the Pope continued the policy of his predecessor: The centralisation of the Church continued with the establishing of general houses for all religious orders in Rome, and the reinforcement of the role of the Nuncios. Missionary activity increased, new dioceses were founded, the Scottish hierarchy was restored, and those in the United States, North Africa, India and Japan reorganised. Leo was also interested in the question of Church unity and was the first to use the expression "separated brethren". He invited the Orthodox and the Protestants to return to the Church's fold. He was particularly interested in the prospect of the conversion of England. Leo also promoted a renewal of Catholic intellectual life and gave much encouragement to the philosophy of St. Thomas Aquinas. He established new criteria for biblical studies, opened the Vatican Archive to scholars of all persuasions, and encouraged studies in natural science and astronomy. In 1878, he condemned socialism, communism and nihilism. In 1884, he issued a strong condemnation of masonry. In his piety, Leo was conservative and traditional. He published eleven encyclicals on the Blessed Virgin Mary and the rosary. He instituted the feast of the Holy Family. Canonisations and beatifications increased during his long reign. A number of extraordinary jubilees was celebrated. During the Holy Year of 1900, Leo consecrated the humand race to the Sacred Heart of Jesus. Leo's pontificate was exceptional by any standards. It brought the Church out of its isolation, conferred enormous prestige and opened new prospects.

255. St. Pius X *(1903-1914)*

The Conclave of 1903 was the last occasion on which a Catholic State directly influenced the election of a Pope. The emperor Franz Joseph exercised a veto on the candidature of Cardinal Rampolla, Secretary of State to Leo XIII. Having made a formal protest, the Patriarch of Venice, Giuseppe Melchiorre, was elected Pope and took the name of Pius. Born to a humble family at Riese, near Treviso, in 1835, Pius had studied at the seminary of Padua. Ordained in 1858, he was appointed assistant in Tombolo and parish priest of Salzano, before being transferred to the diocesan Curia where he acted as Chancellor. Named Bishop of Mantua in 1884, he was promoted to the Patriarchate of Venice in 1893 and created Cardinal. Pius' formation had been exclusively ecclesiastical and pastoral. He had no experience of the Roman Curia nor of the diplomatic world. This was an innovation in the modern history of the papacy. The new Pope was attentive to the religious side of his mission and less so to its political aspects. Assisted by a young Secretary of State, Cardinal Rafael Merry Del Val, Pius embarked on a policy of defending the rights of the Church. The French government abrogated the concordat of 1801 and enacted a law of separation of Church and state. All ecclesiastical goods were transferred to lay associations. The Pope condemned these measures and prohibited the French bishops from making any compromise with the government. The Pope also protested against the separation of Church and state in Portugal. His support for Irish Catholics caused difficulties with the British government, while his support of the Poles led to tensions with Russia. Relations with the Italian government improved under Pius, who began to ease tensions, especially by relaxing the terms of the *non expedit* for the elections of 1904. Catholics were allowed to vote in an election where there was a danger of the election of socialist candidates. Pius X was deeply opposed to socialism. He insisted that Catholic movements should assume a more explicitly religious and less social character. In 1904, the Pope dissolved the *Opera dei Congressi*. Begun in 1875, the Opera was a hard-line movement but internally divided especially because of the democratic ideas propounded by don Romulo Murri. In 1905, Pius replaced the Opera with the *Azione Cattolica* which, under strict clerical control, remained aloof from direct political involvement. The pontificate of Pius X is closely associated with the condemnation of the modernists, which was defined as a "synthesis of all heresies" in the encyclical *Pascendi* of 1907. Modernism was suppressed and an anti- modernist oath was enjoined on the clergy. Pius was a truly reforming Pope. The Curia and the ecclesiastical tribunals were radically reformed, as were seminaries and catechetical instruction. Pius began the work of codifying the laws of the Church, a work brought to completion after his death. The rules for the Conclave were also revised. Pius strongly promoted frequent, even daily reception of Holy Communion. The age for first communion was lowered to about seven years. Pius set in motion a reform of liturgical music which saw the restoration of Gregorian chant. A new edition of the Breviary was published and the reform of the Roman Missal was begun. These initiatives have led many to see Pius as a pioneer of the liturgical movement. A process for canonisation was opened in 1923. Pius XII beatified him in 1951 and canonised him in 1954. His feast day is 21 August.

256. Benedict XV *(1914-1922)*

Born at Genua to a patrician family in 1854, Giacomo della Chiesa held a doctorate in civil law from the university of Genua. He had studied at the Capranica and at the Gregorian in Rome. Ordained in 1878, he entered the diplomatic service of the Holy See and was appointed secretary to Mons. Mariano Rampolla, then Nuncio in Spain. When Rampolla was appointed Secretary of State and Cardinal, della Chiesa remained his secretary. Benedict was named Sostituto of the Secretariat of State in 1901 and retained this post under Cardinal Rafael Merry del Val. Named Archbishop of Bologna in 1907, he was created Cardinal in 1914. He was elected Pope three months later, just as much of Europe went to war. The war dominate Benedict's pontificate. In a letter sent to the belligerent powers, Benedict describe it as a "useless slaughter". Benedict opposed the war from the outset. He adopted a policy of strict neutrality and began an intense diplomatic campaign to halt the war, coupled with a vast programme of relief for prisoners of war. Benedict's position was regarded with hostility by the Allied powers, especially by Italy. It was believed that it had been inspired by a German undertaking to restore the Papal States in the event of a German victory. The Holy See was excluded from participation at the peace conference by virtue of an Italian veto. Pius' appeals for peace had enormous influence among the troops confined to the trenches and among the peasants who were deeply opposed to the war. Although critical of some aspects of the newly founded League of Nations, the Pope supported the initiative and undertook a major reform of the Vatican diplomatic service in order to adapt it to the new world order. Achille Ratti was sent as Apostolic Nuncio to Poland and Lithuania; Eugenio Pacelli was named Nuncio in Germany. The number of countries maintaining diplomatic relations with the Holy See increased significantly. Great Britain reopened relations with the Holy See for the first time since the sixteenth century. France reestablished diplomatic relations in 1921, after Benedict agreed to canonise Joan of Arc. Relations with the Italian state improved dramatically during this pontificate. Benedict authorised the foundation of the Popular Party by don Luigi Sturzo in 1919, thereby repealing *de facto* the *non expedit*. In the hope of promoting a union with the Eastern Churches, he founded the Pontifical Institute for Oriental Studies. After a long process of codification, the *Codex Iuris Canonici* was promulgated in 1917. Benedict was epecially concerned to promote the missions. The encyclical *Maximum illud* 1919 underlined the need to train native clergy and to organise the missions from the perspective of the good of the native populations rather than that of the colonial powers. Benedict died unexpectedly of pneumonia in 1922. Two years earlier, his statue had been erected in Istanbul by the Turkish authorities who described him as "the great Pope of a world tragedy, a benefactor of nations without distinction of nationality or religion".

257. Pius XI (1922-1939)

Born in 1857 to a middle class family in Desio, near Milan, Achille Ratti studied for the priesthood at Milan and Rome, and obtained doctorates in canon law and theology. He was ordained in 1879. Learned and erudite, he entered the service of the Ambrosian Library and became its prefect in 1907. He was an excellent scholar and librarian. In 1911, he became Vice Prefect of the Vatican Library. He was promoted to Prefect in 1914. He was named Apostolic Visitator (and subsequently Nuncio) in Poland and Lithuania in 1918. He refused to leave Warsaw when the bolsheviks invaded. Due to difficulties with some of the the Polish nationalists, he was recalled to Rome in 1921. Shortly afterwards, he was named Archbishop of Milan and Cardinal. His election on the fourteenth ballot of the Conclave of 1922 was the result of a compromise. He imparted the *urbi et orbi* from the loggia of St. Peter's for the first time since 1870. Pius had two eminent Secretaries of State, Pietro Gasparri, and Eugenio Pacelli (from 1930). He immediately began a policy of contracting concordats. During his pontificate some twenty concordats or accords were concluded between the Holy See and various States. Relations with France improved and an agreement was reached on several questions arising from the separation of Church and State in 1905. A «conciliation» was achieved with the Italian government. Guided by Benito Mussolini, negotiations with the Italian government saw the signing of the Lateran pacts of 1929 which consisted of a treaty, a concordat and a financial convention. The independent Vatican City State was established, thereby finally closing the Roman question. The Holy See recognised the Italian State with its capital in Rome. The Italian State indemnified the Holy See for the loss of its territories and reestablished Catholicism as the state religion of Italy, and abolished the equality of religion introduced forty years previously. Pius' pontificate coincided with the rise of the totalitarian regimes in Europe. He concluded a concordat with Hitler, which stemmed Catholic opposition to Nazism and led to criticism of policies of the Pope. The Church's clash with Nazism came in 1937 with the publication of the encyclical letter *Mit Brennender Sorge* which denounced the violation of the concordat, and branded Nazism as anti-Christian. Again in 1937, Pius condemned soviet totalitarianism and its concomitant atheism in the encyclical *Divini redemptoris*. The idyllic relations with Fascism in Italy came to an end in 1931 when Mussolini took measures against the *Azione cattolica,* in his efforts to stem the rise of Catholic associations whose development had been much accelerated following the signing of the Italian concordat. Matters came to head in 1938 when Mussolini adopted Hitler's racist policies and began to align himself with Germany. When Pius died in 1939, a encyclical was in the process of being prepared which sharply condemned antisemitism and the theories of racism. It was never published. In 1933 Pius condemned the separation of Church and state effected in Spain by the left wing republican government. During the Spanish Civil War, which was marked by a bitter left wing persecution of bishops, clergy and Catholics, Pius supported General Francisco Franco in his efforts against the republican government. On several occasions during the 1920s and 1930s he condemned the persecution of the Church in Mexico. Much of the Pope's political policy was inspired by his belief that the Church had to work within society and not from outside of it. In 1922, he reorganised the *Azione cattolica* which was based on the principle of collaboration in the apostolate between the clergy and laity. He greatly encouraged the spread of this movement. Jubilee years were held in 1925 and 1929, and an extraordinary Jubilee in 1933 to commemorate the nineteen hundredth anniversary of the Redemption. He increased the number of public religious ceremonies

147

as well as meetings and pilgrimages. He published many encyclical letters on the subject of Christian education, marriage, and social and economic questions. He beatified and canonised many Saints, including St. Thérèse of Lisieux, Sts. John Fisher and Thomas More, and St. John Bosco. He declared Peter Canisius, John of the Cross, Robert Bellarmine and Albert the Great, doctors of the Church. Pius instituted and promoted the feast of Christ the King. He was deeply committed to the missionary efforts of the Church, following the line of his predecessor which tended to favour the interests of native populations rather than those of the colonial powers. He promoted the formation and ordination of native clergy whose numbers grew significantly during this pontificate. In 1926, Pius consecrated six Chinese bishops. He founded a faculty of missiology in the Gregorian university, and the ethnological and missionary museum in the Lateran, which was subsequently transferred to the Vatican collections. Pius was somewhat diffident towards the ecumenical movement and forbade Catholics from participating at non-Catholic conventions. He rehabilitated some of the modernists and diffused much of the tension that have been occasioned by their repression. Convinced of the necessity to promote Catholic culture, he undertook several initiatives in this area, including the foundation of the Institute of Christian Archeology, the Pontifical Academy of Sciences, the expansion of the Vatican Library and the modernisation of the Vatican observatory. Pius had a particularly close interest in the Catholic University of the Sacred Heart, founded in Milan in 1921. He also inaugurated Vatican Radio, entrusting its technical equipping to Guglielmo Marconi, and was the first Pope to use radio as a means of communication. Pius governed the Church energetically, taking all important decisions to himself.

258. Pius XII (1939-1958)

Eugenio Pacelli was born to a family of lawyers in Rome in 1876. He studied at the Gregorian, the Capranica, and at Sant'Apollinare. He entered the Curia after his ordination in 1899. He was one of the principal assistants of Cardinal Gasparri in the work of codifying the law of the Church. He taught international law at the Accademia dei Nobili Ecclesiastici. He was Nuncio in Germany from 1917 to 1929. Named Cardinal in 1929, he was appointed Secretary of State in 1930 and concluded concordats with Austria and Nazi Germany. He was elected in the third ballot of the Conclave which met shortly before the outbreak of war. He was the third Secretary of State to have been elected since Clement IX. Although circumstances had radically altered, the political policy of the Holy See was very similar to that adopted by Benedict XV during the First World War. Pius XII attempted to obviate the coming conflict by diplomatic means. He wrote to Mussolini pleading in vain to keep Italy out of the war. At the outbreak of war, he declared absolute neutrality. The Vatican *de facto* supported the collapse of fascism (25 July 1943) and the formation of a government under Pietro Badoglio, from whom Pius obtained an assurance that Rome would be declared an open city. Through various Catholic associations, Pius activated an impressive relief programme for prisoners of war. Following the Nazi occupation of Rome on 10 September 1943, Pius offered asylum in the Vatican to refugees, including many Jews. The Church in Italy and in many other European countries gave refuge to numerous Jews, secreting them in convents and other religious institutions. Many of the accusations made against Pius XII by certain historians overlook this important factor, on which there is complete agreement, and concentrate on what are regarded as Pius' veiled and indirect efforts in the face of the

Nazi extermination of the Jews, especially of the Roman Jews which occurred on 16 October 1943. Against such criticisms, the Holy See has pointed to the constraints place on Pius by the necessity of not further endangering both Catholics and Jews in Germany. During the war, Pius made several appeals for peace and the establishment of a new international order, especially during his Christmas messages which were broadcast throughout Europe. He frequently advocated the establishment of democracy based on the principle of «Christian civilisation» as the surest antidote to totalitarianism, especially in its soviet form. Pius completely opposed the idea of the collective responsibility of the German people. He was fiercely anti-Communist and took the personal decision, communicated by a decree of the Holy Office, to excommunicate any Catholics militating in or supporting the communist party. Advantageous concordats were concluded with Spain (1950) and Portugal (1955). Pius created an unprecedented number of Cardinals in two Consistories held in 1946 and in 1953. In an attempt to internationalise the Sacred College, many of the new Cardinals came from different parts of the world and the number of Italians was reduced to about a third of its members. The number of dioceses increased dramatically during this pontificate. Catholic hierarchies were established in several African and Asian countries. Unlike his predecessor, Pius was decidedly favourable to the ecumenical movement, which was formally recognise in 1949. He permitted Catholics to participate in ecumenical debates and meetings. The Pope published several important encyclical letters including *Mystici corporis* (1943) on the Church, *Divino afflante spiritu* (1947) on the renewal of biblical studies, *Mediator Dei* (1950) on the need for liturgical reform, and *Humani generis* (1950) which was theologically very conservative. He canonised thirty-three Saints, including St. Pius X in 1954. Pius held countless audiences, pronounced thousands of discourses which he carefully prepared. He made constant use of radio and television. The Jubilee of 1950 and the Marian Year of 1954 drew unprecedented numbers of pilgrims to Rome. In 1950, he defined the doctrine of the Assumption of the Blessed Virgin Mary, making the first use of papal infallibility since its definition in 1870. Pius encouraged Marian devotion and showed much interest in the apparitions of Fatima, in Portugal. Between 1939 and 1949 he had authorised the excavations under the floor of St. Peter's. At the close of the Holy Year of 1950, he announced that the burial place of the Apostle Peter had been located. By nature authoritarian, Pius reserved decision on many important matters to himself alone. He gained the affection of the Romans when he visited the working class area of the City at San Lorenzo following the allied bombing on 19 July 1943. Although he enjoyed enormous prestige throughout the world at the time of his death in 1958, the affection of the Romans had become somewhat attenuated, partly because of his personal austerity and the isolation in which he lived, and partly because of the unpopularity of those who surrounded him in the Curia.

259. Blessed John XXIII *(1958-1963)*

Angelo Giuseppe Roncalli was born to a peasant family at Sotto il Monte, near Bergamo, in 1881. Having completed his studies at the seminary of Bergamo, he won a burse to study theology at Sant'Apollinare in Rome, where he obtained a doctorate in theology. Named secretary of Mons. Giuseppe Radini Tedeschi, Bishop of Bergamo, he taught ecclesiastical history in the local seminary. He was conscripted during the first World War, acting firstly as a medical orderly and subsequently as military chaplain. In 1921, Benedict XV appointed him to the council of the *Pia Opera* of

Propaganda Fide. During this period, he began an exhaustive study of St Charles Borromeo, the last volume of which was published shortly before his election. In 1931, he was appointed Apostolic Visitor in Bulgaria, and Apostolic Delegate to Turkey and Greece in 1934. During his mission in Istanbul (1941-1944), he worked to provided help to all nationalities. He did much to prevent the deportation of Jews during the Nazi occupation. While Nuncio in Paris (1944-1952) he was obliged to deal with a number of delicate matters ranging from the situation of the Bishops who had collaborated with the Vichy regime to the phenomenon of worker priests. In 1953, Roncalli was created Cardinal and Patriarch of Venice where he governed with solicitude and rigour. At the age of seventy-seven, he was elected Pope on the twelfth ballot of the Conclave. John's was expected to have been a transitional pontificate, but it quickly became an important event in the history of the Church. John convoked the Second Vatican Council, which was intended to bring about a regeneration of the Church through a renewal of doctrine, discipline, and organisation, and to pave the way for union of the separated brethren. His pastoral concern for the diocese of Rome was clearly demonstrated by the convocation of a diocesan Synod which was held in the Lateran in 1960, and served as a preparation for the Council. This was the first pastoral synod in the modern history of the diocese of Rome. It aimed at revitalising the ecclesial life of the City but had few practical effects. John established several commissions and councils in preparation for the Council which opened in St. Peter's on 11 October 1962 in a climate of great openness and with the presence of observers from many non-Catholic Churches. The first session of the Council closed on 8 December 1962. John also began the task of revising the *Codex Iuris Canonici* of 1917 and continued the liturgical reform of Pius XII. He abolished the rule of Sixtus V which limited the number of Cardinals to seventy, and internationalised the Sacred College by raising its members to eighty-seven. He inverted the policy of centralisation and delegated several important functions to the various episcopates. Relations between East and West thawed during his pontificate. In 1962, during the Cuban missile crisis which brought the world to the verge of a nuclear disaster, he made an intervention exhorting both the United States and the Soviet Union to moderation. The Holy See began to initiate various kinds of relations with several communist countries. In 1963, John published an encyclical on peace, *Pacem in terris*, addressed not only to Catholics but to all men, in which he declared respect for the rights of man to be the basis for peace. He appealed for peaceful coexistence between the Western and Eastern bloc countries. Christian unity was another important concern for Pope John. In addition to his own efforts at ecumenism, John met the leader of Anglicanism. In 1960, he established the Secretariat for Christian Unity and entrusted its direction to Cardinal Agostino Bea. In anticipation of the Council's radical appraisal of relations with Jews, he reformed the traditional intercession for the Jews in the Good Friday liturgy. He visited the Roman hospitals and the *Regina Coeli* prison. Although a cultivated and traditional churchman, John always maintained a simplicity and directness of style. John was loved and revered during his pontificate and widely mourned at his death. Pope John XXIII was beatified by John Paul II in 2000. His feast day is 11 October.

260. Paul VI *(1963-1978)*

Giovanni Battista Montini was born to a middle-class Catholic family at Concesio, near Brescia, in 1897. He was ordained in 1920 and moved to Rome where he took doctorates in philosophy, canon law and in civil law. In 1923 he was assigned to the Nunciature in Warsaw as a secretary. He returned to the Secretariat of State in 1924. At this time he was closely associated with a number of student movements, including the *Federazione universitaria cattolica italiana*, of which he was the national spiritual director. He was obliged to resign this position in 1933 because of Fascist opposition to his political opinions, and opposition from conservative ecclesiastical circles. Named Sostituto of the Secretariat of State in 1937, he worked closely with Pius XII, who promoted him to Pro-Secretary of State for general affairs in 1952. Here he played a crucial role in determining the political policy of the Holy See. In 1954, he was nominated Archbishop of Milan. At the time, this was regarded as a move designed to remove him from the Curia. In Milan he threw himself wholeheartedly into the pastoral government of the diocese, paying careful attention to problems such as immigration, labour, and urban expansion. In 1957, he organised a great mission of evangelisation in the diocese. He was created Cardinal by Blessed John XXIII, with whom he worked closely in preparing for the Second Vatican Council, and promoted a line of moderate reform. The Conclave of 1960 was the largest yet held and consisted of eighty Cardinals. He was elected on the fifth vote. The Council was the major task facing his pontificate. He quickly made the Council his own and directed the largest ever assembly of Bishops on a radical course of renewal. He directed the work of the Council with great prudence, favouring innovation, but reserving crucial questions to the authority of the Pope. The Encyclical *Ecclesiam suam* of 1964 set out the main concerns of his pontificate which encompassed not only the renewal of the Church but also dialogue with other Christian confessions, and with other world religions. Two new Secretariats were created: one for non-Christians, the other for non-believers. They were given the task of promoting good relations with other religions and with atheists. In 1963, Paul made a surprise visit to the Holy Land, to which none of his predecessors had returned. Indeed, no Pope had left Italy for more than a century and a half. The Council considered a range of questions including religious liberty, relations with the Jews, ecumenism, episcopal collegiality which was intended partially as a balance to the dogmatic definition of the First Vatican Council of 1870. In 1964, Paul travelled to Bombay and made an appeal on behalf of poorer nations. The Synod of Bishops was instituted in 1965 as a representative assembly of the world's episcopate. Intended as a consultative body, it held five sessions during Paul's pontificate. The declaration *Nostra aetate* on relations with non-Christian religions was approved during the final stages of the Council. It deplored as «odious» all persecutions and manifestations of anti-semitism. On the eve of the closure of the Council (8 December 1965), the excommunications issued against Constantinople in 1054 were lifted, thereby opening a new era of relations between the Church of Rome and that of Constantinople. The Holy Office was reformed and became the Congregation for the Doctrine of the Faith. This foreshadowed the reform of the Curia which Paul had reserved to himself in 1963. Renewal initiatives multiplied: in 1966, the Index of prohibited books was abolished. The Curia was reformed in 1967 with the intent of internationalising it, and making its operation more effective, especially through the development of links with the newly founded episcopal conferences. In 1968, the papal court was abolished. In 1970, the various pontifical

151

armed corps were abolished, with the exception of the Swiss Guards. In the same year, Paul excluded all Cardinals over eighty years of age from the Conclave. This greatly reduced the influence of the Italian Cardinals of the Curia who generally did not share many of the Pope's ideas. The Pope created one hundred and forty four Cardinals, the majority of whom were non-Italians. Paul carried through many of the reforms of the Council, including the liturgical reform which saw the introduction of vernacular languages into the liturgy. These reforms were contested in the more advanced ecclesiastical circles, and opposed in more traditional quarters, including Archbishop Marcel Lefebvre. Paul reiterated the importance of celibacy for the clergy of the Latin Rite in his encyclical *Sacerdotalis coelibatus.* Much criticism was reserved for his condemnation of artificial methods of contraception, which was contained in the encyclical *Humanae vitae* of 1968. In 1970, Paul, who had admitted women to the Council and to the offices of the Curia, took the unprecedented step of declaring St Theresa of Avila and St. Catherine of Siena doctors of the Church. The diplomatic service of the Holy See was greatly expanded during this pontificate. It served to promote world peace and continued the dialogue with the communist bloc begun under John XXIII. Between 1967 and 1970, Paul undertook nine international trips which, for the first time, took the Pope to five continents. In 1975, he celebrated a Holy Year, to which he gave a conciliar stamp. For the first time in history, the celebrations in Rome were preceded by those in the rest of the world. In 1965, he opened the processes for the canonisation of Pius XII and John XXIII, both of whom had come to symbolise opposing ecclesial trends.

261. John Paul I *(August - September 1978)*

Albino Luciano was born in 1912 at Forno di Canale (Canale d'Agorde) near Belluno. He came from a working class family of socialists. Ordained in 1935, he took a doctorate at the Gregorian University in Rome. His first appointment was as curate in his native parish. Subsequently he became vice rector of the seminary in Belluno. Named Bishop of Vittoria Veneto in 1958, he succeed to the patriarchate of Venice in 1969. From 1972 to 1975, he was vice president of the Conference of Italian Bishops. He was named Cardinal in 1973. He was elected on the third count on the opening day of the Conclave. For the first time, the Pope took a double name, in honour of his two immediate predecessors, and reiterated the importance of continuing the reforms of the Second Vatican Council, especially in matters of ecclesiastical discipline. He refused the traditional coronation and quickly won enormous popularity, especially with his addresses. Thirty-three days following his election, he died of a heart attack. Legend has developed around his unexpected death, including a story that he was poisoned so as to obviate his intention of reforming the Vatican Bank. He was the first worker Pope, a simple man who was close to the people.

262. John Paul II *(elected 1978)*

Elected on the eight ballot in the second Conclave of 1978, Karol Wojtyla was born at Wadowice, near Cracow, in 1920. He is the first Polish Pope and the first non Italian since Adrian VI. A sportsman, fascinated by poetry and theatre, he studied literature at the university of Cracow. During the Nazi occupation, he was conscripted for forced labour. At this point he began theological studies. He was ordained priest in 1946 and took a doctorate in theology at the Angelicum in Rome, and another in philosophy in Cracow. He was professor in the seminary of Cracow and at the Catholic university of Lublin. Named Auxiliary bishop of Cracow by Pius XII in 1958, he succeeded to the See in 1964. During these years, he worked closely with the Primate of Poland, Cardinal Stephan Wyszynski, defending the interests of the Church against the communist regime. He also participated at the Second Vatican Council. He was created Cardinal in 1967. He participated in the Synod of Bishops and travelled to various parts of the world. A number of leitmotivs running through his long and important pontificate can be identified. The first, his concern for Eastern and Central Europe. The Pope's efforts in these countries were a significant factor in the events of 1989 that led to the fall of communism and the reestablishment of the Catholic hierarchy. Another important feature of his pontificate has been his concern for visibility and presence throughout the world. Various means have been employed to fulfill this end including vast public audiences at St. Peter's which began shortly after his election and continue up to the present, despite an assassination attempt in 1981. John Paul II has given innumerable addresses, and published countless papal documents, including thirteen encyclical letters. These have touched upon the persons of the Trinity, the social teaching of the Church, the Blessed Virgin Mary, the missions, Christian morality, the defence of human life, ecumenism, and the relationship between faith and reason. The Pope's international travels, almost a hundred in all, have been a basic aspect of his pontificate. He has visited some countries more than once. Significant among them have been his trips to predominantly muslim countries, to Poland, and to the countries of the former soviet bloc. Particularly important were his visits to Cuba in 1998 and to Israel in 2000. John Paul II has performed numerous beatifications and canonisations, often during his apostolic journeys. He has conducted more than half of the canonisations and beatifications performed over the past four centuries. John Paul II has given notable encouragement to Marian devotion which figures largely in his own personal piety. His journeys to Fatima have been particularly significant. The preparations of the Jubilee of 2000 were given special importance. The Pope has often seen this event as fundamental for his pontificate and for his mission, and set it in the context of the reconciliation which the Church needs because of the sins committed by her members in the past. In strict continuity with the Second Vatican Council and with Paul VI, John Paul has frequently expressed regret for the responsibility borne by some Catholics for antisemitism, divisions among Christians, religious wars, inequality and social injustice, as well as intolerance and violence committed in the name of defending the truth. Under his pontificate, there have been frequent meetings of the Synod of Bishops and of the Cardinals. Collegial responsibility for the government of the Church, desired by the Second Vatican Council and developed by Pauli VI, has been repeatedly emphasised. Despite the emergence of new difficulties such as the tensions with the Russian Orthodox due to the reestablishment of the Catholic Church in Eastern Europe, and with the Anglicans on the ordination of women, ecumenical dialogue with other Christian confessions has been very active. With regard to non-Christian religions, the Pope has continued dialogue with Jews and Muslims, and taken new and significant positions with regard to inter religious dialogue as can be seen from his visit to the Roman synagogue in 1986, and from the world day of prayer for peace held at Assisi in 1986 and repeated in 2002. The presence of the Holy See at international level has been enormously strengthened during this pontificate which has seen the opening of diplomatic relations with countless states. In matters relating to Italy, a revision of the 1929 concordat was agreed in 1984. Among the principal concerns of the pontificate, mention can be made of the need for «new evangelisation» in traditionally Christian countries, and in those dominated by the communists, the protection of the family and of human life, especially in the face of abortion, euthanasia and the death penalty, the defence of human rights (especially religious freedom), and efforts to promote peace, justice and development. In political affairs, after spending more than ten years engaged in a critique of communism, John Paul II's attention has turned to provide a critique of the dehumanisation consequent on capitalism and the pure market economy created by globalization. In addition to these activities, which are external to the Church, John Paul II has accentuated the need for doctrinal and disciplinary clarity within the Church, and has lent support to several traditional or conservative groups or movements such as Opus Dei. The pontificate of John Paul II has also seen a revision of the Code of Canon Law for the Latin Church, the codification of the canon Law of the Oriental Churches, and the publication of a revised and enlarged Catechism of the Catholic Church. John Paul II has created an unprecedented number of Cardinals - over two hundred.

Appendix

«Pope Joan»

The story of Pope Joan is a legend lacking any historical basis. It appears to have developed in the twelfth century and was universally known and accepted by the sixteenth century. Many sources refer to it. All the sources agree on the structure of the events recounted: a woman who looks like a man is elected Pope, she is discovered because she gives birth to a child, she is killed by the raging mob. The details, dates and location of the story differ. The story is located somewhere in the high middle ages. According to the *Cronaca* of Martin of Troppau, a Polish Dominican, Joan was born in Mainz and had studied in Athens, disguised as a man. Having come to Rome, her reputation for piety and learning spread, and she was eventually elected Pope in succession to Leo IV in 855, taking the name of John the Angelic. The imposture was discovered during the procession to the Lateran during which she gave birth to a child in the streets between the Colosseum and San Clemente. According to this account, she then set upon by the mob and killed. From then on, the papal procession never again passed through that street. The existence of Pope Joan did have wide acceptance: her bust is included among those of the Popes in the Cathedral of Siena. The legend was believed by Petrarch and Boccaccio. It was exploited by the protestants in their invectives against Roman immorality. In Catholic circles, the legend was regarded with suspicion from the middle of the fifteenth century. It was finally demolished by a French protestant, David Blondel, in a series of studies published in Amsterdam in the middle of the sixteenth century.

The Papal Election

Following the death (or resignation) of a Pope a period known as the *sede vacante* occurs, during which time the ordinary government of the Church devolves on the Sacred College of Cardinals, which above all has the important of electing the new Pope. According to the present rules, Cardinals who reach the age of eighty before the Pope's death, or the beginning of the *sede vacante*, are automatically excluded from the vote. In preparation for the Conclave, all the Cardinals meet in daily session. Having completed the obsequies of the Pontiff, the Sacred College is obliged to proceed to an election within twenty days of the Pope's death (or resignation). The election must take place in the territory of the Vatican City State. The Conclave, which consists of about 120 electors, takes place in the strictest isolation so as to exclude any possibility of external interference or influence. Two thirds of the votes are normally required for election. After the vote, the results are communicated by means of burning the ballot papers in a stove in the Sixtine Chapel. A negative vote is indicated by black smoke - the ballot papers being burned in wet straw. White smoke indicates that an election has taken place. Immediately following election, the new Pope chooses a name and receives the obedience of the Cardinals. The senior Cardinal Deacon announces the election from the loggia of St. Peter's in the usual Latin from, and the new Pope imparts the *urbi et orbi* (to the City and to the world) blessing, indicating that he is Bishop of Rome and universal Pastor of the Church. This complex electoral system is the result of a long historical development, which saw the original right of election enjoyed by the Roman people and clergy gradually reserved to the Cardinals alone.

Chronological list of Popes and anti-Popes

[anti-Popes in square brackets]

St. Peter (martyred in 67)
St. Linus (68-79 circa)
St. Anacletus (o Cletus,
  80-92 circa)
St. Clement I (92-99 circa)
St. Evaristus (99-108 circa)
St. Alexander I (108-119 circa)
St. Sixtus I (119-126 circa)
St. Telesphorus (127-138 circa)
St. Hygnius (138-142 circa)
St. Pius I (142-157 circa)
St. Anicetus (157-168 circa)
St. Soter (168-177 circa)
St. Eleuthterius (177-185 circa)
St. Victor I (186-197 circa)
St. Zephrinus (198-218 circa)
[Sant Hippolytus, 217-235]
St. Calixtus I (218-222)
St. Urban I (222-230)
St. Pontian (230-235)
St. Anterus (235-236)
St. Fabian (236-250)
St. Cornelius (251-253)
[Novatian, 251]
St. Lucius I (253-254)
St. Stephen I (254-257)
St. Sixtus II (257-258)
St. Dionysius (259-268)
St. Felix I (269-274)
St. Eutychian (275-283)
St. Caius (283-296)
St. Marcellinus (296-304)
St. Marcellus I (306-309)
St. Eusebius (April-October 309)
St. Melchiades, (311-314)
St. Sylvester I (314-335)
St. Mark (January-October 336)
St. Julius I (337-352)
Liberius (352-366)
[Felix II, 355-365]
St. Damasus I (366-384)
[Ursinus, 366-367]
St. Siricius (384-399)
St. Anastasius I (399-401)
St. Innocent I (401-417)
St. Zozimus (417-418)
St. Bonifice I (418-422)
[Eulalius, 418-419]
St. Celestine I (422-432)
St. Sixtus III (432-440)
St. Leo I the Great (440-461)
St. Hilary (461-468)
St. Simplicius (468-483)

St. Felix III (II, 483-492)
St. Gelasius I (492-496)
Anastasius II (496-498)
St. Symmachus (498-514)
[Lawrence, 498-499; 502-506]
St. Hormisdas (514-523)
St. John I (523-526)
St. Felix IV (526-530)
Boniface II (530-532)
[Dioscorus, September-
  December 530]
John II (533-535)
St. Agapitus I (535-536)
St. Silverius (536-537)
Vigilius (537-555)
Pelagius I (556-561)
John III (561-574)
Benedict I (575-579)
Pelagius II (579-590)
St. Gregory I the Great (590-604)
Sabinian (604-606)
Boniface III (February-
  Novermber 607)
St. Boniface IV (608-615)
St. Adeodatus I (or Deusdedit,
  615-618)
Boniface V (619-625)
Honorius I (625-638)
Severinus (May-August 640)
John IV (640-642)
Theodore I (642-649)
St. Martin I (649-653)
St. Eugenius I (654-657)
St. Vitalian (657-672)
Adeodatus II (672-676)
Donus (676-678)
St. Agatho (678-681)
St. Leo II (682-683)
St. Benedict II (684-685)
John V (685-686)
Conon (686-687)
[Theodore, 687]
[Paschal, 687]
St. Sergius I (687-701)
John VI (701-705)
John VII (705-707)
Sisinnius (January-February 708)
Constantine (708-715)
St. Gregory II (715-731)
St. Gregory III (731-741)
St. Zachary (741-752)
Stephen II or III (752-757)
St. Paul I (757-767)

[Constantine, 767-768]
[Philip, 768]
Stephan III or IV (768-772)
Adrian I (772-795)
St. Leo III (795-816)
Stephen IV or V (816-817)
St. Paschal I (817-824)
Eugenius II (824-827)
Valentine (August-
  September 827)
Gregory IV (827-844)
[John, 844]
Sergius II (844-847)
St. Leo IV (847-855)
Benedict III (855-858)
[Anastasius, 855]
St. Nicholas I (858-867)
Adrian II (867-872)
John VIII (872-882)
Marinus I (882-884)
St Adrian III (884-885)
Stephan V or VI (885-891)
Formosus (891-896)
Boniface VI (April 896)
Stephan VI or VII (896-897)
Romanus (July-November 897)
Theodoroe II (December 897)
John IX (898-900)
Benedict IV (900-903)
Leo V (July-September 903)
[Cristophorus, 903-904]
Sergius III (904-911)
Anastasius III (911-913)
Landus (913-914)
John X (914-928)
Leo VI (May-December 928)
Stephan VII or VIII (929-931)
John XI (931-936)
Leo VII (936-939)
Stephan VIII or IX (939-942)
Marinus II (942-946)
Agapitus II (946-955)
John XII (955-964)
Leo VIII (963-965)
Benedict V (May-July 964)
John XIII (965-972)
Benedict VI (973-974)
[Boniface VII, 974; 984-985]
Benedict VII (974-983)
John XIV (983-984)
John XV (985-996)
Gregory V (996-999)
[John XVI, 997-998]

Sylvester II (999-1003)
John XVII (May-November 1003)
John XVIII (1003-1009)
Sergius IV (1009-1012)
Benedict VIII (1012-1024)
 [Gregory, 1012]
John XIX (1024-1032)
Benedict IX (1032-1044;
 March-May 1045; 1047-1048)
Sylvester III (January-
 March 1045)
Gregory VI (1045-1046)
Clement II (1046-1047)
Damasus II (luglio-agosto 1048)
San Leo IX (1049-1054)
Victor II (1055-1057)
Stephan IX or X (1057-1058)
 [Benedict X, 1058-1059]
Nicholas II (1058-1061)
Alexander II (1061-1073)
 [Honorius II, 1061-1064]
St. Gregory VII (1073-1085)
 [Clement III, 1080; 1084-1100]
Blessed Victor III (1086-1087)
Blessed Urban II (1088-1099)
Paschal II (1099-1118)
 [Theoderic, 1100]
 [Albert, 1101]
 [Sylvester IV, 1105-1111]
Gelasius II (1118-1119)
 [Gregory VIII, 1118-1121]
Calixtus II (1119-1124)
Honorius II (1124-1130)
 [Celestine II, 1124]
Innocent II (1130-1143)
 [Anacletus II, 1130-1138]
 [Victor IV, 1138]
Celestine II (1143-1144)
Lucius II (1144-1145)
Blessed Eugenius III
 (1145-1153)
Anastasius IV (1153-1154)
Adrian IV (1154-1159)
Alexander III (1159-1181)
 [Victor IV, 1159-1164]
 [Paschal III, 1164-1168]
 [Calixtus III, 1168-1178]
 [Innocent III, 1179-1180]
Lucius III (1181-1185)
Urban III (1185-1187)
Gregory VIII (October-
 December 1187)
Clement III (1187-1191)
Celestine III (1191-1198)
Innocent III (1198-1216)
Honorius III (1216-1227)
Gregory IX (1227-1241)

Celestine IV (October-
 November 1241)
Innocent IV (1243-1254)
Alexander IV (1254-1261)
Urban IV (1261-1264)
Clement IV (1265-1268)
Blessed Gregory X (1271-1276)
Blessed Innocent V (January-
 June 1276)
Adrian V (July-August 1276)
John XXI (1276-1277)
Nicholas III (1277-1280)
Martin IV (1281-1285)
Honorius IV (1285-1287)
Nicholas IV (1288-1292)
St. Celestine V (July-December
 1294)
Boniface VIII (1294-1303)
Blessed Benedict XI (1303-1304)
Clement V (1305-1314)
John XXII (1316-1334)
 [Nicholas V, 1328-1333]
Benedict XII (1334-1342)
Clement VI (1342-1352)
Innocent VI (1352-1362)
Blessed Urban V (1362-1370)
Gregory XI (1370-1378)
Urban VI (1378-1389)
 [Clement VII, 1378-1394]
Boniface IX (1389-1404)
 [Benedict XIII, 1394-1423]
Innocent VII (1404-1406)
Gregory XII (1406-1415)
 [Alexander V, 1409-1410]
 [John XXIII, 1410-1415]
Martin V (1417-1431)
Eugenius IV (1431-1447)
 [Felix V, 1439-1449]
Nicholas V (1447-1455)
Calixtus III (1455-1458)
Pius II (1458-1464)
Paul II (1464-1471)
Sixtus IV (1471-1484)
Innocent VIII (1484-1492)
Alexander VI (1492-1503)
Pius III (September-October
 1503)
Julius II (1503-1513)
Leo X (1513-1521)
Adrian VI (1522-1523)
Clement VII (1523-1534)
Paul III (1534-1549)
Julius III (1550-1555)
Marcellus II (April-May 1555)
Paul IV (1555-1559)
Pius IV (1559-1565)
St. Pius V (1566-1572)

Gregory XIII (1572-1585)
Sixtus V (1585-1590)
Urban VII (September 1590)
Gregory XIV (1590-1591)
Innocent IX (October-
 December 1591)
Clement VIII (1592-1605)
Leo XI (April 1605)
Paul V (1605-1621)
Gregory XV (1621-1623)
Urban VIII (1623-1644)
Innocent X (1644-1655)
Alexander VII (1655-1667)
Clement IX (1667-1669)
Clement X (1670-1676)
Blessed Innocent XI (1676-1689)
Alexander VIII (1689-1691)
Innocent XII (1691-1700)
Clement XI (1700-1721)
Innocent XIII (1721-1724)
Benedict XIII (1724-1730)
Clement XII (1730-1740)
Benedict XIV (1740-1758)
Clement XIII (1758-1769)
Clement XIV (1769-1774)
Pius VI (1775-1799)
Pius VII (1800-1823)
Leo XII (1823-1829)
Pio VIII (1829-1830)
Gregory XVI (1831-1846)
Blessed Pius IX (1846-1878)
Leo XIII (1878-1903)
St. Pius X (1903-1914)
Benedict XV (1914-1922)
Pius XI (1922-1939)
Pius XII (1939-1958)
Blessed John XXIII (1958-1963)
Paul VI (1963-1978)
John Paul I (August-September
 1978)
John Paul II (elected 1978)

157

Alphabetical List of the Popes

[References are to page numbers]